day
by
day
with
Jesus

day by day with Jesus

Daily Devotions
Through the Year

Rudolph F. Norden

Publishing House
St. Louis

Scripture quotations marked TEV are from the *TODAY'S ENGLISH VERSION*. Copyright ©
American Bible Society 1966, 1971, 1976.

Some Scripture quotations in this publication are from the Revised Standard Version of the Bible,
copyrighted 1946, 1952, © 1971, 1973 by the Division of Christian Education of the National
Council of the Churches of Christ in the U.S.A., and used by permission.

Some quotations are from the King James or Authorized Version of the Bible.

Unless otherwise marked, hymn texts are from *Lutheran Worship*, copyright © 1982 by Concordia
Publishing House.

Hymn texts marked *TLH* are from *The Lutheran Hymnal*, copyright 1941 by Concordia Publishing
House.

Some of the meditations in this book were broadcast over Radio Station KFUO, St. Louis, on the
"Daily Treasures" program sponsored by the Lutheran Laymen's League.

Copyright © 1985 by Concordia Publishing House
3558 S. Jefferson Ave., St. Louis, MO 63118
Manufactured in the United States of America

Library of Congress Cataloging in Publication Data

Norden, Rudolph F.
    Day by day with Jesus.

    1. Devotional calendars. I. Title.
BV4811.N63 1985   242'.2   84-23880
ISBN 0-570-03971-1

---

1 2 3 4 5 6 7 8 9 10 MAL 94 93 92 91 90 89 88 87 86 85

*To Gladys, my spouse since 1937,
who joins me in my daily devotions*

Preface

For many years *Day by Day with Jesus*, a yearly series of daily devotions, has been offered to Christian readers. The series was originated by Dr. Walter A. Maier, the Lutheran Hour speaker, and was, on his death, continued by his friend and close associate, Dr. Eugene R. Bertermann, until he himself was called home in 1983. The present devotions are a continuation of this series, if not in the exact title then certainly in the underlying theme: the life in Christ.

In the course of years *Day by Day with Jesus* has taken various forms: first as a prayer calendar with boxed loose pages, then as a bound book. Through the years, however, there has been no change in the Gospel message undergirding every daily devotion. Jesus Christ, who is the same yesterday, today, and forever, has always been "center stage."

The page format in the current book is simple—the same that was used in the International Lutheran Laymen's League radio program "Day by Day with Jesus." Each page contains the date, the Scripture reading, the topic, the meditation, and a prayer suggestion. The latter feature invites leaders in the devotional group to exercise the privilege of prayer by using their own words as they pray *ex corde*—from the heart. Persons using these devotions in privacy may "think" their petitions and thanksgivings, in keeping with the hymn lines: "Prayer is the soul's sincere desire, unuttered or expressed."

These devotions can be used in addition to other materials available. If, for example, some other daily readings are used in the morning, these devotions may be read in the evening, or vice versa.

To mind comes the invitation and encouragement of a hymn Christians have sung for centuries: "Let us ever walk with Jesus, Follow His example pure." The Lord Jesus, having laid down His life for us and then taken it up again, is not only our Exemplar but also the Enabler of Christian service by word and deed, for through His Word He sends the Holy Spirit to guide us into all truth and to help us speak it to one another.

—*Rudolph F. Norden*

Free to Serve

On New Year's Day 1863 President Abraham Lincoln issued the epoch-making Emancipation Proclamation, which declared to states that had left the Union that "all persons held as slaves within such designated States and parts of States are and henceforth shall be free." Thereby some 3,500,000 slaves were declared free.

Years later, soon after America's entry into World War II, President Franklin D. Roosevelt made his "Four Freedoms" speech, holding out to oppressed nations the hope of freedom of speech and worship and freedom from want and fear.

There is another kind of slavery that completely deprives the whole human race of the freedom with which it was originally created: the slavery of sin. No person can by his own efforts free himself from the just condemnation of God's law. Only the Son of God, who was above sin, could do this, and He did. St. Paul tells the Galatians: "Christ redeemed us from the curse of the Law, having become a curse for us." This He did when He died on the cross.

The Holy Spirit, having brought us to faith in the Savior through the Gospel, gives us new life. Thanks to our liberation from the tyranny of sin and from the demands of our sinful ego, we are set free to become disciples of Jesus Christ. We are not draftees but volunteers. We are free to be God's servants and free to serve one another in love. This is the paradox within which Christ's disciples live and find joy: They are freed from sin to become the slaves of Jesus Christ.

Prayer Suggestion

Ask the Lord Jesus to lead you into all truth and thus set you free to serve Him.

God's Time Is a Good Time

Many of us can reminisce along with the author of "When You and I Were Young, Maggie" as he speaks of bygone days. And when he says, "My face is a well-written page . . . but time alone was the pen," this will be true also of us as time etches more lines into our faces.

Time does such things, and much more. It causes change and decay. It affects all human beings, as the hymn declares: "Time, like an ever-rolling stream Soon bears us all away."

Yet time is something good. It is a gift of God, along with other blessings God has entrusted to us: talents, treasures, the truths by which we live. God desires us to be thoughtful stewards in our use of time, recognizing that there is a time to work and a time to rest, a time to plant and a time to harvest, a time to speak and a time to listen—a time to listen to God. St. Paul reminds us: "Behold, now is the acceptable time; behold, now is the day of salvation."

Our Lord Jesus Christ knew the value and importance of time. He said He had to work while it was day, for the night comes when no one can work. We know the work He did: He went about doing good; He proclaimed the Gospel; He healed and helped where there was need. Above all, He endured what the prophet Isaiah calls "the travail of His soul"—great labor and pain—as He walked the road to Calvary with a cross on His back to redeem all people from sin.

Christ gives us not only the example but also the power to turn the time God entrusts to us into a good time as we worship Him and serve one another. And then when we reminisce on bygone days, we can say, "A good time was had by all."

Prayer Suggestion

Meditate on the hymn lines "Take my moments and my days; Let them sing your ceaseless praise," asking God to let this be true in your life also.

Born to Serve

The man in the Bible who had so many misfortunes, Job, at one point didn't think life was worth living. He asked, "Why did I not die at birth?" A little later on he exclaimed, "Man is born to trouble as the sparks fly upward."

"Born to trouble"—that expression seems to fit Jesus of Nazareth. There was trouble in His early childhood when King Herod considered Him a rival to his throne and sought to kill Him. And He Himself did say during His ministry that He had not come to bring peace but a sword, as though He were a born troublemaker. At the end the religious leaders accused Him before Pontius Pilate of being a dangerous man: "We found this man perverting our nation, and forbidding us to give tribute to Caesar, and saying that He Himself is Christ a king."

Was Jesus really born to trouble? Indeed not. His reply to the foregoing charge was: "For this I was born, and for this I have come into the world, to bear witness to the truth." He reminded the Roman governor who was to be His judge: "Everyone who is of the truth hears My voice."

Truly Jesus had not come to make trouble but to serve, declaring in a summary statement: "The Son of Man came not to be served but to serve, and to give His life as a ransom for many." He came to witness to the truth that He was a Servant and the Savior of all mankind.

What if the questions arise in your life and mine, as they did in Job's: "Why was I born? Why do I have all this trouble?" Is there an answer? Yes. Believe in Jesus Christ as your Savior and then do what He did: Serve God and those around you. That's why you were born.

Prayer Suggestion

Pray that God may help you fulfill the purpose for which He has placed you here.

Energized to Serve

During an electrical storm on June 15, 1752, Benjamin Franklin demonstrated with the simple apparatus of a key attached to a kite that lightning is an electrical discharge. Franklin did much in exploring the field of electricity. He explained clearly, for example, that there are positive and negative types of electrical force.

As great and helpful a force as applied electricity is, there is a power even greater—the Gospel of Jesus Christ. Electrical power can illuminate our homes and turn the wheels of industry, but it cannot change a person's heart. Only Christ can do that. By means of His saving Word, the Gospel, He sends His Holy Spirit into a person and makes a Christian out of him or her. All the world's combined armies, navies, and air forces cannot do this, as the prophet Zechariah has well said: "Not by might, nor by power, but by My Spirit, says the Lord of hosts."

By His Word and Spirit Christ changes hopeless, helpless orphans in a sinful world into God's children—into people who know they were lost but now have found pardon and peace. St. Paul writes: "God has delivered us from the dominion of darkness and transferred us to the kingdom of His beloved Son, in whom we have redemption, the forgiveness of sins." What a change!

Alive in Christ, we are energized to serve Him. We now have the stamina and strength, the motivation and incentive to work for Him, to witness to His love, to befriend His brethren in need. What energizes us? Christ's love to us, yes, Christ Himself. St. Paul said: "I can do all things in Him who strengthens me." You and I can say the same.

Prayer Suggestion

Ask that Christ may send you His Holy Spirit to fill your heart with His wisdom and power.

Equipped to Serve

It was on July 20, 1969, that astronaut Neil A. Armstrong stepped from his landing craft onto the moon's surface. He was able to take this giant step for mankind because he was well trained and properly equipped with a space suit and helmet, delicate instruments, oxygen to breathe, and the like.

When God puts His people on earth to take giant steps for Him, He likewise equips them with life-support systems and the proper spiritual tools. This is the equipment available to us, according to St. Paul: "Take the whole armor of God, that you may be able to withstand in the evil day. . . . Stand therefore, having girded your loins with truth, and having put on the breastplate of righteousness, and having shod your feet with the equipment of the Gospel of peace; besides all these, taking the shield of faith, with which you can quench all the flaming darts of the evil one. And take the helmet of salvation, and the sword of the Spirit, which is the Word of God."

With the "sword of the Spirit," the Gospel, Christ's people are well equipped for their own nurture and for the task of missions. The first Christians were but a handful of people—120 men and women in an upper room in Jerusalem. But equipped with the Gospel of salvation in Jesus Christ alone, they were most effective in living for their Lord and proclaiming His saving message.

We today may not have overflowing treasuries, fine church buildings, and the latest technical equipment, but if we have the full Gospel to live by and to share with others, we are alive in Christ. And that means we are well equipped.

Prayer Suggestion

Pray that the Holy Spirit may open your mind to all that Christ has provided to make your life effective.

Jesus Christ, God's Gold Star

During World War I the Scottish singer and entertainer Harry Lauder lost two sons in quick succession. He went to Australia to recover from the shock, to regain his spiritual perspective. Out walking one evening, he saw stars in the windows of homes, signifying the men in military service. He noticed also the gold stars in honor of the fallen. Then he looked up into the evening sky and saw an especially bright star. It reminded him that the heavenly Father, too, had given up His Son for the salvation of all. Lauder, the distraught father, found comfort.

Yes, God lost a Son for our great gain. St. Paul writes: "God did not spare His own Son but gave Him up for us all." At His birth God put a star into the heavens to announce His coming. The Wise Men of the East followed that star and were led to the Christ Child in Bethlehem. The Savior is Himself called a Star. Balaam said in a Messianic prophecy: "A Star shall come forth out of Jacob." That Star came into the darkness of people's lives to give them light.

Jesus Christ, God's only Son, is still our Gold Star, as St. John quotes Him as saying, in the Book of Revelation: "I am . . . the bright Morning Star." No matter how deep our trouble or dark our night, that Star shines. His message is this, as our Lord Himself said to Nicodemus: "God so loved the world that He gave His only Son, that whoever believes in Him should not perish but have eternal life." That Son, indeed God's Superstar in our behalf, is our Day Spring from on high. His light radiates to us in and through His Word, the Gospel. This Word, as St. Peter declares, is "a lamp shining in a dark place until the day dawns and the Morning Star rises in your hearts."

Yes, God gave up His Son, but that sacrifice is not in vain so long as He gains us as sons and daughters who love and serve Him.

Prayer Suggestion

Pray that Christ, the bright Morning Star, may light up your life.

How the Good News Gets Around

In York, England, stands a column dating back to A.D. 71. A part of the headquarters building of the Roman army, it was found on the site later occupied by the York minster, or cathedral. Here the Roman troops in A.D. 306 declared Constantine the Great the Roman Caesar—a most significant act, for Constantine was the first emperor to recognize Christianity as a licensed religion and was himself baptized. The dreadful government-sponsored persecutions were now over.

The Christian faith had come a long way. Caesar Augustus, the emperor when Jesus was born, very likely never heard of the Savior; if he did, he attached no significance to Him. The marvelous growth of the Christian Gospel in the first three centuries came about without the benefit of military force, or government favor, or the prestige of famous scholars, or the use of fast communication and transportation systems.

Then how did Christianity spread? Mostly by word of mouth. One person told another—just as Mrs. Olson in TV commercials used to tell her friends and neighbors about a certain brand of coffee. True enough, the preaching of the apostles was accompanied by signs and wonders—occasional healing and speaking in tongues—but alone these 12 men could not have turned the world upside down for Christ. Not so much the generals but the common foot soldiers of Christ carried His Gospel to the ends of the earth.

That is what Christians still do today. The lines of a hymn say: "If you cannot speak like angels, If you cannot preach like Paul, You can tell the love of Jesus; You can say he died for all." That is effective, more so than the prestige or impact value of a famous man like Constantine calling himself a Christian.

Prayer Suggestion

Say your thank-You to God for all the people who by word of mouth speak the Gospel which also you have heard.

15

Getting a Heart Lift

All of us have marks of a sort, like facial features. Some physical marks, like blemishes in the face, can be removed, perhaps by a face-lift. Other marks are stamped on the mind and heart, and they, although unseen, can be very bothersome and painful.

In Nathaniel Hawthorne's novel *The Scarlet Letter* Hester Prynne's guilt is externalized, for she is made to wear a scarlet A on her garments for all to see. Life was not any easier for guilt-ridden Arthur Dimmesdale, who was inwardly branded. He suffered greatly, because his burden was that he had to appear before people to be what in his heart he knew he was not.

In the Bible, St. Paul was a man who bore marks, inwardly and outwardly. His inner scars stemmed from the time he hated Jesus Christ, persecuted Christians, and killed some of them. This he could never forget. What is more, he had inner wounds because of the very fact that he, like everybody else, was a sinner, and it gave him pain that a negative force in him kept him from doing what he knew was right. The other marks by which the apostle was branded were outward. These were the wounds he endured in the body when he was beaten and stoned for the sake of the faith. He writes: "I bear on my body the marks of Jesus."

We can get rid of inner wounds—the marks on the soul, the unseen but bitter memories of sin. We can do this because Jesus was wounded for all our sins—for our transgressions, digressions, indiscretions. Believe in Him as your Savior and you are saved, you are forgiven, you are inwardly healed. You have received a spiritual heart lift! So good is this spiritual surgery that you have in fact received an entirely new heart.

Prayer Suggestion

Ask God, for Jesus' sake, to lift from you the burden of your sins and cares.

Working and Praying

The tour guide tells people who visit historic Marblehead, Mass.: "The first settlers didn't come here to pray; they came to catch fish." He sought to distinguish these men of the sea from the religious Puritans who settled elsewhere in Massachusetts.

Life was hard for all concerned, also for the hardy men of Marblehead. Many did not survive the shipwrecks and other perils of the sea: pirates, sickness, hunger, and thirst. It is said that the architecture of the houses provided for a high place called the "widow's walk," where the wives of seafaring men waited for their husbands to return—quite often in vain. You can be sure that the women did some praying up there.

In view of life's uncertainties—and its opportunities, as well— it is never enough just to catch fish, just to do one's housework, just to make a *living*; we need to make a *life*, and for that, prayer, reading and hearing the Word of God, growing in faith and Christian love are the necessary ingredients. When working and praying blend properly together, we have Christian vocation.

Our Lord said, "Seek first God's kingdom and His righteousness, and all these things shall be yours as well." Again, "Man shall not live by bread alone, but by every word that proceeds from the mouth of God."

Our Lord and Savior Jesus Christ is Himself the Bread of Life. He is the heavenly Manna come from heaven to nourish the people of God. All that He procured for our salvation by His dying and rising again is communicated through His Word. God's favor, forgiveness, and peace are ours.

Working, praying: It is not an either-or but a both-and.

Prayer Suggestion

Pray that God, through the comfort and guidance of His Word, may fulfill all your spiritual needs.

Rock or Shifting Sand?

God bases His work on rock bottom. The psalmist declares: "Of old Thou didst lay the foundation of the earth"—layer on layer of rock.

The church of Jesus Christ likewise rests on a solid foundation. St. Paul writes: "No other foundation can anyone lay than that which is laid, which is Jesus Christ." The Word of God that Jesus taught and the work of redemption that He wrought—that is the rock on which God's kingdom is built. This kingdom is "the city which has foundations, whose Builder and Maker is God." In it we are safe, as Isaiah said long ago: "The Lord has founded Zion, and in her the afflicted of His people find refuge."

Since God lays solid foundations for what He constructs, shouldn't we do the same in the life we are building from day to day? Our Christian faith is sure, for it rests on Christ's Word and work. Similarly, in our Christian life we *hear* Jesus' words and *do* them. Then we are "like a wise man who built his house upon the rock; and the rain fell, and the floods came, and the winds blew and beat upon that house, but it did not fall, because it had been founded on the rock." That is so much better than building on unstable sand.

What the world offers, not only the underworld but also much of the overworld—tainted riches, the latest technological gadgets, passing pleasures that harm rather than help, rock-and-roll stimulation in every sphere of life—is shifting sand and therefore an unreliable basis for life. To live in and for Christ—that is wisdom, that brings security. Our Lord said: "Heaven and earth will pass away, but My words will not pass away." Every promise of His stands.

Prayer Suggestion

Pray that the Holy Spirit may lead you to a firmer faith in Jesus Christ, in whom lies our security.

The Heavenly Father's Love

While Dr. Perry Mead, Anchorage, Alaska, was operating on victims of the severe earthquake of 1964, he received word that his 12-year-old son was killed trying to rescue his baby brother, who likewise perished. With tears streaming down his face, the doctor carried on with his operations. Before such a brave man—and loving father—we have to rise up and call him blessed.

Much greater is the love of our heavenly Father, who in His incomparable love did not spare His own beloved Son but delivered Him up for us all. People of all times and places had become involved in the catastrophic earthquake of sin, and the heavenly Father was active in His concern and compassion. He did not want any of the victims to perish; He wanted all to be saved and come to the knowledge of the truth. To that end He gave up His own Son, not only by sending Him into this world as a human being but also by giving Him over into the hands of sinners to crucify Him in atonement for sin.

So we exclaim with St. Peter, "Blessed be the God and Father of our Lord Jesus Christ! By His great mercy we have been born anew," for the Father through the Holy Spirit regenerated us. It is God who gives us spiritual life, gives us saving faith in Jesus Christ. And with faith goes hope, as the apostle declares, "born anew to a living hope." This hope is genuine and for real, for it is a *living* hope, a hope supported "through the resurrection of Jesus Christ from the dead."

So whatever aspect of salvation we discuss—Christ's atonement on the cross, His resurrection, our conversion—always it is God the Father of our Lord Jesus Christ who is at work. How great is His love!

Suggestion

Give thanks to God for His great love in sacrificing His own Son in your behalf.

Suicide Is Not the Answer

Since the Golden Gate Bridge spanning San Francisco Bay was opened in 1937, many people have jumped from it to their death. Only God knows what griefs and inner torments drove them to these desperate acts.

We read in the Bible how one of Christ's own disciples, Judas Iscariot, hanged himself because he was overcome by despair at having betrayed his Lord into the hands of enemies who condemned Him to death. Poor Judas! He needed not to have done this, for Jesus would have forgiven him his betrayal, even as He forgave Peter his denial.

Sometimes people overwhelmed by problems get little help from those around them. When so many afflictions had descended on Job—that great sufferer of whom the Bible speaks—his wife suggested suicide, saying: "Do you still hold fast your integrity? Curse God, and die."

It has been said that one out of four persons has at some time or other thought about committing suicide. It is no disgrace to have been so tempted. The devil tempted even Jesus to leap to His death from the pinnacle of the temple.

If you are depressed, don't give up, and don't do anything rash. Don't even think about it. Instead, seek help from people who are competent to give it. Turn to God in prayer, remembering what a Friend you have in Jesus, all your sins and griefs to bear. Instead of jumping from a bridge, leap into the arms of your heavenly Father. He will help you, as St. Paul has written: "He who did not spare His own Son but gave Him up for us all, will He not also give us all things with Him?"

Prayer Suggestion

Ask the Holy Spirit to remove despair from your heart and to give you hope in Christ, your Savior.

Satisfying the Inner Hunger

People today like to talk about food—how to prepare it, where to dine, what kind of nourishment we need to keep healthy. That was the case also in Jesus' day. After the feeding of the five thousand our Lord and the people around Him carried on a running discussion about bread to eat, with the scene shifting from the wilderness to the city of Capernaum.

Christ's purpose in the long discourse recorded in John 6 was to turn minds from bodily food to nourishment for the soul. Preoccupied with earthly bread, the people recalled that their fathers ate manna in the wilderness, crediting Moses for this. Jesus replied, "My Father gives you the *true* Bread from heaven. . . . I am the Bread of life."

Earthly bread is needed to appease physical hunger. But there is another kind of longing that food and drink cannot satisfy—the hunger and thirst of the soul. Jesus Christ, the Son of God, came from heaven to be the Bread broken for us on Calvary's cross so that, believing in Him, we might have forgiveness of sins, the promise of life eternal, and peace with God.

Many of our contemporaries do not realize that only Jesus can satisfy the inner life. So they turn to the occult arts, to the revived superstitions of old, to pagan mysticism, and to eastern philosophies.

Jesus, the Bread of Life, promises: "He who comes to Me shall not hunger." He imparts peace such as the world cannot give. He blesses us with rest for the soul. As we live day by day with Jesus, believing His Word, doing His will, and giving our lives to Him, we too will be well nourished.

Prayer Suggestion

Pray that Christ may satisfy the hunger and thirst of your soul by leading you to firm faith in Him through His nourishing Word.

A Water of Wonders

What a difference water can make! Large parts of the southwest United States were once desert, but now they support flourishing cities and fruitful farms. Irrigation helps keep the breadbasket filled.

Plants flourish when their roots have access to water. The River Jordan is like a green ribbon as it twists its way through the Holy Land. It gives of its water to make the desert blossom like a rose. Billy Graham has called modern Israel "the California of the Middle East."

We need another kind of water, and we have it. It is the water of Holy Baptism—plain water from a tap that has spiritual power when it is "comprehended in God's command and connected with God's Word" (Luther's Small Catechism). It is a water of wonders. It does miracles because the Holy Spirit works through it. It causes a sinner to be born anew, turning him into a saint, that is, one whose sins are taken away because he believes in Christ, the Sin-Bearer. It truly "saves," to use St. Peter's term. It is, as St. Paul tells Titus, "the washing of regeneration and renewal in the Holy Spirit."

But the sacramental water does more. It makes the baptized, believing person a human tree bearing the fruit of the Spirit: love, joy, peace, patience, kindness, goodness, faithfulness, gentleness, self-control. He is, in the words of Psalm 1, "like a tree planted by streams of water, that yields its fruit in its season."

And the church of believers—your congregation—what is it but an orchard of fruit-bearing trees because the water of Holy Baptism flows through it!

Prayer Suggestion

Pray that Christ, through the Gospel in the Bible and the Gospel of Holy Baptism, may become a fountain of living water in your life.

How to Be Right with God

God's righteousness comes to "all who believe," the Bible declares. God's righteousness—the only kind good enough for Him to accept—is the righteousness of Christ, which is ours by faith. Does this seem too easy? Should not a person who wants to be right with God first prove himself worthy of Christ's righteousness by being good and doing good?

If so, the righteousness that meets God's perfect standard would be earned. Then salvation would not be God's gift but a reward.

But God's way is different. He declares a person righteous in His sight apart from any merit system man might devise. Righteousness in God's eyes comes to those who believe—just by their believing in Jesus Christ as their Savior. St. Paul writes in his Letter to the Romans that the righteousness of God is imparted "through faith in Jesus Christ for all who believe." He goes on to say that those who believe "are justified by His grace as a gift, through the redemption which is in Christ Jesus, whom God put forward as an expiation by His blood, to be received by faith."

Too easy? "Cheap grace?" Salvation on another's credit card? It is not too easy if you consider that our justification before God cost Him the life of His own dear Son. Christ paid a high price so that we might now totally belong to Him and serve Him faithfully. We were not declared just and holy in order to take life easy or be spiritually lazy. We were bought with a very high price so that our whole lives might be turned around. We were saved to serve.

Prayer Suggestion

Pray that the Holy Spirit may give you greater confidence in Jesus Christ, through whose righteousness alone you are made right with God.

The Way of the Beatitudes

Our Lord opened His Sermon on the Mount with nine Beatitudes, that is, statements beginning with the word "Blessed." Blessedness means true happiness or bliss—the bliss of being at peace with God.

St. Paul writes: "Since we are justified by faith, we have peace with God through our Lord Jesus Christ." This is the teaching and promise of Jesus as well. He goes to the cross to give His life a ransom for all, and all who accept Him in faith as their Redeemer are assured: "Peace I leave with you; My peace I give to you; not as the world gives do I give to you."

The Beatitudes are addressed to Christ's disciples, to believers in Him. These are persons who have come to faith and are at peace with God. The purpose of the Beatitudes is not to give mankind in general a set of principles or golden rules whereby people can attain to salvation and secure harmony with God and one another. Their purpose is to serve as guidelines for Christians as they grow in holiness, lead Christlike lives, and seek strength and comfort in days of adversity.

The road to true happiness or blessedness, as Jesus outlines it, is not a four-lane highway without obstacles, as though the life of a Christian were only fun and games. No, to follow the King's highway in the footsteps of Jesus involves sacrifices and the surrender of lesser things so that we might gain the greater ones. It means self-denial and the refusal to put one's own interests first, in order to please God and serve the neighbor. Then peace and happiness come as a bonus.

Prayer Suggestion

Ask God to take your life and so fashion it that it may please Him and bring joy to yourself and to others.

Food to Sustain the Soul

In "America, the Beautiful" Katherine Lee Bates thrills to the sight of "purple mountain majesties above the fruited plain." Other countries offer similar sights combining beauty with utility— mountains harboring snow, and valleys where grain is grown for bodily nourishment.

Make no mistake about it: Bread is an essential of life. When there is no food, people die of starvation. In His providential love God provides us with daily bread and all that is needed for the support and wants of the body. Christians don't let a single day pass without thanking God for the blessings He places on their tables. Man cannot live without bread.

Jesus at one time said, "Man shall not live by bread *alone*." That was His reply to Satan, who came to tempt Him in the wilderness, urging Him to forget His obedience to the Father— forget His spiritual commitment, His mission as the world's Redeemer from sin and death. Let Him break His 40-day fast and satisfy His physical hunger by turning stones into bread.

Jesus' statement was quoted from Deuteronomy 8:3, where Moses points out that the people of Israel survived in the wilderness not only because of the manna but "by everything that proceeds out of the mouth of the Lord." Man's spiritual life, his soul and spirit, is sustained by the will and Word of God.

Jesus Christ is the personal Word, the Word that was made flesh, and He proclaims the Word of God for our salvation. He who is the Bread of life declares: "The words I have spoken to you are spirit and life." We are fully nourished when through Word and Spirit we believe in Jesus Christ as Lord and Savior.

Prayer Suggestion

Speak to God in prayer, thanking Him for your daily bread and asking Him to nourish you with Christ's Gospel, the bread of life.

The View from a Mountain

We find ourselves at times in the valleys of mental depression. Then God wants to lead us to mountaintops so that we can see our life in a clearer perspective.

Our worship in God's house is such an experience, for the church is a spiritual Mount Zion set in the midst of our world. A vantage point is given us when special occasions occur: a promotion in our work, recognition of services performed, the celebration of a birthday. When we mark 25 or 50 years of married life or observe other anniversaries, we are standing on mountaintops; we can see from where we have come, where we are now, and where we are going. In fact, not only joyful occasions but also unpleasant experiences—sicknesses, loss, deep disappointments—can give us a better view of life if we rise from the "dumps" and let God show us His love. These are then pauses that refresh, moments when we can say: We lift up our eyes to the hills, from where God's help comes.

To Moses God said when His people were about to enter the land of promise: "Ascend . . . Mount Nebo, which is in the land of Moab, opposite Jericho, and view the land of Canaan, which I give to the people of Israel for a possession." What a thrill it was for Moses to see the land from end to end!

In Yosemite Park there is a spot called Inspiration Point. It offers a spectacular view—the 7,500-foot-high granite monolith called El Capitan, and the Bridalveil Falls. Find your inspiration point in the park of your life! Do this not only when you are up but also when you are down. Faith is the upward look to Jesus the Lamb of God, to Jesus the Pioneer and Perfecter of our salvation. He who gave His life for us and rose again is the High Point of our lives.

Prayer Suggestion

Pray for God's guidance to gain a better perspective on your life as you turn to Jesus.

Blessed Under the Fatherhood of God

Augustus was the Roman emperor when Jesus was born. What sort of persons were the emperors and their consorts? A recent writer gives us this sampling: "Livia was the vicious power behind the throne during the reign of her husband, Augustus Caesar, and that of her son by an earlier marriage, Tiberius. The intrigue and debauchery of those eras, plus that of the infamous Caligula, were recorded by the supposedly imbecilic Claudius, who later became emperor himself." Yet these emperors called themselves divine, and early Christians were sentenced to death for refusing to worship them as gods.

God tells us: "I am the Lord your God. . . . You shall have no other gods before Me."

A terror to those who hate Him, God is the loving Father of all who believe in Jesus Christ, the Reconciler and Redeemer. In steadfast love, which remained unaffected by our disaffection and disobedience, the heavenly Father blessed the human race when He "sent forth His Son, born of woman, born under the Law, to redeem those who were under the Law, so that we might receive adoption as sons." The apostle Paul continues to show how blessed we are: Because we are sons and daughters, "God has sent the Spirit of His Son into our hearts, crying, 'Abba! Father!' " Now we are no longer slaves—no longer outcasts, no longer orphans, no longer victims of tyranny under cruel emperors—but God's sons and daughters; and if His children, then also heirs, heirs of eternal life.

How true, then, the psalmist's words: "Blessed is the nation whose God is the Lord, the people whom He has chosen as His heritage!" Again: "As a father pities his children, so the Lord pities those who fear Him"—who love Him and trust in Him.

Prayer Suggestion

As you pray the "Our Father Who Art in Heaven," consider how God enriches your life under His Fatherhood as He grants your petitions.

Hair Today—Gone Tomorrow?

A Dayton University professor holds that long hair, beards, blue jeans, and the like don't reveal the wearer's true character. After conducting many interviews, he concluded: "If you try to judge a student's politics and attitude by his dress, you will be wrong almost as often as you will be right."

In Bible times long hair and a straggly beard told something about a man. He may have been one who took the Nazarite vow and let his hair grow long as a visible sign of consecration.

Beards were considered signs of manly dignity among the Israelites. Sideburns were "in." By way of contrast, many pagan men "shaved the side of the face between the ear and eye." By their beard one could tell who was who.

Long hair and beards don't have such significance today. Hairstyle is a matter of taste, sometimes a fad. Fads come and go, and so it could well be "hair today and gone tomorrow."

It has always been true, however, that, as the Bible says, "Man looks on the outward appearance, but the Lord looks on the heart." God has no hang-up about hair. He is more concerned that we have "love that issues from a pure heart and a good conscience and sincere faith" (1 Timothy 1:5).

The Christian prays frequently, "Create in me a clean heart, O God, and put a new and right spirit within me." Such a clean heart God gives us when Christ Jesus abides in us—the same Lord who died an ignominious death so that we might have forgiveness and be made a new creation in Him. Are you that kind of a new person?

Prayer Suggestion

Ask God to help you judge others with true Christian love and to keep you from being misled by outward appearances.

Jesus Has It All

Many North Americans, notably young people who have dropped out of the church, profess that they benefit from instruction in oriental religions. While being on a "religion kick" is undoubtedly to be preferred to drug addiction, the question needs asking: Why not the Christian religion?

The instruction given by Jesus Christ is on record in the Sermon on the Mount and other utterances found in the four gospels. It is truly helpful.

Is it inner peace that people desire? Jesus not only talks about peace but actually imparts it: "Peace I leave with you; My peace I give to you; not as the world gives do I give to you."

Is it harmony with God people seek? Jesus not only discusses such harmony but also conveys it: "I am the Way, the Truth, and the Life."

Is it freedom from the prison of self that people are looking for? Jesus not only extols freedom verbally but also outlines a simple program for achieving it: "If you continue in My Word, you are truly My disciples, and you will know the truth, and the truth will make you free."

Is it relief from the burdens of life that people desire? Jesus not only speaks of such relief but actually grants it: "Come to Me, all who labor and are heavy laden, and I will give you rest."

Are people troubled because they know they did what was wrong, left undone what was right, and can do nothing to make restitution? Jesus not only has words of wisdom but also deeds that bring salvation: "The Son of Man came not to be served but to serve, and to give His life as a ransom for many."

So, turn to Jesus Christ. He has it all.

Prayer Suggestion

Ask the Father to send you the Holy Spirit that He may open your heart and mind to the gifts Jesus Christ has provided to meet all your needs.

The Basis of Contentment

From Croatia came Nikola Tesla to seek his fortune in the United States. He was poor. On board ship he sat against the smokestacks to keep warm. He made good in America, especially in perfecting electrical inventions. When He returned home for a visit, his mother asked, "How is America treating you?" "Fine," said her son, adding that could make $10 million in royalties from his inventions. "That is not what I mean," his mother said. "Nikola, are you getting enough to eat?"

"If we have food and clothing, with these we shall be content," writes St. Paul. God has promised us daily bread, which is not only the flour product baked in ovens, but what is needed for the support and wants of the body.

Jesus said we should not worry about what we shall eat, drink, and wear, for the heavenly Father knows that we need these things, and He will provide them. God has not promised a rose garden of life's luxuries, pleasures, and riches. So the main question for us is not: "Nikola [or whatever our name], are you making millions?" but "are you getting enough to eat." Enough food, clothing, and shelter—this is the sufficient basis for contentment.

In His love God gives us more, not only in that most of us have many extras but especially in that He has given us His Son, Jesus Christ, to be the Bread of life, well knowing that we do not live from earthly bread alone. When our faith is fixed on Jesus as our Savior from sin and as the Provider of "soul food," then we are truly well supplied. Then we have every reason to be content and to thank God daily for His many blessings.

Prayer Suggestion

Ask God to make you content in your personal fellowship with Christ, His Son.

Gateway to a New Life

Many people, in the course of the everyday grind, reach a point of exhaustion. They feel trapped in a humdrum existence that has no goal and leads nowhere. Nothing would please them more than to break out of the old routine and start life afresh.

Emigration to America used to—and often still does—offer new opportunity. Ellis Island in New York harbor symbolized entry into a better life for the poor and oppressed. During a period preceding World War I, this United States government station admitted more than 16 million people. The record for one day was 11,747. Some immigrants, of course, were disillusioned.

The Gospel of Jesus Christ is the true gateway to a new life. The Gospel brings faith and spiritual rebirth. Holy Baptism, which is the Gospel made visible by the water, unites us with our Savior, making us full shareholders in His redemption and giving us power to walk in newness of life.

What a change takes place! The chains of selfishness are broken. Evil desires and lusts give way to delight in the Lord and love for Him and for those whom He loves. Despair is overruled by hope. The materialistic goals of life— moneymaking and the pursuit of self-gratifying pleasures—yield to a new spiritual ori-entation, as St. Paul experienced it: "Forgetting what lies behind and straining forward to what lies ahead, I press on toward the goal for the prize of the upward call of God in Christ Jesus."

Let us be realists. Not all who entered the country at Ellis Island found all their fond hopes fulfilled. Not all who come to Jesus, hoping to find heaven here on earth, will find the new life in Christ satisfying. But if serving God is their purpose and heaven above is their hope, they will find discipleship just what they were looking for.

Prayer Suggestion

Ask God to help you find fulfillment by living *in* and *for* Christ.

The Road That Leads to Life

In Missouri's Elephant Rocks State Park, so named because the boulders in it resemble elephants, there is between two boulders a narrow passageway called "Fat Man's Squeeze."

Jesus said in the Sermon on the Mount: "Enter by the narrow gate." He is speaking in spiritual terms, of course. Discipleship—this thing of believing in and following Him—is not easy. It requires self-denial. Salvation, of course, is free, having been earned by Jesus Christ when He walked the painful way of the cross. But what follows—the life in His footsteps—Christ has not pictured to us as a pleasure trip along a primrose path. It is beset by difficulties because the way leads through a sinful world, and we who walk this way are sinful still.

Christian life is like an obstacle course, not unlike a race to be run or a contest to be won. Therefore the New Testament writer urges us to "lay aside every weight, and sin which clings so closely, and let us run with perseverance the race that is set before us."

The narrow gate, the rough path, the passage referred to as the "Fat Man's Squeeze" are apt word pictures telling us to avoid becoming spiritually overweight with the cares, worries, and pleasures of this life.

Always to be kept in mind is the goal toward which we are heading. Let the road be difficult, we can manage, because we know that it leads to the place where we want to be: the Father's house of many mansions.

It is a blessed company that travels this way. Theirs is a pilgrimage of faith bringing them into Christ's fellowship, for now and forever.

Prayer Suggestion

Pray for patience, that you may complete your journey on Christ's road of life.

Faithful to Our Calling

Most people believe that clergymen follow a danger-free calling. But in historic Old Mines, Mo., where lead mines were opened in 1726, a visitor finds this interesting footnote on the gravestone in the cemetery: "Rev. James Gaffrey, drowned in the Meramec River, February 7, 1856, making a sick call."

A footnote to this footnote is: This man of God was faithful in the performance of his pastoral duties. This tribute is for all Christian persons who are faithful in their calling: businessman, clerk, salesman, teacher, nurse, physician. By serving God and their fellow human beings with their entrusted talents, they are good stewards. St. Paul declares that God asks all stewards to be faithful—not eminently successful, not universally recognized, not loved by everyone, but *faithful.*

Let's face it: Most people hold nonglamorous jobs, and their everyday lives seem routine. But what they are and do can be most purposeful and meaningful. To use a current expression, they can find self-fulfillment, that is, find joy and contentment, in knowing that they are living far beyond selfishness—living, in fact, as a credit to their Creator and sharing His love with those who need it. This is filling a most important role.

Jesus Christ, the Son of God, was, as has been said, "the Man for others." These are His very words: "The Son of Man came not to be served but to serve, and to give His life as a ransom for many." Not only did He set a good example, but He also made it possible for us to attain greatness in service. He made us the recipients of His redeeming love, set us free from the chains of selfishness, and empowers us by His Holy Spirit to be faithful in our calling.

Prayer Suggestion

Pray that God will help you find joy in your life's work by serving others.

33

Living in Hope

Poets are not always happy, carefree persons. Often their hearts are heavy as they reflect on life. This was true of Sara Teasdale, born in St. Louis, Mo., August 8, 1884. Her eight volumes of verse reveal personal suffering. Her friends thought that her 1933 volume *Strange Victory* sounded a more hopeful keynote. In her poem "Grace Before Sleep" she included others in the sharing of peace and contentment at eventide.

But, alas, 1933 was also the year when her peace and hope ran out, and she took her own life in New York City.

People are far from perfect, and we ourselves have our failings, but we must cling to hope—hope springing eternal in the human breast. Hope has to have a basis; otherwise it may have a here-today-gone-tomorrow quality, as do so many human feelings.

God's love in Jesus Christ is the ground for hope. The psalmist asks himself: "Why are you cast down, O my soul, and why are you disquieted within me?" And he answers: "Hope in God; for I shall again praise Him, my Help and my God." We can say this to ourselves and to one another because God says we should, and this word of God is backed up by His action in Christ, His Son. As St. Peter writes: "Blessed be the God and Father of our Lord Jesus Christ! By His great mercy we have been born anew to a living hope by the resurrection of Jesus Christ from the dead." We have a living hope because Jesus lives.

So let us all, especially those of us who are sensitive to the problems of life as was the poetess Sara Teasdale, take heart. God is in control. We hope in His mercy and are sustained.

Prayer Suggestion

Pray that God may increase your faith, hope, and love.

When the End Is the Beginning

For many people age 65 is the end—the end of their employment. Since the job has largely determined the purpose and program of their lives, its termination is nearly synonymous with the end of life itself. But for Laura Ingalls Wilder of Mansfield, Mo., age 65 marked the beginning of the most fruitful period of her life—in fact, the beginning of a whole new life. At that age she began writing her nine books about rural life, among them *The Little House on the Prairie*. She died in 1952 at age 90.

In our relationship to God, the end of one kind of life is the beginning of another—a better—one. In apostolic times many people made the transition from a life of sinful paganism to one of piety and of service to God. As the unconverted they were "dead in trespasses and sins" (KJV). There was no spiritual life in them. But when God called them to faith in Jesus Christ, a new life began.

This happened not only in apostolic times. Take the case of John Newton, author of the hymn "Amazing Grace." In a church in England this epitaph is found: "John Newton, clerk, once an infidel and libertine, a servant of slavers in Africa, was, by the rich mercies of our Lord and Savior Jesus Christ, preserved, restored, pardoned, and appointed to preach the faith he had long labored to destroy."

Coming to the new life in Christ is just as amazing and miraculous as the resurrection of Christ from the dead. In fact, because our Lord, having atoned for sin by His death, rose again, we are enabled to become spiritually alive and will on the Last Day be raised to life eternal. If there is to be a life of holiness, it is necessary for the old sinful life to end. Its end is the beginning of a life that extends from here to eternity.

Prayer Suggestion

Pray that the Holy Spirit may through the Gospel lead you to the new, worthwhile, fruitful life in Christ.

Righteousness Exalts a Nation

After a seemingly strong bell tower in Venice fell with one mighty crash—fell because for years unseen insects had bored through the timbers—Edwin Markham wrote the poem "The Hidden Adversary." He feared that likewise "senate and citadel and school and shrine" could fall because the termites of greed, ease, and all their "crawling progeny" were at work.

The writer of Proverbs declares: "Righteousness exalts a nation, but sin is a reproach to any people." This applies not only to open and obvious crimes but also to secret sins—to hypocrisy in high places, to white-collar greed and dishonesty, to laziness and indifference of all sorts, to the I-don't-want-to-get-involved attitude that lets evil-minded people take over.

Markham lamented that with the crash of the tower not only a building fell, but with it a thousand years of art and architecture that a culture had produced. When a nation's civic institutions fail, more is always lost than those particular institutions. With them perish the supports of the good life, and then the good life itself. Therefore the stress needs to be on moral righteousness.

This righteousness begins with individuals. In his book *Peace of Mind* Joshua Loth Liebman wrote: "No reconstructed society can be built on unreconstructed individuals." Only when individual citizens are righteous can a nation be righteous. From the Christian perspective, righteousness comes about when people who by faith clothe themselves with the perfect righteousness of Christ practice righteousness in everyday life.

Prayer Suggestion

Pray that our country's citizens, including ourselves, grow in personal righteousness.

Patient Waiting

The main character in William Saroyan's play *The Time of Their Lives* expresses impatience: "We wait. The more and longer we wait, the less there is to wait for. We spend 23 1/2 hours out of a day waiting for a half hour of some important activity."

Waiting is part of life. We spend many hours in waiting rooms. We wait for spring, summer, fall, or winter. We wait when other persons are late for appointments.

The Bible speaks of waiting. The psalmist bids distressed people to wait patiently for the Lord. Old Testament believers waited for the promised Messiah to come. God's patience waited in the days of Noah for sinners to repent. The compassionate father in Jesus' parable waited for the prodigal son to return.

People today must wait, and you may be one of them—perhaps in a hospital. Waiting is bearable for Christians because, whatever their situation, they have something good to wait for. The restoration of health, so that we can return home and resume our daily duties—that is worth waiting and praying for.

Hope enables us to be patient, not because it is seen but, as St. Paul stresses, because it is unseen. In his Letter to the Romans he says: "If we hope for what we do not see, we wait for it with patience." Christians, in life and in death, have hope, because in their hearts they have Jesus. Jesus went the way of suffering.

"In Jesus," wrote John in the Book of Revelation, he shared "the patient endurance." Truly, Jesus, the Lamb of God, was patient and enduring amid His suffering and dying for us. From Him we receive strength to be patient. For His coming we wait! His coming now in the Word, and His coming in glory on the Last Day to take us home.

Prayer Suggestion

Pray that God grant you patience as you await His help.

The King and You

Nowadays kings and queens, as nominal heads of government, exercise only ceremonial power. But time was when kings had real authority, for better or for worse. We read of them in history and also in the Bible: Nebuchadnezzar, Pharaoh, Herod.

Kings were not the same in their power. Some were but kinglets, while others were mighty emperors. The question may arise: Who is (or was) the greatest king? Who is the king over all kings? When we think how the mightiest rulers of all ages now lie in dust along with their fallen empires, it is evident that the answer to "Who is the greatest?" cannot be sought among mortal men.

The title "King of kings and Lord of lords" belongs to God. In the Bible we read that it is borne by both God the Father and God the Son. St. Paul refers to the former as "the blessed and only Sovereign, the King of kings and Lord of lords, who alone has immortality." According to the Book of Revelation Jesus Christ bears this title also, for St. John writes of His enemies: "The Lamb will conquer them, for He is Lord of lords and King of kings."

Jesus is King, but not in any political sense. His kingdom is spiritual. It has to do with His rule of grace and love in the hearts of all who believe in Him as their Savior from sin.

What is important is that you and I acknowledge Him as the King who rules over our lives. Is it hard to serve Him? The play *The King and I* is set in Bangkok, Siam, during the 1860s, and it portrays the vast cultural differences that separate King Mongkut from Anna Leonowens, the Englishwoman who had come to teach his children.

No such barriers exist between Christ and us, for He is one of us. We can confidently say: "Lord Jesus, You are my King," for we know that He loves us.

Prayer Suggestion

Ask Christ to come into your heart to fill you with His love and to guide you into all truth.

Good News to Tell

In our age of instant communication it is hard to understand why good news is sometimes so long delayed. Letters that could bring good cheer and courage to another are not written. Words of love remain unspoken, and this failure in communication leaves the other person in misery or doubt. A telephone call that could convey important information is not made. The result is unnecessary suspense and agony for someone.

It reminds us of an incident in United States history. A peace treaty ending the War of 1812 was signed in Ghent, Belgium, on Christmas Eve, 1814. But word did not get to the new world very quickly, with the result that the Battle of New Orleans was fought on Jan. 8, 1815. Hundreds of men unnecessarily lost their lives.

The outcome may not be as tragic in present-day breakdowns in communication. Yet the results can be serious. When the Christian missionary Dr. E. Stanley Jones spoke to a mother in India about the God of Christianity—the God who in love sent His Son Jesus Christ as Savior—she replied: "I always knew there had to be a God like that. Speak to my children about Him; for me you are too late."

Jesus wants the good news of salvation to be proclaimed among all nations, and in those nations He wants love shown to all in need: the sick, the poor, the despondent. The Gospel of Christ's redemption and resurrection is too precious to be kept a secret. At the empty tomb on Easter morning the angel said to the women: "Go quickly and tell His disciples that He has risen from the dead." Why should the disciples continue to mourn His death when He was alive?

You and I have all kinds of good news to tell—about favorable developments, about our changed feelings, about our love for someone, about God's love to us in Christ. Let's tell it!

Prayer Suggestion

Pray for thoughtfulness in telling others the good Word.

"I Want to Be Me"

In an age of the regimented life, when personal names give way to numbers, it is understandable why many people are heard to say: "I am my own man, my own woman," "I want to do my own thing," "I want to be me." For many, a highly individualized life-style ensues.

Now indeed God wants you to be you. He does not want you to try to be someone else, for that would make you a mindless imitator, an impersonator, a copycat. You have to be you, a unique person. The TV commercial of an insurance company stated, "There's nobody else like you." This is true. God made you that way—unique, distinctive, with talents all your own. You have no exact duplicate; even so-called identical twins are distinctive.

What is more, when God made you, when He redeemed you, reclaiming you through the atoning merit of His Son Jesus Christ, He entered into an I-You relationship with you. Even now He sends the Holy Spirit to create faith in you and constantly makes you a new creation in Christ. This faith is yours. No one but you can be saved through this faith. With every gift of God to you goes personal responsibility, with judgment passing on to you—not to somebody else—for its misuse. Yes, in God's sight you are you. He planned it that way.

When we serve the Lord Jesus Christ, we do not lose our identity and individuality. On the contrary, our true self is enhanced, for we have escaped the narrow prison of self and are free to devote ourselves and all our endowments to the loving service of Jesus Christ and His people. Now you can really say, "I am me."

Prayer Suggestion

Pray that the Holy Spirit may help you to become your true self by removing everything false and by renewing you in the image of Jesus Christ.

Sharing Joys and Sorrows

Little Mary, sent on an errand, came home late for supper. When her mother asked about it, Mary said, "I met Sue along the way and saw she had a broken doll." "Did you help Sue fix her doll?" the mother volunteered. "No," Mary replied, "I helped her cry."

Without the sympathy of those near and dear to us, this world would be a cold place indeed. St. Paul urges participation in the joys and sorrows of those around us when he writes, "Rejoice with those who rejoice, weep with those who weep." We are closely knit to one another, like the members of a human body. A headache brings distress to the whole body—the whole person—not only to the head. When a stomach ulcer has healed, the whole system, not just the stomach, feels relieved.

As members of Christ's body, Christians are no different, as St. Paul points out: "If one member suffers, all suffer together; if one member is honored, all rejoice together." This is true sympathy, which means, literally, "feeling with" another.

The distresses and problems our friends experience are far more serious than broken dolls. Their home may lie in ashes after a fire. Their hearts may be broken because of a death in the family. Their lives may be shattered by a bitter divorce. We may not be able to mend the fractures, but we can be a comfort by participating in their sorrow. We can be there; we can take the edge off things by assuring them that "all things work together for good to them that love God" (KJV)—to those who place their life into the care of a God who loved them so much that He gave His own Son to die for them. Be a friend to someone who needs you!

Prayer Suggestion

Pray that God may send you as His representative to bring the good cheer and comfort of the Gospel into someone's life.

A Spiritual Heart Transplant

You would expect a man who has lost a son and a wife to assassins' bullets to be bitter and filled with the kind of hate that prompted these murders. But Dr. Martin Luther King Sr., a Christian, was not that kind of man. He said, "I carry no ill will in my heart against any man. I shall never stoop enough to hate anybody."

To forgive one's enemies is to follow in the footsteps of Jesus Christ, who prayed on the cross, "Father, forgive them; for they know not what they do."

But how can any normal, flesh-and-blood person transcend himself, overcome his natural feelings, and forgive his enemies when every fiber of his being calls for revenge, for getting even? Who is equal to our holy Lord's performance and to His instruction to us to love our enemies and pray for them?

This no one can do nor wants to do unless he or she has had a spiritual heart transplant. Those whom the Holy Spirit has led to the foot of Jesus' cross, convincing them of God's great love for them, are new creations in Christ. They are twice-born people; they have a new heart, mind, and will. They have received new power to do what to the unconverted is impossible. They can forgive not only their friends but also their enemies. They can give love for hate.

This is what the love of God can do in a person. St. Paul writes: "God shows His love for us in that while we were yet sinners Christ died for us. . . . While we were enemies we were reconciled to God by the death of His Son." Believing this with all our heart, we are both willing and able to love our enemies.

Prayer Suggestion

Pray that God may create in you a clean heart and renew a right spirit within you so that you can forgive your enemies.

Life from the River

Historians say that during a 40-year period in the 1800s there were 81 steamboat explosions on the Missouri River, causing 4,104 deaths. Rivers themselves can also be very destructive, especially when they spill over their banks and cause floods.

But rivers, despite man's pollution, are also life-giving, like the Nile in Egypt. So it is with rivers in a spiritual sense, with the water of life flowing in and through the Gospel. In a mission hymn we sing: "Blest river of salvation, Pursue thine onward way; Flow thou to every nation, Nor in thy richness stay" (*TLH*).

The river of salvation shares its richness with all who come to Jesus Christ to receive the water of grace, of forgiveness, of life everlasting. He Himself was baptized in the Jordan River to fulfill for us all righteousness. In the Sacrament of Baptism, which He instituted, He conveys to us all that He has earned on the cross. Baptism is the means through which the Holy Spirit creates and strengthens faith in Christ, the Savior.

So if you are a thirsty desert wanderer, hear this: "There is a river whose streams make glad the city of God," make glad the individual who has lost the way in the wilderness of sin. You too can be "like a tree planted by streams of water, that yields its fruit in its season." All who come to Christ receive from Him the living water that quenches the thirst of the soul and becomes in them "a spring of water welling up to eternal life."

This is God's standing offer: "Ho, everyone who thirsts, come to the waters," come to Jesus Christ, who speaks to us in the Gospel.

Prayer Suggestion

Take all your burdens to the Lord in prayer, asking Him, for Jesus' sake, to refresh you with His love.

Talking with God

We are told: "The Lord used to speak to Moses face to face, as a man speaks to his friend." Also the reverse is true: Moses spoke to God in direct, intimate terms. It was a dialog: God speaking to Moses, and Moses conversing with God in prayer.

In *Fiddler on the Roof* Tevye, the hard-pressed milkman in the Russian village of Anatevka, is accustomed to talk to God on a friendly, familiar level. At one time he wants to refer to something in the Bible, and he declares, "Lord, Your Book says—well, You ought to know; You wrote it."

God is pleased when we speak to Him in prayer as children address their beloved father or mother—with boldness and confidence, with words of simple meaning. In public worship the assembled congregation may wish to observe a kind of formality as its members come before their great King. But in private prayer we can speak to God with informal, friendly intimacy. We can say, "Abba, Father."

We have no reason to be afraid of God. Christ Jesus has taken away our sin, which had caused our estrangement from God. St. Paul tells the Ephesians: "God has destined us in love to be His sons [and daughters] through Jesus Christ, according to the purpose of His will, to the praise of His glorious grace which He freely bestowed on us in the Beloved. In Him we have redemption through His blood, the forgiveness of our trespasses."

Because we are on good terms with God through faith in His Son, we can talk to Him as we would talk to a friend. We encourage you to do this. God wants you to talk with Him, walk with Him, and remind Him that you are His own.

Prayer Suggestion

Speak now to God in your own words as you make your needs known to Him and as you thank Him for His goodness to you.

Your Welcome to Christ

Homer, who lived at about the time of Isaiah, was a great epic poet among the Greeks. It is said of him: "Seven cities claimed old Homer dead/ In which the living Homer begged his bread."

Towns and cities like to bestow honor on former residents, living or dead, *after* they have found fame and success in the world. On occasion they may plan a special homecoming celebration to say nice things to them. The folks at home like to bask in reflected glory. Supposedly the hometown is to be credited with producing an outstanding individual.

If this is so, why was Nazareth so inhospitable to its "native son" Jesus? And why did Jesus say: "No prophet is acceptable in his own country"?

Gaining a reputation in the world at large is not the same as gaining it in one's hometown. The local people are inclined to say: "This person is just as we are. We know his abilities, his circumstances, his family. Surely he can't be someone special."

Further, the people of Nazareth seemed to feel slighted because Jesus had brought fame to Capernaum and other cities by doing His mighty works there instead of in Nazareth. They overlooked that it was their unbelief that kept Jesus from proclaiming His Word and doing His deeds of love in their midst.

Unbelief always shuts the door to Christ, who in love died for us and rose again that He might share eternal life with us. His is a standing offer of grace: "Behold, I stand at the door and knock"—at your door. Do ask Him in! You'll be glad you did, for He brings many blessings.

Prayer Suggestion

Pray that the Lord Jesus may come into your heart and home with all the blessings of His love and stay with you.

The Folly of Tempting the Tempter

When in the fuel crisis of the '70s oil-exporting countries succumbed to the temptation to raise the price, a United States Senator reminded them: "The meat of the gazelle may be succulent indeed, but a wise gazelle does not boast of it to lions." To press one's luck in the face of another's misfortune is to court trouble.

Christians need always be on the lookout lest they invite trouble. They need to show great wisdom over against the devil. St. Peter compares their great spiritual enemy to "a roaring lion" who prowls around, seeking someone to devour. How foolish it would be for people to expose themselves to him unnecessarily, or to flaunt before him their virtues, good qualities, and attainments in holiness, for that would only whet his appetite. It would be tempting the Tempter.

We do well to remember what St. Paul wrote: "Let anyone who thinks that he stands take heed lest he fall. No temptation has overtaken you that is not common to man. God is faithful, and He will not let you be tempted beyond your strength, but with the temptation will also provide the way of escape, that you may be able to endure it."

Far from playing games with the devil, we are called on to "resist him," always firm in the faith. Faith in Jesus Christ, who conquered the devil by His death on the cross and announced this victory by rising from the grave, is the only sure shield against Satan. That's why St. Paul urges us to take "the shield of faith, with which you can quench all the flaming darts of the Evil One."

Prayer Suggestion

Pray that God may keep you safe against the devil's temptations by strengthening your faith in Jesus Christ.

We Are All on God's Welfare

Quite a few families, especially those living in the decaying inner cities, are on public welfare. Welfare rolls are not regarded as honor rolls. Yet people unable to work because of sickness, old age, or unavailability of jobs should not consider it a disgrace to be on welfare.

In a wider sense, we are all on welfare—God's welfare program. Everything we have comes from God. He provides daily bread through the wisdom, strength, and health He gives us for our work. He blesses our efforts. Besides food, God supplies us with clothing, shelter, fuel, medicine, water to drink, air to breath, rain, and sunshine. The psalmist exclaims: "Thou openest Thy hand, Thou satisfiest the desire of every living thing." In the final analysis it is God who supports us.

St. James includes all gifts, physical and spiritual, when he writes: "Every good endowment and every perfect gift is from above, coming down from the Father of lights."

God's greatest gift for our welfare in time and in eternity was His Son, Jesus Christ, who denied Himself to the utmost that we might have great spiritual riches. St. Paul states: "You know the grace of our Lord Jesus Christ, that though He was rich, yet for your sake He became poor, so that by His poverty you might become rich."

Thanks to Jesus Christ, our Savior from sin, we are on God's spiritual welfare program; we have the forgiveness of sins, a place in God's family, eternal life. Could we ask for more?

Prayer Suggestion

Thank God for daily bread and for your salvation in Jesus Christ, who is the Bread of Life.

God's No-Fault Insurance

Much has been said and written about no-fault automobile insurance. Under this plan, at least in smaller accident cases, each company takes care of its client's costs without trying to determine whose fault the mishap was.

How is it with our lives in general—with the things we do, the words we speak, the thoughts we think—is anyone of us ever totally without fault? Obviously not. The Bible declares: "All have sinned and fall short of the glory of God."

There was only One in this world who was altogether without fault, and that was Jesus Christ. He once challenged His enemies: "Which of you convicts Me of sin?" None did, because none could. Even Pontius Pilate, the pagan Roman official and judge, declared after his examination of Jesus: "I find in Him no fault at all."

The faultlessness of Jesus Christ is to the good of all of us, who are all guilty of sinning. Because He is the faultless, sinless Lamb of God who took on Himself the guilt and penalty of our sins, we are declared to be faultless and are free of punishment. God's law has been satisfied, for St. Paul writes: "Christ is the end of the Law, that everyone who has faith may be justified."

God Himself stands behind this offer, this guarantee, of His forgiving grace. He tells us that if we believe in His Son as our Savior, we are assured of salvation.

This is, if we want to call it that, God's no-fault insurance. It means, in the Bible's own words: "There is therefore now no condemnation for those who are in Christ Jesus." Accept Jesus as your Lord and Savior and you too, come what may, are fully covered.

Prayer Suggestion

Take your burdens, faults, and guilt feelings to the Lord in prayer, believing that for Jesus' sake you are forgiven.

"The Devil Made Me Do It"

"The devil made me do it" is a favorite line of a woman character invented by a well-known TV comedian. If, for example, the husband asks his wife why she spent so much money on a new dress, her reply is, "The devil made me do it."

In reality the line was first spoken by Eve after the sinfall. The Lord asked, "What is this that you have done?" Eve replied, "The serpent beguiled me, and I ate."

To say, "The devil made me do it" falls right into line with present-day claims that the individual is at best only partly responsible for his deeds. Having all but eliminated personal accountability, we have well rehearsed our culprits to plead that they cannot be held responsible for what they do because "drugs, drink, the bad environment, or poverty made me do it."

"The devil made me do it" is a line Jesus could have spoken, although in an altogether different sense. Why did Jesus have to go to the cross to bleed and die on our behalf? The devil made it necessary for Him to do this, because the Tempter succeeded in deceiving Adam and Eve in the Garden of Eden. While Satan's temptation did not take them off the hook, it is true that Satan did play the important role here, as St. John stresses in the words, "The devil has sinned from the beginning." He it was who led the human race into sin. Because humanity's sinfulness, the Son of God had to come from heaven to save us. Yes, the devil made Him do it.

Thank God that Jesus Christ did come to redeem us! Through His death He destroyed "him who has the power of death, that is, the devil." Now the devil can no longer make us do what pleases him.

Prayer Suggestion

Ask the Lord Jesus to draw you closer to Him, for in His presence you are safe from Satan.

Exorcise or Exercise?

In the first century A.D., God gave extraordinary power to the apostles to heal and to expel evil spirits in Jesus' name. Whether God still gives such power today to certain Christians is a much-debated question. Certainly God could do so if He so desired or deemed it necessary. Whatever extraordinary powers and gifts the Holy Spirit may bestow today, one thing is sure: They are always to be exercised in and with the saving Gospel of Jesus Christ—never apart from it. The apostles were not primarily healers or exorcists but preachers of the Gospel.

When spoken, "exorcise" is easily misunderstood as "exercise." Although they are different words, they have something in common. Exorcise means to drive out, and exercise in its root meaning denotes to drive on. There is an even closer connection, namely this: The more we exercise the power inherent in the Word and the Sacraments, the less opportunity demons will have to enter human beings.

Through the means of grace—Word and Sacraments—the lordship of Jesus Christ is established in our hearts. We belong to Him. He is our one and only Lord, for He purchased us with the price of His own blood. Through Holy Baptism we were brought to faith in Him as well as strengthened, confirmed, and sealed in this faith. We declared our allegiance to Him and at the same time renounced the devil and all his works and ways.

This is the kind of "exorcism" that takes place when we exercise ourselves in obedience to our Lord's command: "Baptize them in the name of the Father and of the Son and of the Holy Spirit." That really sends the devil packing!

Prayer Suggestion

Pray that God for Jesus' sake sends you His Holy Spirit to give you faith and love.

His Trumpet Sounded No Retreat

In a Springfield, Ill., park one can read this inscription: "I cannot conceive how a man could look up into the heavens and say there is no God." So said Abraham Lincoln, whose birthday we observe on February 12.

As a boy growing up in the country, Lincoln had many opportunities to note how God has revealed Himself in nature. But he learned much more from a higher source: the Holy Scriptures, of which he was a diligent student. He said: "I believe that the Bible is the best gift which God has ever given to men. All the good from the Savior of the world is communicated to us through this Book." His public and private utterances were replete with expressions from the Bible.

Faith in God, who spoke to him in the Bible, gave Lincoln the strength of character he needed as President during critical times. He stood on the principles of love and truth when many of his countrymen were carried away by their emotions. This is plain from his Second Inaugural: "With malice toward none; with charity for all; with firmness in the right as God gives us to see the right, let us strive on to finish the work we are in, to bind up the nation's wounds." From this commitment his trumpet never sounded retreat.

The slavery from which Lincoln wanted people to be free typifies the slavery of sin and Satan in which all people were held and from which Jesus Christ set us free. The Book that Lincoln studied and loved bears witness to this truth: "The wages of sin is death, but the free gift of God is eternal life in Christ Jesus our Lord."

Prayer Suggestion

Ask God to give you the strength that comes from rightly hearing, reading, marking, learning, and inwardly digesting the Holy Scriptures, which testify to us of Jesus Christ, our Savior.

Missing in Action?

Those in military service who are tentatively unaccounted for are called MIAs, which stands for "Missing in Action." Some MIAs will be located and found to be alive. Others, after a stipulated period, will have to be presumed dead.

Of Jesus' disciples at the time of His arrest in Gethsemane it has to be said that they were not so much missing in action as missing the action entirely. In the critical moment they all forsook Him and fled.

By and by the disciples found each other again and continued in fellowship with each other—that is, all of them except Judas Iscariot, who had hanged himself, and doubting, unbelieving Thomas. On the evening of Easter Day, when the risen Savior revealed Himself to the 10 disciples, Thomas was not there. He was unaccounted for. One might say that he was "missing in action."

This was tragic, for on that occasion Thomas missed out on the peace Christ had come to bring. He missed out on a special bestowal of the Holy Spirit as the Lord commissioned His disciples to proclaim the Gospel of the remission of sins. Thomas was not only missing *in* action; he was missing *from* the action.

We deprive ourselves of many blessings when we absent ourselves from worship services, where Christ reveals Himself in His Word. Consider how much action we miss: communion with God through Christ, instruction in the Word, consolation and inspiration from the singing of hymns, fellowship with others, and the closing benediction that sends us joyful on our homeward way.

Instead of being MIAs, it is so much better to be where God's action is—and also our action of serving Christ and His brethren.

Prayer Suggestion

Pray that you may be a disciple who follows Jesus to where the action is: His cross, where He died for you, and His empty grave, from which He rose to give you eternal life.

Violence: Cause and Cure

Violence, which so marks our modern age, is as old as the sinful human race. Cain, the first son ever to be born, resorted to violence when he killed his brother Abel. The Bible tells us that at Noah's time "the earth was corrupt in God's sight, and the earth was filled with violence." Given a human race evil at heart, it comes as no surprise that corruption should gain the upper hand and that the earth should be filled with violence.

The use of violence to gain one's end at the expense of another is clearly a sin. No excuse can be made for it. Poverty does not justify it. Injustice received, as wrongful as that is, does not sanction violence. In a limited number of cases one may have to consider extenuating circumstances, but violence, terrorism, and bloodshed can never be approved as morally permissible steps by which the individual hopes to attain his goals, however noble they may seem to be.

If violence springs from moral corruption, there can be only one effective way to overcome it, namely by removing the corruption. This kind of spiritual surgery only the Holy Spirit can perform through creating faith in the Gospel of Jesus Christ. Only He can remove the stony heart and replace it with a new heart that delights not in violence but in loving the neighbor and serving him—even if he is an enemy. That kind of love can come only from Him who first loved us and gave His Son Jesus Christ to die for us.

Violence? No. Rather this: "Love your enemies and pray for those who persecute you."

Prayer Suggestion

Give thanks for the peace God has given you in Jesus Christ, and pray that it may never be disturbed by sinful violence done *to* you or done *by* you.

Believing the Unbelievable

A respected scientist wrote: "In the world there is nothing to explain the world"—where it came from, why it is here, where it is going. We are living in a universe of mysteries.

This is so not only with respect to the vast heavenly bodies orbiting in space but also in regard to little creatures. For example, a turtle, without benefit of geography lessons or sophisticated instruments, can leave its feeding grounds off the Brazilian coast, swim 1,400 miles, and unerringly reach its destination: Ascension Island, a small speck of land halfway to Africa. How remarkable!

If so much in our natural world defies understanding, shall we reject transcendent truths in the spiritual realm?

Jesus said to Nicodemus: "If I have told you earthly things and you do not believe, how can you believe if I tell you heavenly things?" The answer is most obvious: No one can accept as true what God says in His Word unless the Holy Spirit opens the heart and mind and leads a person to faith. Thank God, we can believe and accept by faith what reason cannot comprehend.

The great truth that staggers the mind is God becoming incarnate in Jesus Christ to redeem all people from death and sin. Jesus said to Nicodemus in the same conversation: The Son of Man was to be lifted up on the cross so that "whoever believes in Him may have eternal life." To many people this seems incomprehensible and utterly fantastic. But Jesus does not ask us to figure things out with our mind. He asks us to believe in Him with our heart.

Prayer Suggestion

Ask the Spirit of God to lead you into all truth, especially the truth that Christ Jesus came into the world to turn your life around so that you may serve Him.

Hoping in God

Plutarch, an ancient Greek author, wrote: "A depressed person looks on himself as a man whom the gods hate and pursue with their anger. Now a far worse lot is before him; he dares not employ any means of averting or of remedying the evil, lest he be fighting against the gods. The physician, the consoling friends are driven away. 'Leave me,' says the wretched man, 'let me, the impious, the accursed, the hated of the gods, suffer my punishment.' Awake, he makes no use of his reason; asleep, he enjoys no repose from his alarm." So far Plutarch.

Such a person, to say the least, is in a bad way. He is compounding his troubles. St. Paul wrote about the heathen who cling to their gods, reminding the Ephesian Christians that they were once "separated from Christ . . . having no hope and without God in the world." But what a change had come into their lives, now that they were "members of the household of God, built upon the foundation of the apostles and prophets, Christ Jesus Himself being the Cornerstone!"

Far from supposing that this or that evil has struck us as a punishment for our sins—and that we dare not seek relief lest God grow still more angry with us—we are confident that for the sake of Jesus Christ all our sins are forgiven. Christ was punished in our stead. Therefore our sufferings cannot be a punishment for sin, for by faith in Christ our sins are forgiven.

God loves us, and we can come to Him in prayer with all our problems. "All things work together for good to them that love God." When troubled, we say with the psalmist: I "hope in God; for I shall again praise Him, my Help and my God."

Prayer Suggestion

Give thanks to God for His forgiveness and for His acceptance of you and your loved ones into His family.

Deeds That Outlive Us

On the day he was inaugurated as President of the United States, William Henry Harrison contracted pneumonia and died 31 days later.

Some people don't live long enough to enjoy what they have spent a lifetime to acquire. That was the case with the wealthy landowner whose fields had yielded a plentiful crop. He didn't have enough granaries to store his grain; so he planned to build larger barns, and then he would say to himself: "You have ample goods laid up for many years; take your ease, eat, drink, be merry." But that night he died. He had to leave everything behind.

Some things in life are worth achieving, however, for they follow us into eternal life. Jesus had this in mind when He said: "Lay up for yourselves treasures in heaven." And St. Paul adds to that: "If then you have been raised with Christ, seek the things that are above, where Christ is, seated at the right hand of God."

What are such things? Surely everything that makes for peace with God through faith in Jesus Christ and, as a result of that, everything that makes for peaceful living with others and that helps them find peace with God through the Gospel. What we do for the least of Christ's brothers and sisters because we love Him and them are deeds that outlive us. These deeds of faith and love Jesus will recall on Judgment Day, and He will say: "As you did it to one of the least of these My brethren, you did it to Me."

The doers of such deeds are truly blessed, although they themselves have long passed away. They shall "rest from their labors, for their deeds follow them."

Prayer Suggestion

Pray that God grant you the wisdom to choose what is good in His sight and the strength to do it.

Bread for the World's Hungry

During the Great Depression, which for some of us is an unpleasant memory and for others an unknown experience, many people had to line up at public soup kitchens and join bread lines. It was then that people fervently prayed, as Jesus directed them in the Lord's Prayer, "Give us this day our daily bread."

Bread baked in ovens is the staff of life. We usually serve it with our meals. Without it we can't make sandwiches. How delicious the aroma of freshly baked bread!

Yet bread—and this goes for all foods—cannot sustain life indefinitely. It cannot prevent death; in fact, if people overindulge in food, it can become the cause of death. Jesus reminded His hearers, according to John 6: "Your fathers ate the manna in the wilderness, and they died."

By contrast, our Lord proclaims Himself as the Bread that is both living and life-giving: "I am the living Bread which came down from heaven; if anyone eats of this Bread, he will live forever."

Christ is our *living* Lord, the eternal Son of God. As St. John wrote: "In Him was life, and the life was the light of men." He is also our *life-giving* Lord. As earthly bread gives us physical life and energy, so from Christ comes full, complete life—life in Him in this world as we believe in Him as our Savior and serve Him, and eternal life in the world to come.

Not as a phantom Christ but as One who had flesh and blood did He offer Himself up on the altar of the cross that He might give life to the world. Yes, the hungry of this world need food, but above all they need Christ, the living Bread.

Prayer Suggestion

Pray that Christ, the Bread of Life, may through His Word and Spirit satisfy your hungry, weary, restless heart.

Man Proposes, Christ Disposes

At one time in Jesus' ministry—this in an uninhabited area—there was a crowd of some 5,000 needing food. Three persons entered prominently into the situation: Philip, Andrew, and Jesus.

The first we'll call *Philip the Estimator.* When Jesus consulted Him about procuring bread for the multitude, the wheels in his mind started turning. He calculated that 200 denarii (a denarius was a day's wage for a workman) wouldn't begin to buy enough food. It is not wrong to estimate. In government, society, and the church we need businessmen, treasurers, and financial secretaries who figure costs. They shouldn't stop with a money count, however, for life is more than a matter of dollars and cents.

The second was *Andrew the Reporter.* This disciple reported, "There is a lad here who has five barley loaves and two fish." The contents of a boy's lunch bag were a sufficient means for Jesus the Almighty to feed the five thousand, but Andrew didn't realize this. He backed off from his report by adding: "But what is that among so many?" Do we not today often overlook assets at hand, thus indicating that our faith lags behind our assessment?

The third person involved in this situation was *Jesus the Provider.* He took the loaves and fish, multiplying them miraculously. With them He fully satisfied all these people, just as in another wilderness God provided manna from heaven. We need this lesson for our lives today. We may have wants and needs, tensions and troubles. But we don't despair. The Son of God went to the cross to give His life for us. He will give also the lesser blessings we need.

Prayer Suggestions

As you pray, "Give us this day our daily bread," ask God, for Jesus' sake, to bless you with everything you need to meet life's crises.

Traveling Light

Jesus sent His witnesses out two by two, both the 70 disciples and the 12 apostles. While on these missions, before our Lord's ascension and the Pentecost event, they were to live not only from hand to mouth but also from handout to mouth. They were to "take nothing for their journey except a staff; no bread, no bag, no money in their belts; but to wear sandals and not put on two tunics." They were to trust that God would provide food and lodging through the people who accepted their message.

After Pentecost the apostles again went out on a lifelong mission. Once more these messengers of Christ traveled light, as Peter remarked to a lame man at the temple who begged for alms: "I have no silver and gold." But the apostles were supplied with something far more precious than money—with the Gospel and with special power to heal the sick and to exorcise demons. They called on sinners to repent and to believe in Jesus as the only Savior from sin and death.

Every Christian does well to travel light, unencumbered by "the cares and riches and pleasures of life." Not wealth itself but the love of it is heavy baggage for life's journey, which is also a mission journey, for all Christians are Christ's witnesses in and to the world. The necessities of life, basically food, clothing, and shelter, are a sufficient ground for contentment. If God gives more, that is all the more reason to be thankful, for then we have the means with which to glorify God by helping others.

How to travel light? Get rid of life's cares and worries; you have a heavenly Father who cares. Get rid of the *love* of money, which is the root of all evil, and be a good steward over the possessions God has given.

Prayer Suggestion

Give thanks for everything God has given you, asking Him also to direct you in its right use.

Mad at God?

In his novel *The Blood of the Lamb* Peter De Vries describes the grief and rage of a widowed father whose daughter had died of leukemia. Not realizing how serious her condition was, he brought along a cake to give to her. After his daughter's death he left the hospital, took the cake and hurled it against the face of a statue of Christ in front of a nearby church.

People may be mad at God for various reasons: death in the family, bitter disappointments, a succession of failures. They had hoped and prayed for help, but all seemed to be in vain. So they hate God, and whatever anger is directed at Him strikes also Jesus Christ, His Son. So things are thrown at pictures or statues of Christ, church buildings are burned down, and Bibles are torn up.

It is, of course, nothing new for people to be angry at Christ and throw things at Him. During His life on earth His enemies several times cocked their arms to throw rocks at Him, spat in His face, beat a crown of thorns into His scalp, and nailed Him to a cross.

But let not *our* tempers flare against God when things don't seem to go right in our lives. Also in instances when it seems our hearts must break with grief, God is still with us and with those over whom we grieve. He is not hateful or indifferent toward us. He loves us—each one of us personally—with an everlasting love. He proved it when He gave up His own Son, Jesus Christ, to give up His life for our salvation. His loving arms still support us, also and especially in hours of grief.

Prayer Suggestion

When you have suffered a great loss, ask God not only to keep resentment out of your heart but also to strengthen you in the belief that all things work together for good to those who love God.

Portrait of a Righteous Man

George Washington, first President of the United States and acclaimed the father of his country, was a Christian man. Visitors at his tomb near his Mount Vernon home see these words of Jesus: "I am the Resurrection and the Life." Nearby is the grave of a relative, Judge Bushrod Washington, about whom these words are inscribed: "A sincere Christian, doing in all things the will of his Master and resting his hope of eternal happiness alone on the righteousness of Jesus Christ."

This inscription reechoes the faith of Washington, as well as the faith of another man who is a spiritual father to all believers: Abraham. Of him St. Paul writes: "Faith was reckoned to Abraham as righteousness." The righteousness of which the apostle speaks was the righteousness of Christ, the perfect righteousness, which God accepts and which is ours by faith.

But for Washington, as for Abraham, there was another kind of righteousness, a righteousness that meets the moral standards of upright people. "Civil righteousness" we call it. It forms the basis of our life together as citizens of the community, state, and nation. This righteousness, in the words of the Biblical Proverbs, "exalts a nation." It gives a country moral and spiritual strength.

As Christian citizens we honor George Washington as a righteous man—righteous in the sight of God because of his saving faith in Jesus Christ, and righteous in the sight of a moral people for his upright principles and leadership in war and peace. We honor his memory not only by naming cities after him, giving him his place in history, or celebrating his birthday, but also by walking in his footsteps.

Prayer Suggestion

Along with thanking God for giving us men like Washington, also ask God to grant us such civic leaders today.

Content for Empty Lives

Someone asked a group at Duke University why students were regularly watching a soap opera on TV. One of the students replied, "It's the only constant in our lives." Life cannot be meaningful if it has nothing more to feast on than the crumbs and fragments of human experiences offered in the frothy daytime serials.

Many people are aware of an emptiness in their lives. Women whose grown children have left home speak of an "empty nest syndrome." Such emptiness is closely related to loneliness and boredom.

It helps nothing when hollow, hungry men and women, sometimes at great expense, turn to substitutes for true soul food—to sensuous pleasure or the mad pursuit of wealth, or to alcohol or drugs. Isaiah asks, "Why do you spend money for that which is not bread?" Others, not knowing how to satisfy spiritual hunger, seek comfort in physical foods. They overeat and have weight problems. Jesus would say to them, "Man does not live by bread alone."

What content can we find for empty lives? Our Lord Jesus Christ said: "I came that they may have life, and have it abundantly." The abundant, hunger-satisfying, joyful, and purposeful life begins with the acknowledgment of the fact of sin, which separates us from fellowship with God. Realizing that only the great and merciful God who loved us in Christ can put meaning into our lives, we turn to Him for forgiveness, for the peace Christ has procured for us on the cross, and for purposefulness in life by serving Him and His brethren. Such "soul food" is available to us in great supply, as St. John wrote: "From His fullness have we all received, grace upon grace." This grace is meant for each one of us.

Prayer Suggestion

Pray that God through His Holy Spirit may lead you along the road with Jesus Christ, with whom there is an abundance of all we need: Peace with God, a place in God's family, and many opportunities for discipleship.

How to Pass the Test

The ancient Egyptians believed that a dying person had to pass a test given him by the gods before he could pass into the next life. According to the *Book of the Dead* he was to say, "I have always shunned evil; I have given bread to the hungry, water to the thirsty, clothes to the naked, a ship to the stranded; to the orphan I was a father, to the widow a husband, to the roofless I gave a home."

It is deeply ingrained in human nature to consider one's good works a passport to heaven. Jesus quotes people as saying to Him on Judgment Day,: "Lord, Lord, did we not prophesy in Your name, and cast out demons in Your name, and do many mighty works in Your name?"

If good works paved the way to eternal life, we would be our own saviors and would need no Christ. But St. Paul testifies: "Not by works of righteousness which we have done, but according to His mercy God saved us." Again, the same apostle: "We hold that a man is justified by faith apart from works of law."

Of course, faith in the redeeming, sin-forgiving merit of Jesus Christ will be active in works of love. On the Last Day Jesus will say to the believers: "Come, O blessed of My Father, inherit the kingdom prepared for you from the foundation of the world; for I was hungry and you gave Me food, I was thirsty and you gave Me drink, I was a stranger and you welcomed Me, I was naked and you clothed Me, I was sick and you visited Me, I was in prison and you came to Me." It is not by these good works that we are saved but by the faith that produces them.

How will you pass the test on Judgment Day? "Believe in the Lord Jesus, and you will be saved." This is God's own answer.

Prayer Suggestion

Pray that God the Holy Spirit may strengthen your faith in Jesus Christ, your Savior, and make it a faith that works by love.

What Is the Price on Your Head?

After some coal mine explosions in southeast Kentucky that took the lives of 26 men, some rather expensive safety measures had to be taken. These would raise the price of coal. But said one of the miners, "If it saves one man's life, it will be worth it."

Jesus sets a very high price on a human life. He asks, "What is a man profited if he shall gain the whole world and lose his own soul? Or what shall a man give in exchange for his soul?" (KJV). According to the arithmetic of Jesus, one life—one immortal soul—is worth more than the wealth of the whole world. If a man possessed billions of dollars, yes, all the riches of the universe, he could not with this price redeem himself from sin and death. How valuable is each person!

There is only one price that could be offered for each one's redemption, and that is the life of the Son of God. As St. Peter wrote: "You were ransomed . . . not with perishable things such as silver or gold, but with the precious blood of Christ, like that of a lamb without blemish or spot." Likewise St. John: "The blood of Jesus His Son cleanses us from all sin."

Two truths present themselves for our devout consideration. First, no human being, no matter how sick or poor or despised he may be, is cheap; he is precious—more valuable than all material wealth. Second, salvation is not cheap, for it cost God's Son His very life.

So, think highly of yourself, especially when you feel depressed. Think highly of the cost of your redemption: the very blood of the Lamb of God.

Prayer Suggestion

Pray that God may always keep you mindful that you were bought with a price—the blood of Jesus Christ, God's Son.

Stairway to Our Home Above

Some years back the U. S. Army ordered two-story houses built in Manila, Philippine Islands, as homes for military personnel. The carpenters had the houses built up one story, with stairways to the second floor, when it was decided that these should be only one-story houses. So it came that these units had stairways that led nowhere, only to the ceiling.

The Bible teaches that life is lived not only in this world, as though we resided in earth-hugging, one-story bungalows. There is a here and a hereafter. There is a second story: the Father's house of many mansions. What is more, God provided a stairway so that we could reach our home above. He sent His Son to endure the consequences of our sins, all the way to death on the cross. The redeeming merits of Jesus Christ were to be the means whereby all God's children could come home to Him in heaven.

But what if Jesus Christ had indeed suffered and died but had not risen again? What if there had been no hereafter for Him, but the grave in Joseph's garden had remained His final, unending resting place? Would it not follow, as far as we are concerned, that there is no resurrection, no hereafter, no heaven above? And would not God's plan of salvation be a stairway leading nowhere?

True, all this would follow. But all is changed because Christ Jesus *did* rise from the dead. And He ascended to heaven, there to prepare a place for us. In Christ we now have the one and only stairway, a true Jacob's ladder, leading us to the stars—to heaven above. Come, join us in climbing Jacob's ladder!

Prayer Suggestion

Ask that the Holy Spirit may through faith keep you in fellowship with Jesus Christ, for He is the Way to the Father.

On Whose Side Is God?

In his novel *Doctor Zhivago* Boris Pasternak tells about two soldiers, one in the Red Russian and the other in the White Russian army. While they were bitter enemies, they also had something in common. Both wore around their necks a locket containing these words of Psalm 91: "He who dwells in the shelter of the Most High . . . will say to the Lord, 'My Refuge and my Fortress; my God, in whom I trust.' " Had there been a confrontation between these two men, whose prayer for survival would God have heard? Whose life would have been spared?

Questions like this arise whenever there is a war which involves Christians on both sides. People ask, "Is God on our side?" When asked this during the Civil War, Abraham Lincoln turned the question around and said it was more important to ask, "Are we on God's side?"

Those who are on God's side—who bow to His will, believe His Word, stand on His revealed truth—have God on their side even if that fact is not at once evident.

St. Paul carries the thought further: "If God is for us, who is against us? He who did not spare His own Son but gave Him up for us all, will He not also give us all things with Him?" If God is for us, we need fear no human opposition. Toward the end of Romans 8 the apostle adds: "We are more than conquerors through Him who loved us. . . . Nothing will be able to separate us from the love of God in Christ Jesus our Lord."

Perhaps you are in conflict with someone. You ask: Is God on my side or on my opponent's side? You may not be able to answer that, but you can make sure that you are on the side of God by trusting fully in His Son Jesus Christ.

Prayer Suggestion

Pray that God may guide you, so that in every situation you may follow His will as revealed in His Word, the Holy Scriptures.

Only the One Jesus Saves

Did you know that another Jesus—besides of Nazareth—is mentioned in the Bible? Toward the close of his Letter to the Colossians, St. Paul extends greetings also in behalf of "Jesus who is called Justus." For that matter, the name occurs many times in the Bible in its Hebrew form: Joshua.

Even in our times, especially among Spanish-speaking people, "Jesus" often is a man's given name. An example is Jesus (pronounced hay-SOOS) Alou, a Christian major league baseball player.

What's in a name? In the case of Jesus Christ the answer is: A great deal, in fact, everything. The name given to the Son born of Mary was carefully chosen by God Himself. To Joseph He said in a dream: "You shall call His name Jesus, for He will save His people from their sins." The name Jesus means Savior—Savior from sin and its consequence: death.

True to His name, Jesus of Nazareth, the Son of God, came to seek and save the lost. He came to give His life a ransom for all. To Him—and to Him alone—we look for salvation, for St. Peter testifies: "There is salvation in no one else, for there is no other name under heaven given among men by which we must be saved." No other Gospel but that of Jesus Christ is the good news of our peace with God.

Who saves? Not fellow human beings and fellow sinners like Joshua of the Old Testament or Jesus called Justus in the New Testament. Only Jesus Christ is the Savior. Do you know Him? Has He entered your life?

Prayer Suggestion

Pray that for you "Jesus" may not only be a name or a word, but a real Person who blesses you with peace and forgiveness, and who wants to participate in your life.

Jesus Wept Here

"Washington slept here" is a claim made in behalf of many places visited by tourists. In the Holy Land are places where Jesus slept: in Bethlehem as a baby, in Nazareth as a youth, in Capernaum as a man. He slept in a boat during a stormy crossing of the Sea of Galilee. All of this shows that our Savior was a true man, not a make-believe human being.

As for our faith, it is even more important to know that Jesus wept here. Near Jerusalem tourists can visit a small chapel called *Dominus flevit,* which is Latin for "The Lord wept." It supposedly marks the spot where Jesus wept over Jerusalem as He said, "Would that even today you knew the things that make for peace!"

Again, the shortest verse in the Bible—John 11:35—tells us: "Jesus wept," namely at the tomb of His friend Lazarus, the brother of Mary and Martha.

The fact that Jesus wept shows that He cared, and still does! He cares deeply about sin, especially the sin of unbelief. He cared so much that He shed not only tears but also His holy, precious blood to break the hold sin has on the human race.

One who can shed tears is good to have as a friend. And that is what Jesus is to us: our best Friend, our Savior, our self-offering High Priest who, as the Letter to the Hebrews states, is able "to sympathize with our weaknesses," for He was "in every respect . . . tempted as we are." Jesus is greatly concerned about our sorrows. He can sympathize with us because He shared human feelings, including the feelings of distress and defeat.

Jesus shared all the ups and downs of our life, also death itself. Now we can share His victory as our resurrected Savior and Lord.

Prayer Suggestion

Express your prayerful gratitude to the Savior for His compassion and love as He participates in your joys and sorrows.

Thankful for Little Blessings

Richard Queen, a hostage released by the Iranians for health reasons, recalled how thankful he was when transferred from a dark basement cell to one where he could catch a glimpse of sunshine coming through a crack in the bricks.

In times of want we appreciate little blessings. A little water is precious to a thirsty desert wanderer. Air to breathe is a lifesaver to a suffocating person. A piece of bread, even without butter or marmalade, is a godsend to starving people.

Isn't it regrettable that we take so many of God's gifts for granted—those small, everyday gifts of His—becoming gratefully aware of them only when we have lost them! This applies to things like a flower, a tree, drops of rain, clean air; it applies to a few words spoken in love, a letter, a good book to read, and that increasing rarity: a morally clean movie or TV program.

God's little blessings, when strung together, become a chain of pearls. They add up to great ones. Large or small, they are given us to enjoy. We show thankfulness amid such enjoyment when we share these gifts, however unpretentious: a cup of cold water, a morsel of food, a garment—and for people's inner needs, which are just as keen: the sunshine of a smile to one in the dungeon of despair, a word of encouragement, a friendly hand on the shoulder.

Those who have learned to appreciate God's little gifts can be expected to be thankful also for His greater ones, yes, for the greatest Gift of all: His Son, Jesus Christ, "who for us men and for our salvation came down from heaven" (Nicene Creed) as the Bearer of love divine. In the words of St. Paul, we exclaim: "Thanks be to God for His inexpressible gift!"

Prayer Suggestion

Pray that God may open your eyes, mind, and heart to His many blessings and make you thankful for them.

Restored Through a Tree

In New England—and perhaps elsewhere—people often planted a tree to mark a family event: a birth, a marriage, a death. As a rule, trees outlive people, and they are therefore a continuing, living memorial.

Trees are God's gifts, providing us with fruit, shade, ornamentation, and wood for burning and building. The poet Joyce Kilmer thought that he would "never see a poem lovely as a tree." From the very beginning, human life was linked to trees.

A tree—the tree of the knowledge of good and evil—was the downfall of Adam and Eve in that they ate of its forbidden fruit. The wages of this sin of disobedience was death in the fullest sense.

But God did not permit things to stay that way. His Son, Jesus Christ, to whom St. Paul refers as the Second Adam, went to another tree—the tree of the cross—to redeem the human race from sin and the power of Satan. This thought is beautifully balanced out in the Holy Communion liturgy during Lent: God "on the tree of the cross . . . gave salvation to mankind that, whence death arose, thence life also might rise again and that he [Satan] who by a tree once overcame likewise by a tree might be overcome, through Jesus Christ our Lord."

Saved by a tree, we now serve God the way a tree serves us, that is, by yielding fruit—the fruit of the Holy Spirit: "love, joy, peace, patience, kindness, goodness, faithfulness, gentleness, self-control."

In staying close to Christ through prayer and the use of His Word, each one of us "is like a tree planted by the streams of water, that yields its fruit in its season."

Prayer Suggestion

Pray that the Holy Spirit may increase your fruitfulness in all good works.

The Serpent, a Sign of Sin and Salvation

Although only an estimated 10 to 12 people in the United States die annually of snakebites, we fear and hate snakes. The publication *Summer Safety* tells outdoor vacationers: "Leave them alone, and they won't bother you."

Our aversion to serpents is in part due to what the Bible says of them. It was as a serpent that Satan came to Adam and Eve and tempted them into sin. In the Book of Revelation Satan is called "the dragon, that ancient serpent."

While the serpent is associated with sin and Satan, it is remarkably true that it is also a symbol of salvation. While the people of Israel were en route to the Promised Land, their camp was at one time invaded by fiery, poisonous serpents, and many people perished. Then God directed Moses to fashion a bronze serpent and elevate it on a pole. The snakebite victims who looked upon this serpent survived.

In His night conversation with Nicodemus, Jesus referred to this event, saying: "As Moses lifted up the serpent in the wilderness, so must the Son of Man be lifted up, that whoever believes in Him may have eternal life." Jesus had in mind His being lifted up on the cross for the salvation of all sinners. Our Lord came back to His crucifixion reference at another time, saying: "I, when I am lifted up from the earth, will draw all men to Myself."

The cross of Christ is like a mighty magnet that draws people to the Savior. You might think it would be the other way around: people being repelled by the accursed tree of the cross. But not so. The cross has drawing power because it testifies to the love of God, who gave His own Son into death that we might live. The uplifted bronze serpent in the wilderness foreshadowed this.

Prayer Suggestion

Pray for a faith that always looks up to Jesus, the Lamb of Calvary.

Jesus, Victim and Victor

Madame Marie Curie, a physical chemist in France, and her daughter, Irene, worked on radioactive materials in the hope of finding—among other things—a treatment for cancer. For this they paid a great price, for both of them died of leukemia.

Human beings often become the victims of the very enemy they seek to conquer. So we praise them for their heroism and self-sacrifice, hoping that their efforts helped to save others.

In the battle against sin and Satan, human beings, themselves sinful and thus subject to death, could not prevail. Only the sinless Son of God, having assumed human flesh and blood as Substitute for all sinners, was capable of winning the victory. For this He had to pay the price of His own life. But He did effect salvation. Through His death He was able to "destroy him who has the power of death, that is, the devil, and deliver all those who through fear of death were subject to lifelong bondage." By becoming the Victim, Jesus became the Victor—for us.

Now we are relieved of the agony of trying to save ourselves. Indeed, "Could my zeal no respite know, Could my tears forever flow, All for sin could not atone, Thou must save, and thou alone." And Jesus did so. Now there is no need for us to undertake the "mission impossible" of do-it-yourself salvation, for Jesus Christ has already won our peace with God. We can take comfort, for by trusting in Jesus we are right with God. This is written in Scripture: "Since we are justified by faith, we have peace with God through our Lord Jesus Christ." He bids us come to Him to find rest for our souls. What other response can we give than this: "O Lamb of God, I come, I come"!

Prayer Suggestion

Start out by thanking Jesus, your dearest Friend, for laying down His life for you.

"Learn to Love Them"

It is not hard to love our friends and to return their favors. Much the same can be said about loving people who have the same cultural background that we have. But things get more difficult when we get in contact with people who are different — people on the wrong side of the railroad tracks, people who do not share our views, people whom we may consider a nuisance. A property owner inquired of an agricultural expert how to get rid of dandelions. The latter replied, tongue-in-cheek: "Learn to love them."

When applied to "undesirable" people, this is a hard lesson to learn and to translate into practice. But that is what our Lord wants us to do: Learn to love them! Jesus said: "Love your enemies and pray for those who persecute you."

What about your relation to people who at work, in community life, in school, even in church and home, get on your nerves? Learn to love them and to favor them with words and deeds that proceed from love. Love does wonders for them and for you.

Learning to love the unloved and unlovable would be difficult—in fact, impossible—without help from God. Jesus realized this, saying that when we love our enemies we are the sons and daughters of our heavenly Father. Here is where the family resemblance shows: like Father, like children! The Father "makes His sun rise on the evil and on the good, and sends rain on the just and on the unjust." What is infinitely more, He sent the Sun of Righteousness, His own Son, to die for the sins of all. He also gives us the Holy Spirit to work faith, thus engendering both the willingness and power to love others.

What about you and the people in the garden of your life who are more like dandelions than daisies—more like rogues than roses? For Jesus' sake, learn to love them!

Prayer Suggestion

Ask God to help you to love others, even your enemies.

Christ Suffered for Us

Three times a week the members of a religious group in New Mexico whip themselves on their backs with scourges of knotted cords. Why? The leader declared, "We do penance to unite ourselves to the Passion of Christ. It is as a way of seeking reparation for our sins and the sins of the world."

While the zeal of such people is great, one has to say that it is entirely misguided and mistaken. St. Paul said of a religious group of his time: "I bear them witness that they have a zeal for God, but it is not enlightened"—it is "not according to knowledge" (KJV).

The truth of the matter is that self-flagellations or other attempts at earning God's forgiveness are not only unnecessary but also sinful. They are unnecessary, for Jesus Christ has already atoned for our sins by His suffering and death. Isaiah declares: "He was wounded for our transgressions . . . and with His stripes we are healed." St. John writes: Christ "is the expiation [the satisfaction, the propitiation] for our sins, and not for ours only but also for the sins of the whole world." Christ is indeed the Lamb of God that bears the sin of the world. God does not collect twice for the same debt. He does not punish twice: His Son and His believing sons and daughters for their sins.

Not only is self-punishment for sin unnecessary, it is also sinful in that it takes away from the grace and glory of Christ as the only Savior. It is presumptuous for people ever to think that they can fully or partly do Christ's work, for that would—fully or in part—make His suffering and dying superfluous.

This is the Gospel: Christ has fully atoned for our sins. Believe this! Thank God for this! Then go and strive to sin no more.

Prayer Suggestion

Pray for the peace of mind that comes from trusting totally in the atoning work of Christ.

One for All, All for One

Since such record-keeping began in 1889, 177 mountain climbers, vacationers, and tourists are known to have lost their lives on Mount Rainier.

Jesus climbed another mount—Mount Calvary—and on it He died. But He was not the only one to lose His life there. How many more died? Perhaps something like 177? Or even 144,000? No, many, many more. In fact every sinner who ever lived, lives now, or will ever live died on Mount Calvary, because Jesus died there in everyone's place. St. Paul writes: "We are convinced that One has died for all; therefore all have died."

Jesus ascended what the Christian poet calls "Calvary's mournful mountain" to be crucified, but not for His own sake, for He committed no sin—no sin ever in thought, word, or deed—for which He needed to die. He went there as the Lamb of God who takes away the sin of the whole world, as the Substitute of all people to endure the penalty for sin: death. And since He died in behalf of all, it is in God's eyes as though all had died.

Now heaven's door is open to all—to all who believe in Jesus Christ as their Redeemer. Now all are reconciled and have peace with God. To possess it wholly and to enjoy it they need only accept salvation as God's gift. What is more, Christ died so that we might live. His climb of Mount Calvary was not a death march but a life march. The apostle declares: "He died for all, that those who live might live no longer for themselves but for Him who for their sake died and was raised." Are you alive in Him?

Prayer Suggestion

Pray that through faith in Jesus Christ you may more and more die to sin and live in Christ and for Christ, who for you died and was raised.

The Entwining Cross

"Behold, how good and pleasant it is when brothers dwell in unity!" writes the psalmist. How true! Canada's song "The Maple Leaf Forever" declares that the maple leaf entwines "the thistle, shamrock, rose"—these are the emblems of Scotland, Ireland, and England—and that "ties of love" bind all its people together, no matter where they came from. The need for people and nations to be joined together in unity is great in our time.

All the while there is a unifying factor that exceeds ethnic bonds, and that is common allegiance to God, who, in St. Paul's words, "hath made of one blood [that of Adam and Eve] all nations of men" (KJV). To bring about such an allegiance on the basis of saving faith, Jesus instructed His followers to gain other followers by proclaiming the Gospel and baptizing them in the name of the Triune God.

Our Lord wanted the Word preached to all because He died for all and rose from death. All who believe in Him as their Lord and Savior are God's children, and to one another they are brothers and sisters in the faith. The cross on which Jesus died unites and entwines them all, regardless of economic and social status, as St. John in the Book of Revelation, having seen the vision, praises Christ for having ransomed them all for God.

As Canada's maple leaf, entwining the thistle, the shamrock, and the rose, symbolizes national unity, so the cross of Calvary entwines all persons who constitute the people of God.

Prayer Suggestion

Pray that the Holy Spirit may help you so that you glory in nothing so much as the cross of Christ.

Don't Repeat the Crucifixion!

In the new Coventry Cathedral in England is a sculpture of the crucified Christ that Helen Jennings fashioned from the metal of a crashed automobile. The implication is that man crucifies man, not only in a holocaust such as destroyed the original cathedral but also on a smaller scale through careless driving.

When you consider that Christ identifies with every human being—for He loved and died for everyone—it is not far-fetched to see in the reckless, irresponsible homicide on the highways, especially when drunkenness is involved, a reenactment of Christ's crucifixion.

Our Lord is concerned about the way we deal with our fellow human beings, especially those whom the world rejects as the least but whom He honors as brothers and sisters representing Him. All people were made in God's image; their life is sacred. In the moral code given to Noah after the Flood God said: "Whoever sheds the blood of man, by man shall his blood be shed; for God made man in His own image."

How different it is when along life's highway we are the successors of the Good Samaritan, showing love and concern for the human casualties of man's inhumanity to man, be that inhumanity induced by haste or by hate!

While in a sense people do crucify Christ anew, as the poignant sculpture in the Coventry Cathedral suggests, the real crucifixion of Jesus Christ, thank God, will never be repeated. With regard to Christ's dying on the cross to save us all, the Bible says: "He did this once for all when He offered up Himself." But what happens all too often, as the writer of the Letter to the Hebrews says in another context, is that people through sinning, whether willful or careless, so to speak "crucify . . . the Son of God afresh and put Him to an open shame" (KJV). This crucifixion we must not repeat!

Prayer Suggestion

Pray that God may give you a new appreciation of human life—your own and the next person's.

Enabled to Serve

The death and resurrection of Jesus Christ are of the greatest significance for every one of us. Because He laid down His life for us, we are now both willing and able to lay down our lives for the brethren. Few of us may ever get into a position to give up our bodily lives for others. But of Aquila and Priscilla, that husband-and-wife team which helped him so much, St. Paul said that for his life they "risked their necks." Things like that may not happen to us, but we are called on often to practice self-denial and to give of our time, treasure, and talents in behalf of those who need our love. We gladly do this because Jesus did it for us.

And there is Christ's resurrection. It too has the greatest meaning for us. Because He rose from the grave fully alive, our faith is valid and full of new vigor. The risen Savior enables us, by the power of the Gospel in His Word and our Baptism, to rise daily from the deadness of sin and to "walk in newness of life."

How wonderful to be alive in Christ so that we might serve Him and all His brothers and sisters among whom we live! Had our Lord not died nor risen again, we would still be spiritual corpses. But all that is changed now, for the God of peace "brought again from the dead our Lord Jesus, the great Shepherd of the sheep, by the blood of the eternal covenant."

The Lord who was dead but now lives, as the writer of the Letter to the Hebrews goes on to say, will "provide you with every good thing you need in order to do His will." Are you alive in Christ?

Prayer Suggestion

Pray that the risen Christ may live in you and renew your life from day to day.

The Mount That Gives Life

During its 2,400 years of recorded history Mount Etna, the volcano in Sicily, has with its eruptions killed about a million people.

The Bible speaks of a mountain that kills in a spiritual sense: Mount Sinai, where amid quaking, lightning, thunder, and black smoke the law of God was given—the law that says, "You shall" and "You shall not"; the law that says, "Do this and don't do that and you will live"; the law that says, "The soul that sins shall die." And we are all sinners.

Thank God, there is another mount, a mount that gives life. While Mount Etna has taken its toll of human life with its *lava,* Mount Calvary has given, and still gives, life to millions with its *love*—the life-giving love of God in Jesus Christ. For our Lord Mount Calvary was a mount of death, but for all who believe in Him it is a mount that gives life, full life here and eternal life hereafter. Jesus said: "I came that they [His sheep, His followers] may have life, and have it abundantly." Again, in the words of Jesus: "Because I live, you will live also." Again, in the words of St. John: "In Him was life, and the life was the light of men." This life, which Christ communicates to us through His Gospel, the Good News of redemption from sin, was earned on Mount Calvary.

What is our response? We take to the hills, not to the hills of any kind of religion or religious cult, but to the only hill that can give life—Calvary, the hill that stood outside the walls of Jerusalem. The hymn writer makes plain what we mean: "My faith looks up to Thee, Thou Lamb of Calvary, Savior divine" (*TLH*).

Prayer Suggestion

Simply tell Jesus that you need Him, that you want to be in His forgiving presence, and say: "O Lamb of God, I come, I come!"

Jesus' Intercessory Prayer

In John 17 we have a long prayer of Jesus in our behalf. In His intercession, as in His total redemptive ministry, He is our High Priest, the divine Middleman, the Mediator between God and us. He speaks to the Father about our welfare.

Down through the long corridors of time Jesus sees the continuous procession of people who believe in Him because of the apostles' message. Like runners in a relay race, Christ's witnesses have handed the torch of the Gospel to generations after them. Consequently there is today a great host of Christians.

Our Lord is concerned that those coming out of "every nation and tribe and tongue and people" be one and be able to say, as the familiar hymn has it: "All one body we, One in hope and doctrine, One in charity." Such unity can come about only if we are one in God. That is surely one reason why Jesus prays: ". . . that they also may be in Us."

The perfect example of the believers' oneness with God and with one another is the union of the Father and the Son, as Jesus also says to the Father: " . . . even as Thou, Father, art in Me, and I in Thee." In John 10 Jesus declares: "I and the Father are one."

Our growth in Christian unity comes about as the Holy Spirit through the Word "gathers . . . the whole Christian church . . . and keeps it with Jesus Christ in the one true faith" (Luther). This is the continuing Pentecost in church and world, and it comes about because Jesus, our High Priest, continues to make intercession for us. This is our Lord's unfinished work, and it will continue until the last sinner has been saved. We make His prayer come true when we live day by day with Jesus.

Prayer Suggestion

Pray that you and the members of your family may remain one in Christ.

Ranks of Friends

The creatures in nature all seem to have ranks of enemies. On the Fiji Islands, for example, the enemy of copra crops is the rhinoceros beetle. The natural enemy of the larvae of this beetle is the wasp. The enemy of the wasp, in turn, is the bulbul bird.

People, too, have ranks of spiritual enemies. The common enemy is Satan, but he uses various agents, demonic and human. He tempts this one with pleasure, another with worry, another with uncontrolled temper, another with strong drir'· The devil and his demons carefully pick their targets, adjustiny their temptations to fit each individual. A high-minded scholar, for example, may not be vulnerable to greed. So the devil tempts him with fiery darts of doubt.

Christians, by the same token, have tiers of friends—their parents, first of all. They have natural brothers and sisters to support them spiritually, and these are backed up by the brothers and sisters in the faith. Beyond human friends, ranks of angels stand ready to serve us, and these are supervised by archangels, Michael and Gabriel among them. Backing them up in their friendship to us, of course, is the King of the angels, of whom we sing in a Christmas carol. He is Jesus Christ, the Son of God, who proved His love and friendship by laying down His life for our salvation. With right we sing: "What a Friend we have in Jesus, All our sins and griefs to bear." But there are two more divine Friends: God the Father, who sent His Son to redeem us, and the Holy Spirit, who supports us within.

Ranks of enemies we have, yes, but they "can harm us none" (Luther), because we are surrounded by friends and are loved by Jesus, our dearest Friend.

Prayer Suggestion

Give thanks to God for your friends: human, angelic, and divine.

The True Story of Salvation

Sir Arthur Conan Doyle, a mystery writer, invented the fictitious character, Sherlock Holmes, who represented the champion of good versus the forces of evil. When came the time to discontinue this detective, the author had him fall to his death in a mortal struggle with his enemy, Professor Moriarity, at Reichenbach, Switzerland.

A much greater death struggle took place between Jesus, the woman's Seed, and the devil, as prophecied soon after the sinfall. But this was not a fictitious combat invented by one or more Biblical writers. The participants, too, were very real.

The question is frequently asked why it was at all necessary for the Son of God to enter the cosmic arena to do battle against an enemy who can't even be seen. The answer is given by St. Paul: "Sin came into the world through sin, and so death spread to all men because all men sinned." Again, St. John: "The devil sinned from the beginning. The reason the Son of God appeared was to destroy the works of the devil."

Now, as real as sin is real, so real is salvation from sin. And as every sin is an act of evil, so is salvation God's great act of love and goodness, as the Bible states, "God shows His love for us in that while we were yet sinners, Christ died for us."

This is the Gospel—the greatest story ever told; it is not fiction, not a mystery story, but the clear revelation of God's amazing grace. You don't have to be a detective to figure it out. You never have to wonder where you fit in. When God declares that *whoever* believes in Christ has forgiveness and eternal life, then that all-inclusive word "whoever" is God's invitation to everyone. God puts you and me into His great Love Story, promising in the Scripture that He will never write us out of the script.

Prayer Suggestion

Pray that God may ever keep you in His love and make you a doer of love to others.

The Word Among Us

Samuel L. Clemens, better known as Mark Twain, was a man of many words, spoken and written. At the village of Florida, Mo., where he was born in 1835, a sign says: "He cheered and comforted a tired world." The small, two-room house in which he was born later served as a grain bin and cow shed.

A much greater impact was made by Jesus Christ, who not only spoke the Word of God to cheer and comfort a tired world; He Himself was the Word. He was born in a cattle shelter, a stable, in the little town of Bethlehem. St. John writes at the beginning of his Gospel: "The Word was made flesh and dwelt among us." As the Word, Jesus was God's message of love and salvation, of grace and truth, wrapped up in human flesh.

Jesus, the Word personified, also spoke, applied, and fulfilled the Word of God. He was the Prophet and Teacher come from God. The people heard Him gladly; they clung to His gracious words. As He expounded the Word of God, they noticed that He spoke with vigor and freshness, as one having authority, as one who knew what He was talking about. While He did preach the Law, which called for repentance, He above all cheered and comforted a tired world with the Gospel, saying: "God so loved the world that He gave His only Son, that whoever believes in Him should not perish but have eternal life."

How blessed we are to be able to hear Christ's Word and to keep it! He tells us: "The words that I have spoken to you are spirit and life." His promise holds firm: "I am with you always, to the close of the age." Books and pamphlets come and go, but His Word abides forever. It is written on human hearts.

Prayer Suggestion:

Pray that Jesus may live *with* and and *in* you with His cheering and comforting Word.

A Love That Surpasses Knowledge

When the great artist Tintoretto tried to capture the ocean on his canvas—the ocean with its power and mystery, its constantly changing moods—he said he was tempted to throw down his brushes, declaring, "The sea grows always greater; nobody can paint it."

Who can with the mind understand—and with words describe—God, who is eternal, all-knowing, all-powerful, present everywhere? The apostle exclaims, and we with him: "O the depth of the riches and wisdom and knowledge of God! How unsearchable are His judgments and how inscrutable His ways!" Even more incomprehensible is the love of God that reaches out to people to bless them when they are so undeserving! Consider the words of St. Paul: "Perhaps for a good man one will dare even to die. But God shows His love for us in that while we were yet sinners, Christ died for us."

The love of God in Jesus Christ does indeed exceed our knowledge, but we can grasp it with believing hearts. We can say "Good Lord, I cannot comprehend Your being, nor Your great wisdom and power I glimpse in Your creation of earth and sky, sea and mountains, fields and forests. Much less can I understand why You should so love me as to send Your only Son to befriend me with forgiveness, peace, life eternal. But I can and do accept these great gifts of Your love, and I hope eternity is long enough for me to sufficiently thank You!"

What Tintoretto said of the sea: It "grows always greater; nobody can paint it," we can say of God's amazing grace: It grows always greater; we cannot describe it adequately, but we can believe it, accept it, and thank God for it.

Prayer Suggestion

Ask the Holy Spirit to give you more and more insights into God's saving love in Christ.

The Bible: Guide to Eternal Life

The Swedish dramatist Johann Strindberg was given to skepticism and criticism, not only toward society but also the Christian church. As an agnostic he made himself obnoxious to many people. However, shortly before he died (in 1912) he said: "Every personal grudge is now gone; I have settled with my life; my accounts are closed. The Bible is the only true guide."

The Bible is an anvil that has worn out many a critic's hammer. The Bible is the tool with which the Holy Spirit forges and fashions living faith in the Savior Jesus Christ, and through that faith He produces fruit.

The Word of God as written in the Bible proclaims the forgiveness of our trespasses, reconciliation with God, and peace with Him in Christ. On the basis of God's forgiveness we can forgive those who trespass against us. We can say with Stringberg in his last moments: "Every personal grudge is now gone." As persons at peace with God, we are at peace with others and with ourselves.

The Bible, as the great Swedish playwright said, "is the only true guide." It leads us to an upright life, for "all Scripture is . . . profitable for teaching, for reproof, for correction, and for training in righteousness." If it is asked: "How can a young man [or anyone else, for that matter] keep his way pure?" the answer of the Bible is: "By guarding it according to Thy Word."

Even more important, the Holy Scripture is our true guide to life eternal, as the hymn declares: "How precious is the Book Divine, By inspiration given! Bright as a lamp its doctrines shine, To guide our souls to heaven." The Bible is our true guide because it bears witness to Jesus Christ, the one true Savior.

Prayer Suggestion:

Pray for the light of God's Word to shine on you and guide you along life's way.

You: A Letter from Christ

In the evening edition of a Chicago newspaper a letter was published asking for help in behalf of people in drought-stricken Madras, India. It was not a good time for such an appeal, since it was a national election night and people were listening to the returns. Yet the response to the letter was such that 38 CARE packages could be sent.

The power of letters is demonstrated even more effectively in the Bible. The apostles wrote epistles, or letters, to teach and exhort, to comfort persecuted Christians, to settle bitter disputes, to plead for victims of famines. To this day Christians throughout the world still read these divinely inspired letters and through them grow in the faith.

Quite often the most effective letters are not those that are *written* but that are *lived.* St. Paul tells the Corinthians: "You yourselves are our letter of recommendation, written on your hearts, to be known and read by all men; and you show that you are a letter from Christ delivered by us, written not with ink but with the Spirit of the living God, and not on tablets of stone but on tablets of human hearts."

How wonderfully stated! You and I who believe in Jesus as our Savior, who confess and live and practice this faith, are Christ's letters to the world. Through faith-in-action we let our light shine, so that people can visualize what Christianity is and then join us in glorifying the Father in heaven.

There are people, hidden away in many places, who may not have received mail for months, no good news, no messages of concern. But when you visit them and speak the comfort of God's Word, they are receiving a letter from Christ.

Prayer Suggestion

Pray that Christ may write His love message on your heart and help you share it with others.

Christians—God's Salt and Light

Samuel L. Clemens (Mark Twain) was not a religious man. He once asked his wife no longer to read her devotions in his presence. That makes all the more noteworthy what he said about Christian missionaries in Hawaii—people whose motives and methods others have impugned: "Missionaries have made honest men out of the nation of thieves; instituted marriage; created homes; lifted woman to the same rights and privileges enjoyed elsewhere; abolished infanticides; abolished intemperance; diminished licentiousness; given equal laws, whereby the chief's power of life and death over his subjects is taken away; in a great measure abolished idolatry; have well educated the people."

"If anyone is in Christ, he is a new creation," writes St. Paul. When you are in Christ, you have faith in His redemption in your behalf; you grow more like Him in your life. The Holy Spirit, having converted you through the Gospel, enlightens you so that you become Christ's active disciples—the salt of the earth and the light of the world. Salt is a preservative and adds zest to eating food. Light is God's gift to dispel darkness, as St. Paul tells the Philippians: "Be blameless and innocent, children of God in the midst of a crooked and perverse generation, among whom you shine as lights in the world."

Where Christians have been, there are higher moral standards. Marriage is honored. The sick and aged are cared for. Hospitals and schools are opened. The essential task of Christians is not social reform but the proclamation and application of the Gospel. Improved conditions come about as a fruit of the Gospel, and it all begins with individual Christians living their faith where they are.

Prayer Suggestion

Pray that by your acts of faith the world may become a better place in which to live.

Our Response to God's Mercy

A Serbian writer has declared, "By using our hands we become strong; by using our brains, wise; but by using our hearts, merciful." This is well said, for it stresses a priority in personal growth. Mercifulness gives proper balance to physical and mental development. But what needs to be added is the prompting and enabling force to be merciful.

Jesus, by word and deed, stressed mercifulness. He said, "Blessed are the merciful, for they shall obtain mercy." Again, "Be merciful, even as your Father is merciful." Jesus performed merciful acts when He healed the sick, cast out demons, and comforted the bereaved by raising the dead. His greatest act of mercy was performed when He laid down His life on the cross for the salvation of the whole human family.

Christ's great love is to draw a response from us, as St. Paul declares, "I appeal to you . . . by the mercies of God, to present your bodies as a living sacrifice, holy and acceptable to God, which is your spiritual worship." We use our hands to serve Him and all who need our love. We use our minds to grow in wisdom and knowledge so that we can the better worship Him. Best of all, we use our hearts so that mercifulness may prompt all we think, feel, say, and do.

We serve God with our bodies when we let our hands move at the impulse of His love; our feet as messengers of His Gospel; our voice, to sing; our lips to be filled with His messages; our intellect, to give direction to our deeds of mercy. This is serving God with our bodies. This is our response to God's mercy to us.

Prayer Suggestion

Pray for God's help for becoming more merciful in the everyday situations of life.

Only Christ Can Still Our Thirst

In 1943 a B-24 Liberator bomber apparently missed its north African base at Benghazi after a bombing raid and crash-landed deep in the Libyan desert. The crew members, having parachuted to earth, knowingly or unknowingly headed for an oasis. Although lacking drinking water, one walked 120 miles, another 111, another 80. But none of them made it; all perished.

Sometimes even Herculean efforts at survival are not enough. This is true especially in a spiritual sense. No person on earth can provide the water of life for the soul. Whatever guilt-stricken sinners may try to do to be right with God and have His forgiveness is insufficient. The hymn writer speaks for us all: "Not the labors of my hands Can fulfill Thy Law's demands; Could my zeal no respite know, Could my tears forever flow, All for sin could not atone; Thou must save and Thou alone."

What we cannot attain or obtain by our own best efforts, that God grants us freely and abundantly for Jesus' sake. Our Lord and Savior suffered for our sins, including excruciating thirst on the cross, so that we might be well supplied with the water of life. He declared: "Whoever drinks of the water that I shall give him will never thirst; the water that I shall give him will become in him a spring of water welling up to eternal life."

These words of Jesus promise not only that His Word of the Gospel will provide present relief in quenching our soul thirst, but also that it will continue to be an effective source of living water. Thus He indicated the power of the Word to sustain both faith and the assurance of salvation. How blessed it is to be refreshed by Jesus' Word!

Prayer Suggestion

Ask Jesus to quench your soul thirst with the promises of His Gospel.

On Keeping One's Spiritual Youth

In March of 1967, in eastern Canada, an 11-year-old boy (Ricky Gallant) died of "old age," a sickness known as progeria. His symptoms were those of a 90-year-old man: senility, hardened arteries, balding, wrinkled skin.

Moses wrote in Psalm 90: "The years of our life are threescore and ten, or even by reason of strength fourscore." This is more or less the expected life span of average persons, thanks to the present-day availability of proper food, rest, and medical care. As the years mount, the weaknesses of old age keep step. Clock and calendar take their toll as far as the body is concerned. "Staying young" bespeaks an attitude of the mind.

There is another dimension to keeping one's youth, and that is daily renewal and growth in Christian faith and life. The psalmist blesses the Lord for His many favors: forgiving his sins, healing his diseases, redeeming his life from destruction, crowning his life with a steady flow of love and mercy, satisfying him with good things. What is the result? The psalmist replies: "So that your youth is renewed like the eagle's."

The starting point of the Christians' continuing youth is God's forgiveness of their sins. For the sake of Jesus Christ, God cancels the sins of all who are united with the Savior by faith. Such closeness to Christ as the one who died and rose again leads to a daily "replay" of Christ's action in their lives: Every day they die to sin and rise to a new life in the likeness of Christ. This is spiritual renewal, this is the retention of spiritual youth and vigor.

Prayer Suggestion

Ask the Holy Spirit to keep you young and strong in the faith.

In Partnership with God

When astronaut teams get ready for space flights, the members carefully rehearse the work each one has to do. Cooperation is necessary also for our life together in this world, as David R. Scott, commander Apollo 15, has stated, "The earth has a crew like a spacecraft, and for the mission to be successful, the crew has to work together."

It is important that the members of Christendom work together. Christ is the Head, and Christians are the members of His body—His eyes, ears, mouth, hands, feet, and the like. The whole body is served when each member does its proper part.

But there is another kind of cooperation that St. Paul stresses. He reminds the Philippians that they have "partnership in the Gospel," and the Corinthians, that they are "workers together with God." This does not mean that people can cooperate with God in coming to faith and in effecting their salvation. The apostle shuts the door to this idea when he says in the verse immediately preceding the statement about working together with God: "For our sake God made Him [Jesus Christ, His Son] to be sin who knew no sin, so that in Him we might become the righteousness of God." A religion of salvation by good works cannot be harmonized with the religion of salvation by grace, which the Bible teaches.

But Christians do have the role of working together with God. Their faith in Jesus Christ yields fruits, and the desire to be a partner with Christ in the spreading of the Gospel is one of them. This means to be workers together with God in doing His will, in performing works of mercy, in being the heart, mouth, hands, and feet in God's behalf. Doing this, we become a crew in the spacecraft of this work, whose members not only work together with others, but together with God.

Prayer Suggestion

Pray for greater desire and skill in being God's instrument for good.

In the School of Humility

"I will tell you the secret of the true scholar. It is this: Every man I meet is my master in some point, and in that I will learn from him." So said Ralph Waldo Emerson.

What can we learn from Jesus? If you want lessons in military science, politics, or philosophy, don't go to Him. Our Lord did not come to teach in these fields. But He does have a specialty, that is, humility, and in this He is our Master Teacher. He tells us: "Learn from Me, for I am gentle and lowly in heart."

From whom could we better learn humility than from the Son of God who was born in a stable of a poor virgin? Our best Teacher? Who but the Creator and Owner of the universe, who said He had no place where to lay His head? Who but the King of the daughter of Zion who rode into Jerusalem on a mule? Who but the one whose lifeless body was taken off the cross and laid in another man's grave? Indeed, Jesus Christ, who came to be the Servant of servants in order to give His life a ransom for all sinners. St. Paul tells us that He took "the form of a servant . . . And being found in human form He humbled Himself and became obedient unto death, even death on a cross."

The school of humility in which Jesus is the Teacher is open to everyone willing to become a disciple. One becomes gentle and lowly in heart through faith in Christ as the complete Savior. Faith in Him enables us to lay aside all forms of pride and arrogance and to follow in the footsteps of Jesus. After washing the disciples' feet He said: "You call Me Teacher and Lord; and you are right, for so I am. If I then, your Lord and Teacher, have washed your feet, you also ought to wash one another's feet." He means: Serve one another.

Prayer Suggestion

Pray for a stronger faith in Jesus and for willingness to learn humility from Him.

Jesus Is Honest with Us

In *Alice in Wonderland*, Lewis Carroll has the queen pay Alice a compliment for not being able to see something. Said the queen: "Such marvelous eyesight, to be able to see nothing, and at this distance, too!"

In life, people often try to turn negatives into positives, a disability into an ability, a vice into a virtue. This creates delusion, especially in the area of religion, where positive value is often ascribed to irreligion, or moral values to immorality. And they succeed in leading others into such delusions. The sect of the Nicolaitans, of which the New Testament speaks, had people believing that the way to treat the flesh was to exhaust it with pleasure, the appealing part being that one could have all that fun while subduing the flesh—like to eat one's cake and have it, too. St. Paul writes about people who exchange the truth for a lie, and how as a judgment "God sends upon them a strong delusion, to make them believe what is false." What a false wonderland to live in!

Alice and all her brothers and sisters of all ages are truly in wonderland when they have come face to face with Jesus, who, having come from God, is the Truth and speaks the truth. In the Gospel of John especially is this fact stressed. The truth as Jesus speaks it hurts when it exposes sin and guilt. But in doing this, Jesus is honest with us. This is necessary so that we may know our need for Christ and thus welcome the healing balm of the Gospel. The truth of salvation is this, as Jesus spoke it: "God so loved the world that He gave His only Son, that whoever believes in Him should not perish but have eternal life."

To have peace with God in Christ—it's wonderful because it's true!

Prayer Suggestion

Ask the Holy Spirit to lead you into all truth as it pertains to Jesus, your Savior.

Doing the Greater Works

About the year 1907 a man from Oklahoma went to Kansas City for a roping contest. There he saw houses heated by radiators, buildings seven stories high, and the like. So in the musical named after his state he repeats the refrain: "That's about as far as they can go."

But people do keep going and doing greater works. Jesus encourages them to do this especially in their spiritual lives, and He is the one who by His great works enables us to do likewise. When the future disciple Nathanael was surprised at the things Jesus knew about him, our Lord said to him: "You shall see greater things than these." Again, when people marveled because Jesus had healed a man, He again said that "greater works" would be done. The greater works that were yet to come were His self-offering on the cross for our salvation, His resurrection, His return to the Father, His sitting at God's right hand, His sending of the Holy Spirit, and, as a work yet to be done, His coming to judgment and the ingathering of the saints.

Jesus said that those who believe in Him would likewise do works greater than they had done before, yes, some works even greater than His own. Think of our power of outreach, thanks to the media of mass communication. In one broadcast we can reach more people than Jesus reached in all His travels. Or, think of the greater opportunities we have to grow spiritually—Bible study groups in all churches.

No Christian today will take up the song of Oklahoma and say: "That's about as far as we can go." Through Christ they can do His great works, even greater ones.

Prayer Suggestion:

Ask God to make you an instrument for doing great works of love.

Increasing Your Capacity

It is said that a snail can pull nearly 400 times its own weight—the equivalent of a 10-pound baby pulling an automobile.

How much can human beings bear? Legend has it that Atlas is carrying the whole world on his shoulders. Sometimes it seems that a world of problems, pains, and griefs is resting on us. Then it would be nice, we think, if we had the capacity to pull or carry a load many times our own size. But that goes beyond the limits of human strength. Besides, we have access to something better: help from God.

To St. Paul, whose strength was depleted by a special ailment called "the thorn in the flesh," God promised: "My grace is sufficient for you, for My power is made perfect in weakness." God's grace is love that cares, compassion gone forth on an errand in our behalf, strength to compensate for our inability. It is the same love that sent His Son, Jesus Christ, into the world to do what human beings, individually and collectively, were unable to do: make them right with God through the Atonement. This love did not cease when Jesus ascended into heaven. It still issues forth, as from an inexhaustible fountain. It is there for you if you will but tap this resource by coming to God in faith and extending your hand to receive His gift.

If you are lying on a bed of sickness, or facing surgery, or experiencing family problems, or are at the end of your rope in a financial crisis, pray to God for help. You may not receive an immediate answer in keeping with your wish, but you will receive this as God's gift: a great carrying capacity.

Prayer Suggestion

Ask God to give you great endurance while burdens rest on you.

God, Developer of Persons

People who knew Winston Churchill as a boy hardly thought of him as the future prime minister of England. One who later looked back to Churchill's boyhood was his dancing teacher, who said, "I used to think he was the naughtiest boy in the world."

Similarly those who saw the boy David watching his father's sheep at Bethlehem hardly thought of him as the future king of the twelve tribes of Israel. The prophet, Samuel, did not think so either, but God told him: "The Lord sees not as man sees; for man looks on the outward appearance, but the Lord looks on the heart."

Human vision and human judgment are limited. We observe outward aspects and conduct, and draw conclusions accordingly. But God knows the heart. He knows what was, what is, and what will be. He recognizes every person's potential, and like a potter He shapes him or her as His instrument. Our Lord Jesus showed great patience with His twelve recruits, incapable as they were at first, because He foresaw their aptitude for being apostles with the help of the Holy Spirit.

God knows that you and I are sinners, with many failings even after we have come to faith in Jesus Christ. But He bears with us, helps us, guides us, teaches us, and gives us power to grow up as His sons and daughters. If someone were to ask: "God, why do You work with these people so much?" we can hear Him say: "I created them, and My Son redeemed them, not with gold or silver, but with His holy, precious blood."

Prayer Suggestion

Thank God for not giving up on you but giving you many opportunities to grow.

The Gospel: Our Tradition

Some people like change for the sake of change. A magazine publisher once wrote: "Modernists have been competing with one another in a mad rush to make the Hall of Fame in their complete break with tradition."

Every change involves a break with tradition, and sometimes that is necessary. Not all opinions, beliefs, and customs handed down by preceding generations are worth keeping. Sometimes they involve error, as St. Peter points out when he refers to the "vain conversation [way of life] received by tradition from your fathers." Likewise Stephen, told his accusers: "You always resist the Holy Spirit. As your fathers did, so do you."

But there is another concept of tradition. It refers to the faith delivered to the saints. St. Paul received this tradition of the Gospel from others: "that Christ died for our sins in accordance with the Scripture, that He was buried, that He was raised on the third day in accordance with the Scripture."

The truths of the Christian faith that others had handed over to him, these the apostle passed on, saying: "Brethren, stand firm and hold the traditions which you were taught by us, either by word of mouth or by letter."

The traditions of which St. Paul speaks are the teachings of the Gospel concerning the forgiveness of our sins through Christ. These teachings and beliefs are our permanent legacy, our precious treasure, for us to have, to use, to hold, and for us to pass on to succeeding generations. This tradition gives strength, stability, and continuity to our lives and to the lives of people coming after us.

Prayer Suggestion

Pray that God may guide you as you prove all things, keeping what is good.

An Important Little Prayer

Sometimes a little flower goes unnoticed because it stands in the shadow of a big tree.

Such is the case with a little prayer we find in Luke's gospel: "Lord, teach us to pray." It is overshadowed by the great Lord's Prayer immediately following it. In fact, it was in response to this little prayer that Jesus taught His disciples the "Our Father" prayer.

Let there be no mistake about it: the Lord's Prayer is an excellent prayer. It covers our spiritual and physical needs. It is well structured—with an introduction, a main body of seven petitions, and a conclusion, or doxology. But this should not cause us to overlook the little "sleeper" prayer tucked away at the beginning: "Lord, teach us to pray."

The disciples voiced a very proper request. They did not ask: "Lord, give us a prayer we can *recite*." Nor this: "Teach us someone else's words in which we can pray." But this: "Teach us to pray. Teach us from the Word of God and through the Spirit of God what our prayer concerns should be. Teach us by Your example in what attitude we should pray—why we can pray to God at all, pray with confidence, and pray in such a way that our own will is subordinated to the will of the heavenly Father." This prayer request Jesus answered.

Our Lord still answers us when we say to Him: "Lord, teach us to pray." He still teaches us to pray in firm confidence and in His name. He is our Redeemer, our Reconciler, who made peace with God in our behalf. This is what He tells us: "Come before your heavenly Father and simply state your requests—in your own words. Tell Him Jesus sent you."

Prayer Suggestion

Ask for the help of the Holy Spirit in directing you how to pray.

Personal Talents for the Common Good

After Marguerite Higgins of the Chicago Sun-Times returned from Communist China, she reported that people, housed in communes, were put into great work pools and often assigned to jobs indiscriminately. She wrote: "Thus a poet may be set to digging ditches, a pianist to working a small blast furnace, a farmer to making nails."

It is a waste of human talents when, as the saying goes, square pegs are forced into round holes. It is not what God, the Giver of all gifts, wants. He did not create a body demanding that people walk on their hands, see with their ears, or breathe with their livers. It isn't fair to deny the members of the body their proper function, and it isn't practical. So it is with the members of society and of the church.

God's will is that all persons function with their individual gifts for the common good. This principle applies also to the special gifts of the Spirit, as St. Paul writes: "To each is given the manifestation of the Spirit for the common good." Then he lists them: utterance of wisdom, the gift of healing, prophecy, speaking in tongues, and the like.

No less the gifts of God—although not as spectacular—are these: friendliness, musical talent, leadership, ability to counsel and console, teaching skill, to say nothing of the special knack people have with tools and utensils. As members of Christ's body, the church, Christians use—and are given the opportunity to use—these personal endowments to serve Christ and one another. Our Lord said of Himself: "The Son of Man came . . . to serve and to give His life a ransom." He did this when in our place He died to redeem us from sin. He gives us His love, so that we can begin to love as He loved us.

Prayer Suggestion

Ask God to help you use your entrusted talents more fully to glorify Him and to serve Him and one another.

A Love That Serves

In his long poem *Evangeline*, Longfellow tells the touching story of an 18th-century French girl who was separated from her lover, Gabriel, when the English moved the French colonists out of Acadia (Nova Scotia). Put on a different ship, Evangeline was never able to find her betrothed again. Finally landing in Philadelphia, she put meaning into her life by ministering to the sick and needy. Longfellow said of her: "Other hope had she none, nor wish in life, but to follow meekly, with reverent steps, the sacred feet of her Savior."

This is well stated. So often people, young and old, are deeply disappointed in love and in life. Their fondest dreams don't come true. Love is unrequited; loved ones pass out of our lives. Though we yearn to be reunited with them, this does not come to pass.

What do we do? Become drop-outs? Grow bitter and feel sorry for ourselves? Turn to drugs and drink? Evangeline shows us a better way in that she turned to a life of service. As Longfellow said, she followed meekly and reverently in the steps of her Savior. Our Lord said of Himself: "The Son of Man came not to be served but to serve, and to give His life a ransom for many." The apostle Peter says of Him: "He went about doing good and healing." He goes on to say in his First Epistle: "To this you have been called, because Christ also suffered for you, leaving you an example, that you should follow in His steps."

Not only is Jesus our Example, He is also our Enabler, giving us the willingness and strength to do as He has done, and that is to devote our lives to serving Him and His own.

Prayer Suggestion

Pray that every disappointment in life may heighten your love for Jesus.

On Saying and Doing

Saying and doing belong together. It does no good to promise a lot of things and then not carry them out. It is a commendation of character when people's words are as good as their bond. We know we can rely on what they say, for deeds will follow.

In the Book of Exodus we read about the many times when King Pharaoh of Egypt promised to let the Israelites go, only to change his mind when the plagues subsided. In his play *The Green Pastures*, Marc Connelly has Moses upbraid Pharaoh for this, telling him, "You been givin' a lot of say-so and no do-so."

Jesus knew about vacillating human nature—how good intentions often fall short of achievement. He referred to some who piously say "Lord, Lord!" but then fail to fulfill the heavenly Father's will. On another occasion He spoke of two sons whom the father wanted to work in his vineyard. One said, very politely, "I go, sir," but didn't go. The other promised nothing, in fact, he declared his unwillingness to go. But he proved better than his word. He went after all and did what the father wanted.

There is another Son—He whom the heavenly Father sent—to work in the vineyard of this world. He is Jesus Christ, who not only said He would go to serve and to give His life a ransom for all sinners, but also did it. Christians, who by adoption are likewise the sons and daughters of God, let their family resemblance show when they keep their promises—when their say-so is accompanied by their do-so.

There is a time to speak, and there is a time to do.

Prayer Suggestion

Ask for the help of the Holy Spirit to speak and do what pleases God and helps people.

Born Anew—To Grow

In many sections of the country, forestry workers remove the old pine trees and replace them with seedlings. Such places are called "regeneration areas." The forest, so to speak, is given a new birth, with new life following.

"Regeneration" is a term used also in theology, referring to spiritual conversion, to internal rebirth. The expression stems from Jesus' conversation with Nicodemus, with our Lord saying: "Unless one is born anew, he cannot see the kingdom of God . . . Unless one is born of water and the Spirit, he cannot enter the kingdom of God." The apostles pick up on this to explain the means, or media, for regeneration. St. Peter wrote: "You have been born anew . . . through the living and abiding Word of God." And St. Paul said: "God saved us . . . by the washing of regeneration and renewal in the Holy Spirit." He was referring to Baptism.

What sort of change is regeneration? It is this: the individual has had a change of heart, with the Holy Spirit turning him or her from the love of sin to faith in, that is reliance on, Jesus Christ, who by His dying and rising again redeemed us from sin and gave us the promise of eternal life. After conversion, there follows a new life—not perfection, to be sure, but a process of Christian growth.

The illustration of the renewal of a pine forest is helpful here. The old, dead wood of sin, selfishness, lust, and greed is cut away. And always new seedlings are planted, the seedlings of Christian faithfulness, hope, and love. As the seedlings grow, the forest is renewed. So it is with persons who are born anew and who throughout life are daily renewed in their personal Christianity as they live it at home, at school, at work, in community living, and in their church life.

Prayer Suggestion

Ask God to renew your faith and kindle love in your heart through His Word and Spirit.

"They Also Serve . . ."

"They also serve who only stand and wait." So said John Milton, the English poet, over 300 years ago. That saying helps put enforced inactivity into a perspective of purpose. In some periods of one's life, standing and waiting are appropriate. The important thing to be kept in mind is that persons who stand and wait are not wilful idlers. It may be part of their job. The members of a fire department are not forever fighting fires. Sometimes they seem to have nothing more to do than to play horseshoes. But they are on the job. They are there to serve when duty calls.

Perhaps your job doesn't seem interesting because you haven't enough to do. You want to be where the action is. But you are on duty, to answer the telephone or to wait on customers. We cannot always create an even flow of work. During quiet times keep in mind: "They also serve who only stand and wait."

After his conversion, St. Paul was anxious to plunge into his work as Christ's witness and missionary. But things didn't seem to work out. He met resistance, a wall of suspicion, and even outright hostility in Damascus. In Jerusalem he met the same obstacles. So he went back to Tarsus, his home town, and also spent quiet time in Arabia. St. Paul knew what it meant only to stand and wait—wait for the time when Christ would call him into active service. Then all the preparing he had done came in handy. He writes: "Christ lives in me, and the life I now live in the flesh, I live by faith in the Son of God, who loved me and gave Himself for me."

So whether you are standing and waiting or perhaps even lying on a sickbed as you recover your strength, keep in mind: "They also serve who only stand and wait."

Prayer Suggestion

Ask God for patience when life's big opportunities to serve seem to be slow in coming.

See the Whole Picture of Christ

The following anecdote, obviously fictitious, has a point worth noting. A man, accustomed to reading a chapter from the Bible before going to sleep, one night felt so tired that he decided to read only one verse. The verse that he happened upon read: "And Judas went and hanged himself." That won't do, thought the man; so he turned to another verse, which read: "Go and do thou likewise." By this time the man was convinced that he had better return to reading a whole chapter.

The lesson in a larger sense is this: Avoid "one verse" Christianity. You need to see the truths of God's Word in their larger context. Signs along a highway that say in utmost brevity: "Christ Saves," or "Christ Is Coming Again" mean something to Christians, but they lack the larger context necessary to bring a message to those who don't know Christ.

When Jesus said: "Search the Scriptures," He had in mind that we should study the whole Bible—not just a verse here and there. The whole Bible testifies of Christ, and it does so in many places. It bears witness that He is true God and true man. It declares that His blood cleanses us from all sin. It proclaims that He was given over into death on the cross for our transgressions and was raised for our justification. All these truths must be seen in a total picture, and this calls for comprehensive Bible study—not just a snatch of it here and there. That would make for piecemeal Christianity.

The Bible doesn't say everything in one verse. So we take the verses together and study them in context, so that we might grow in the grace and knowledge of our Lord Jesus Christ.

Prayer Suggestion

Pray that the Christ of the Bible reveal Himself to you in the fullness of His love.

Learning to Know Jesus Better

A rich man in France, called "the miser of Marseilles," was hated for seemingly not caring about people. But when, upon his death, his will was opened, these stipulations were found: "Poor people have trouble [getting] fresh water. I leave all my wealth to build an aqueduct." When this became known, the people hailed him as "the savior of Marseilles."

"Do not pronounce judgment before the time," St. Paul tells us. He himself had been the victim of premature judgment, and so had Jesus Christ, his Lord. One of the first disciples to be told about Jesus was Nathanael, who misjudged Him by saying: "Can anything good come out of Nazareth?" After he got to know Jesus, he said: "You are the Son of God! You are the King of Israel."

Many contemporaries of Jesus were at first offended at Him, particularly when they noted that He was poor and humble, and had no intention of setting up an earthly kingdom. By God's grace some of them, after they understood His mission and saw it fulfilled with His resurrection, believed in Him and called Him the Savior of the world.

"Judge nothing before the time" is good advice. We need to learn more of Jesus before putting Him down. We need to come to know Him as our dearest Friend. We learn of Him, as He told us, "Do not judge by appearance, but judge with right judgment." He tells us not to be quick to judge others or to ascribe wrong motives to them, as did the people of Marseilles. There is much we don't know about other people—what they are at heart, their true intentions, what good they plan to do. It is for us to withhold judgment and to give them the benefit of the doubt.

Prayer Suggestion

Pray that you may come to know Jesus better and to enjoy His love.

Living in God's Sunlight

Edgar Allen Poe, well-known author of "The Raven" and other poems, had various idiosyncrasies. For one thing, he loved the night—the only time he would go out. During the day he would stay indoors, drawing the curtains of the room and lighting candles.

Some people are fond of darkness because it covers their misdeeds, as Jesus said: "Everyone who does evil hates the light, and does not come to the light, lest his deeds should be exposed." But nothing is gained by lurking in the shadows. The Bible speaks of the works of darkness as "unfruitful."

Christians have come out of the night of sin, guilt, and fear; they live in the sunlight of God's love. Jesus, the Light of the world and the Sun of righteousness, shines on them. On Easter morning, after His rest in the grave, He arose in all His glory as living proof of His victory over sin and death. In Him, as the apostle declares, God "delivered us from the dominion of darkness and transferred us to the kingdom of His beloved Son, in whom we have redemption, the forgiveness of our sins."

How wonderful, to live openly and honestly in the light! God's people have nothing to hide; their sins are taken away, forgiven, forgotten. St. Paul reminds them: "Once you were darkness, but now you are light in the Lord; walk as the children of light!" In the light of the Gospel we all—men, women, young people, children—can grow as God's plants and bear fruit. We don't have to sit in our darkened rooms, as a morose and moody Edgar Allen Poe, but we can come out into the sunlight and enjoy ourselves, for in Jesus Christ we have peace with God, peace with fellow human beings, peace with ourselves.

Prayer Suggestion

Ask God to enlighten you, so that you may bask in the sunlight of His grace.

The Life Unending

If you have traveled in the State of Israel, you may have heard the greeting or toast: *Le-chaim!* It means, "To life!"

A this-is-the-life theme runs through the words of Jesus as recorded by St. John in his gospel. Our Lord spoke often of life, notably on how the full and abundant life in Him, who is Life Personified, is to be attained.

One long discourse of Jesus on life occurred after He had miraculously fed a multitude in the wilderness from five barley loaves and two fish. Wanting to stress that people do not live by earthly bread alone, He in the synagog in Capernaum continued the discussion on the higher life He promised to give as the Bread from heaven. This higher life could be theirs by believing in Him as the One whom God had sent for the salvation of all people to satisfy their spiritual hunger. He would give them life, and not only life for a while, but eternal life!

Every person who in his or her flesh-and-blood existence in this present world believes in Jesus Christ as Savior "has eternal life," said Jesus. He or she has it in the present tense—here and now. What is more, Jesus promises to raise him or her up on the last day. Then begins the enjoyment of everlasting life in its fullness. Now we have a foretaste of it.

Through His Word—the Word that is present also in the Sacraments of Baptism and Holy Communion—our Lord imparts and strengthens faith in the forgiveness of sins, the resurrection of the body, and the life everlasting.

Prayer Suggestion

Thank the Lord for giving you life, and ask that He may give you more of the abundant life in Him, who is the Way, the Truth, and the Life.

Believing Without Seeing

By nature all people hail from Missouri, the "Show Me" state. They quote the old adage: "Seeing is believing," or "I've got to see it to believe it." But seeing is not always believing. When Jesus Christ was here on earth in the flesh, many saw Him, heard Him, even touched Him. But that didn't lead to faith.

And, reversing the terms, believing is not always seeing, for faith can exist without sight. What St. Paul says of hope applies to faith as well: "It was by hope that we were saved; but if we see what we hope for, then it is not really hope. For who hopes for something that he sees?"

The apostle Thomas had demanded empirical, tangible proof of Jesus' resurrection. To seeing-is-believing he added touching-is-believing, for he said, "If I do not see the scars of the nails in His hands and put my finger where the nails were, and my hand in His side, I will not believe." Unless these conditions were met, Thomas said he would not believe. This was more than doubt; it was unbelief.

But on being confronted by Jesus, Thomas returned to faith. He confessed, "My Lord and my God." The risen Lord was pleased to receive him again into the company of the apostles, even as He was glad to restore Peter to his apostleship. But He comments, also for our benefit: "Do you believe because you see Me? How happy are those who believe without seeing." This believing without seeing is no delusion. It is firm faith, created by the Holy Spirit. It rests not on feelings or our senses, but on the Word of God.

You can trust this Word, for it lives and abides forever. It leads you to Jesus Christ, the Savior, who is the same yesterday, today, and forever.

Prayer Suggestion

Pray that God may grant you the vision of faith so that you may see Jesus Christ more clearly.

Hope Addicts

School children still read Joaquin Miller's poem "Columbus." It is about the first mate repeatedly coming to Columbus with questions: "Admiral, what shall we do? What shall I say to the men because of this or that hazard on the ocean? What shall we do when hope is gone?" And always the Admiral's answer is: "Sail on! Sail on! Sail on, and on!" America was discovered because Columbus and his crew would not give up.

Discouragements come often as we sail on the sea of life. At times it seems that even hope is gone—the hope of recovering serious losses, the hope of being able to finish a task, the hope of ever being able to walk again. When then? Columbus, who made it across the ocean in his three small, frail ships, would tell you: "Don't quit! Sail on, even when it seems that hope is gone!"

Hope is a flower we can pluck out of God's garden. God wants it to spring eternal in the human breast. In the Bible He brings us many messages of hope. He has the psalmist ask: "Why are you cast down, O my soul, and why are you disquieted within me?" He finds a good answer: "Hope is God; for I shall again praise Him, my Help and my God."

There is a solid foundation for the Christian's hope, and it was stated by St. Peter: "Through Jesus Christ you have confidence in God, who raised Him from the dead and gave Him glory, so that your faith and hope are in God." The situation seemed hopeless when Jesus, the sinners' Substitute, was nailed to a cross, died, and was buried. But hope was restored when the heavenly Father raised Him from the dead. Now there is hope for all of us.

Prayer Suggestion

Pray that God may renew your hope when things seem to go badly for you.

Adding Love to Justice

"Steadfast love and faithfulness will meet; righteousness and peace will kiss each other," writes the psalmist. If you want to know what this means, think of this story told by the poet Longfellow in one of his works.

A certain town was very proud of its statue of justice with its perfectly balanced scale. Elsewhere in town it happened that a servant girl was accused—and executed for—stealing a string of pearls from her mistress. By and by came a storm and knocked over the statue of justice. And what was found in one of the pans of the scale? A bird's nest, and in the nest the string of pearls. An innocent girl was executed.

We have to be careful that we don't make false accusations. Jesus had this in mind when He said: "Judge not . . . condemn not." Most instances of bearing false witness do not occur in formal courts of law, but in everyday situations in home, workshop, school, even church. In church? Yes, even there—when false motives are ascribed to church member, officer, and pastor; when a judgment is made on the basis of outward appearance; when things that somehow disappear from church premises are said to be stolen by So-and-So.

The preventive to bearing false witness is a good, healthy dose of Christian love, love that is everything that St. Paul says it is in 1 Corinthians 13, love that according to Romans 13 "does no wrong to the neighbor."

From what source does such love flow? Only from the love of God, who gave His only Son to be the Savior of all. St. John writes: "We love [God and we love one another] because He first loved us."

Justice? Yes! But let it be tempered by mercy and love.

Prayer Suggestion

Pray that only truth may dwell in your heart and cross the threshold of your lips.

Don't Let Grief Get the Best of You

Jane Pierce, wife of U. S. President Franklin Pierce, was practically a recluse in the White House. She was grieving over her son, Banny, who was killed in a train wreck. Her grief was intensified by a feeling of guilt; she imagined that she had neglected her son. In her distraught state of mind she wrote notes to her dead son, asking him to forgive her for not having loved him more.

Into everyone's life rain must fall, not only in gentle drops but sometimes in a deluge. To grieve and to show grief is a normal reaction. This is better bottling up one's sorrow.

Quite often guilt feelings are added to grief. A voice within says: "It was your fault that this happened. You didn't love enough!" Of course, all of us could have done more, loved more, cared more. But the feeling of our inadequacy should not get the best of us. What can we do?

In the midst of every adversity we have hope, because our faith is in God and in His Son, Jesus Christ. St. Paul writes: "We know that in everything God works for good with those who love Him." Jesus Christ endured the agony of death to give us the hope of everlasting life, thus removing the sting of grief and also taking away our guilt. He forgives all that we have left undone in showing love to others. God tells us through the apostle Paul that our dear departed ones are peacefully asleep in Christ, so that we do not grieve as others do who have no hope.

In the midst of grief we thank God for the comfort of His Word. When we do that, we have turned a corner; we have begun to control grief.

Prayer Suggestion

Ask your Lord to help you cope with grief by comforting you with His Word.

Amazing Grace

People close to Abraham Lincoln said he was not a practicing Christian when he first entered politics or even when he became President of the United States, nor when his son died. But he did become one when he saw all the graves at Gettysburg. After that he got up at 4 a.m. every morning to read the Bible and pray for an hour.

God often prepares people for faith through some shocking experience. He, so to speak, prepares the ground for the seed of His Word. He lets harrowing experiences enter our lives or, as the psalmist declares: "The plowers plowed upon my back, they made long their furrows." Then the Holy Spirit comes to us in the Gospel, inviting us to come to Christ, the Healer of wounds. He does even more: He takes us by the hand, leads us to the Savior, and gives us the strength to believe in Him.

St. Paul was certainly one who was shocked out of his wrong-headedness and turned around when he was converted near Damascus. After that he lived for Christ and bore witness to Him. He praised the grace of God.

John Newton, according to an inscription in one of England's famous old churches, was once an infidel and libertine, a servant of slavers in Africa, but was by the rich mercy of our Lord and Savior Jesus Christ preserved, restored, pardoned, and appointed to preach the faith he had long labored to destroy. After his conversion he wrote the hymn:

> Amazing grace! How sweet the sound
> That saved a wretch like me!
> I once was lost, but now am found,
> Was blind, but now I see.

Ever so many of us can join Abraham Lincoln, St. Paul, and John Newton in thanking God for His amazing grace.

Prayer Suggestion

Pray that every experience of life may lead you closer to Christ.

The Church Survives

Millions of people saw the televised marriage of Prince Charles to Lady Diana in historic St. Paul's Cathedral in London. The edifice occupies a site where once a pagan temple stood. In A.D. 607 King Ethelbert built a Christian church there, which burned down in A.D. 1086. Next came a cathedral that was destroyed in the great London fire of A.D. 1666. The present structure was designed by the great architect, Sir Christopher Wren.

Many ancient churches were not so fortunate as to be rebuilt. They lie in ruins, as we see them in our inner cities. But the true church lives on, as Bishop Brundtvig states in his hymn: "Built on the rock the church doth stand, Even when steeples are falling." How foolish are arsonists who, mad at God or at Christianity, set fire to church buildings! That does nothing to stop the cause and course of the Christian Gospel.

Jesus Christ is the Rock on which the church rests. He is the Cornerstone, having become the Head because He loved the church and gave Himself for it. Although ascended into heaven, He still builds and upholds the church on earth through His Word and Spirit. The truth of the Gospel is the foundation of the church, and the gates of hell cannot prevail against it.

At some future time, if the world lasts long enough, St. Paul's Cathedral in London may lie in dust. But the Gospel that St. Paul proclaimed lives on from age to age—the same Gospel you and I hear and believe today.

A metropolitan newspaper pictured a cornerstone as the only remnant of a once beautiful church that had become the victim of the headache ball. Inscribed on the cornerstone were these words from the Bible: "Behold, the tabernacle of God is with men." This is still true: God dwells among us, even when a given church has been shut down.

Prayer Suggestion

Pray that Christ may bring many more people into His church.

When Wealth Can't Help

On April 15, 1912, John Jacob Astor, one of the heirs of the great Astor fortune, went down with the luxury liner *Titanic*. A little more than three years later—on May 7, 1915—Alfred Vanderbilt, also a wealthy man, perished when the *Lusitania* was sunk. All the money in the world could not save these men from death by drowning. In that critical moment the poorest man on solid ground was better off than they.

Wealth can do many things for those who own or control it. It enabled Abraham to do much good: raise a private army to save his nephew Lot and others from the marauders, give the tithe to Melchizedek, priest of the Most High God, and practice a generous hospitality. Is it not wrong to be rich. What does matter is how riches are obtained and what one does with them later.

While wealth has its proper uses, one thing it cannot do: buy peace with God. With it we cannot purchase salvation.

There is no need for making any attempt at saving oneself that way, for Jesus Christ has redeemed us. He has paid the price, and it was not gold or silver but His holy, precious blood and His innocent suffering and death. Rich person, poor person—Jesus has paid the price for the salvation of all.

There is something we can do with our wealth, not in order to be saved but *because* we are saved: be good, responsible stewards of it, for it has been entrusted to us by God in order to glorify Him and to help the poor. Above all, we can use it for the proclamation of the Gospel in the world—the Good News that Jesus Christ has purchased and won all people from the misery of sin so that they might joyfully serve Him.

Prayer Suggestion

Pray that God may enrich you with faith in your Savior Jesus Christ.

A Compliment from God

James Boswell, well known in English literature for his accurate biography of Dr. Samuel Johnson, was less factual when writing about himself. While studying law in Holland he kept a diary, and these were some of his entries: "Yesterday you did delightfully. You did not commit one fault in any respect the whole day." Again: "Yesterday you did just as well as you could wish. Upon my word, you are a fine fellow."

These are self-congratulations, self-compliments. We find them also in the Bible. Once a young man came to Jesus, claiming to have kept all of God's commandments perfectly from childhood. He asked, "What do I still lack?" The Pharisee in the temple prayed, "God, I thank Thee that I am not like other men." Then he recited his good works, as if to say: What a fine fellow I am!

It is one thing to seem righteous and good in the eyes of people or in one's own eyes, but quite another to be righteous and good in the eyes of God. Instead of complimenting ourselves, or patting ourselves on the back for being such good people, we confess our sinfulness, put our trust in the forgiving, redeeming merit of Jesus Christ, and serve Him faithfully. Then we are giving all glory to God, as did St. Paul, who said, "By the grace of God I am what I am." Then our compliment will come from God.

Prayer Suggestion

Ask for the Holy Spirit's gifts of humility, faithfulness, and truthfulness.

On Whose Side Is Your True Self?

When Michael Faraday, the great English physicist, was a boy, he at one time thrust his head through an iron fence and wondered whether his true self were on this or on the other side of the fence.

It is a question people must often ask themselves: What side am I on? What part of me is on a given side: my head, my mind, my body, my heart? We cannot, of course, split ourselves down the middle and say: A part of me is for this cause, but the other part is for a contrary cause. Neither is it possible in the long run to straddle the important issues of life.

After many of the Israelites had worshiped the golden calf, Moses said, "Who is on the Lord's side? Come to me." And the prophet Elijah asked, "How long will you go limping with two different opinions? If the Lord is God, follow Him; but if Baal, then follow him."

It is said when the Alamo in Texas was under siege, the question of whether to fight or to surrender was settled when the commander drew a line and asked all who were for defending it to cross to his side of the line. They all did, even a wounded man who had to be carried across.

Jesus said, "No one can serve two masters; for either he will hate the one and love the other, or he will be devoted to the one and despise the other. You cannot serve God and mammon."

Thank God, the Lord Jesus did not hesitate, did not halt between two opinions, but for His last journey set His face steadfastly and resolutely toward Jerusalem, where He knew He would suffer, die, and rise again for the salvation of us all. That's why we are on His side.

Prayer Suggestion

Pray that God may give you the courage always to be on His side.

116

God's Word: True and Sure

A Chicago art dealer attended an auction in New York, where he bought an oil painting for $100. Later on an expert pronounced it an original portrait of Lucrezia Borgia painted by Bartolomeo Veneto (1486–1519). Immediately the appraised value shot up to $100,000. Much depends on whether an art work—and the money by which it is bought and sold—is authentic.

This is above all true of Holy Scripture. If it is counterfeit, it is worthless—like three-dollar bills, or play money. If it contains only human wisdom, it may have some value for the teaching of morals. But instruction in morals can be given also from the writings of Plato, or Marcus Aurelius, or Ralph Waldo Emerson. If the Bible is man's word, it belongs into the $100 category of pictures.

The proper appraisal of Holy Scripture comes only when we recognize it as the authentic Word of God written by penmen whom the Holy Spirit inspired. Because Holy Scripture is authentic, Christian missionaries can preach a sure Gospel, as did St. Paul, who writes: "We impart this in words not taught by human wisdom but taught by the Spirit."

The message of the Bible is addressed to people of all times and places in testimony of the way of salvation alone by faith in Jesus Christ, the Son of God who became man to die for the sins of the world and give people new life. "The Sacred Writings . . . are able to instruct you for salvation through faith in Christ Jesus." Also for you is the Word of God a lamp for your feet and a light to your path. Holy Scripture is the true and sure Word of the apostles and prophets.

Prayer Suggestion

Pray that you may come to know Jesus better as a true Friend.

117

What the Water of Baptism Can Do

When Jiang Qing, wife of Mao Tse-tung, and other Gang of Four members were convicted for furthering the destructive Cultural Revolution, a Communist newspaper in China stated that the "pouring out of the waters of the Yangtze River could not wash away their crimes."

It is true: the combined waters of the Yangtze, Ganges, Amazon, Mississippi, and other great rivers cannot wash away one sin. If to these waters one were to add the flood of tears shed because of sin, one would have to say with the hymn writer: "All for sin could not atone."

There is a water that can wash away sin: Holy Baptism. True, the water in itself cannot cleanse sin. But it can do it when the Word of God is added to it—the Word of the Gospel, the Word that bears witness that Jesus lived, suffered, died, and rose again for our salvation, the Word of the baptismal formula given by Jesus Himself: Baptize them in the name of the Father, and of the Son, and of the Holy Spirit.

Water from the faucet can wash away sin because through it and the added Word the Holy Spirit creates faith in hearts and minds He makes entirely new. So Christ's spokesmen testify— St. Peter on Pentecost Day: "Repent and be baptized everyone of you in the name of Jesus Christ for the forgiveness of your sins"; Ananias, a devout disciple in Damascus to Saul the Pharisee: "Rise and be baptized, and wash away your sins"; St. Paul: "God saved us . . . by the washing of regeneration and renewal in the Holy Spirit." And Christ Himself taught that by rebirth through water and the Spirit we enter God's kingdom.

Throughout life our baptism is in effect. Everyday we can draw strength from it to walk in the newness of life.

Prayer Suggestion

Pray every day that you may remain and grow in your baptismal grace.

Road or Balcony Religion?

A prominent churchman has said, "There are two kinds of religion: of the road and of the balcony."

Balcony religion means standing or sitting on an elevated place from where one can watch a parade or look on while others work. People of this type are spectators or benchwarmers, very content to let George or Georgia do the witnessing and working for Christ. The mother of James and John wanted her sons to have balcony seats—seats of honor and power—when she said to Jesus: "Command that these two sons of mine may sit, one at Your right hand and one at Your left, in Your kingdom."

The religion of the road is one of service to Christ and His people. St. Paul was "one for the road" when he became the apostle to the Gentiles. Of course, not all Christians can be traveling missionaries. So they are Christ's disciples on the highways and byways of their lives: at home, in school, at work, in the community, in church. They are doers of the Word and not hearers only. The hymn says: "If you cannot speak like angels, If you cannot preach like Paul, You can tell the love of Jesus, You can say He died for all." This is religion of the road.

To keep things in perspective: sitting in church or in Bible study groups to learn God's Word is very necessary, and of this, Mary of Bethany, who sat at Jesus' feet and heard His Word, is our example. Her sister Martha, at the time an activist in the kitchen, should have been doing this, too. Hearing, yes, but then we translate the Word into action, becoming doers of it in all aspects of Christian living. That is turning balcony religion into road religion.

Prayer Suggestion

Ask that Christ may make you a hearing *and* doing disciple.

Don't Panic!

"Gallows humor" originally meant that a person about to be hanged retained sufficient composure as to voice a joke or a bit of humor. It can prevent a feeling of panic. An injured man, trapped for seven hours under debris when portions of a Kansas City, Missouri, hotel collapsed, said when rescued: "My Timex is still running."

It is not good to go to pieces when evil strikes. How much better if with the help of God we retain self-possession! A setback does not mean that it is the end of the world for you—so don't panic! And when a real catastrophe strikes, people can render more effective help, to themselves and to others, if they keep their heads and their presence of mind.

One way to help prevent panic is to prepare for an eventuality. You plan ahead as to what you will do if such and such should happen. To be forewarned is to be forearmed.

The Bible contains much good advice about obviating panic. St. John writes, "There is no fear in love, but perfect love casts out fear." But how does one obtain that kind of love? The apostle has said earlier: "God is love, and he who abides in love abides in God and God abides in him." God extended His love to us when He gave His dear Son, Jesus Christ, to sacrifice His life so that we might be redeemed from sin and the fear of death and be enabled to live for Him—confidently, joyfully, and contentedly.

When God's love-in-Christ takes hold of you, fear must fade away. Peace with God in life and in death shuts the door to panic. "Let not your hearts be troubled; believe in God, believe also in Me," said Jesus.

Prayer Suggestion

Pray for a greater measure of the love of God that casts out fear.

Christians Are Changed People

Conversion—the act of the Holy Spirit in bringing us to faith in Jesus Christ—is an in-depth event. It changes the heart, making a believer out of an unbeliever, a friend of God out of an enemy. Conversion is regeneration, new birth.

Mere outward reform is not conversion, nor is the improvement of habits, nor the cosmetic change in the outward appearance. Skin-deep face-lifts can impress people, but not God. Scripture says: "Man looks on the outward appearance, but the Lord looks on the heart."

Civilization—the maintenance of peace and order in the community—is of the utmost importance. But it is not Christianity, for it is often a surface thing. Once after nights of burning, looting, killing, and stone throwing in England's cities, Prime Minister Margaret Thatcher said, "Civilization is a thin veneer indeed." It doesn't take much scratching of the surface to find underneath the raw impulses of human nature.

That's why Christian conversion is so necessary, not only for a better life in this world but in preparation for the life to come. It makes Christians, children of God, out of sinners. It makes for people who have peace with God because their sins have been forgiven through the redeeming work of Jesus Christ, who died that all people might live—live eternally. Writes St. Paul: "If anyone is in Christ, he is a new creation; the old has passed away, behold, the new has come."

It is a fruit of faith when improvements in our world come about. T. S. Eliot has well said: "No community can become a Christian community unless it is a community of Christians."

Prayer Suggestion:

Pray that Jesus may live in your heart and make your life genuinely fruitful.

Grounds for Joy

Sometimes, when a despondent person stands on the ledge of a tall building and threatens to jump, the crowd below, always eager for a thrill, eggs him or her on to leap to death. What a sad commentary on human nature! What a lack of regard for a human life!

It was different when a young man from St. Louis once prepared to jump from Eads Bridge into the Mississippi River. When the police and his mother had persuaded him to give up his suicide attempt, the crowd on the wharf below cheered. People were glad that he had changed his mind. They gave him a hand.

It is a little bit of heaven on earth when regard and concern for human life is shown. People who care about the well-being of a distraught person are on the side of the angels. Jesus said, "I tell you, there is joy before the angels of God over every sinner who repents."

There are grounds for joy also here on earth when someone *repents* or, as the New Testament Greek has it, changes his mind. As soul accountants, and as our brothers' and sisters' keepers, we ought to do what we can to persuade people to correct the error of their ways. And we ought to rejoice when an alcoholic decides to seek help, when a prodigal son or daughter returns home, when present-day publicans and sinners repent and turn to Jesus for salvation.

Jesus, the Friend of sinners, came to seek and to save the lost. He gave His life on Calvary's cross so that all people might turn to Him and live. His standing invitation is: "Come to Me, all who labor and are heavy laden, and I will give you rest." To that our response should be: O Lamb of God, I come, I come. And when someone else comes to Him, we ought to give that person a hand, not only in applause but in assistance.

Prayer Suggestion:

Pray that God may lead you to someone in need of your friendship.

Life's Ups and Downs

St. Paul writes, "I know how to be abased, and I know how to abound. In any and all my circumstances I have learned the secret of facing plenty and hunger, abundance and want."

Another man who knew life's ups and downs was Ulysses S. Grant. He reached high points as a winning general in the Civil War and as a two-term President of the United States. But he also had his low points: failure as a Missouri farmer and real estate man, bankruptcy in the banking and brokerage business in New York because his partner absconded with the money, unjustified implication in the Whiskey Ring Scandal of 1874, death by cancer.

Undoubtedly all of us have been on life's roller coaster. We experience a sense of euphoria and hope when things go well. Then something happens to dash our hopes and crush us to the ground. What can we do?

We go to those who have traveled the route before us and draw strength from them. Better still, we go directly to Jesus Christ, of whom the Biblical writer states: "[Look] to Jesus the Pioneer and Perfecter of our faith, who for the joy that was set before Him endured the cross, despising the shame, and is seated at the right hand of the throne of God."

Now, that is really going from the lowest to the highest point. And we can do likewise if we are united with Him and can say with the hymn writer: "My faith looks up to Thee, Thou Lamb of Calvary, Savior divine (*TLH*)." When that is our response, we can say with St. Paul, the ups-and-downs apostle: "I can do all things in Him who strengthens me."

Prayer Suggestion:

Pray for God's guidance to keep your life on even keel during times of elation and distress.

Reading the Word of God Together

The well-known writer and poet Robert Penn Warren and his wife, also an author, read to one another. They began with Homer, continued with other Greek authors, and followed that with the Bible.

Many blessings come from reading the Word. St. Paul declares that the Holy Scriptures are profitable, not only for teaching and for guidance in righteousness but, above all, for their testimony concerning salvation through faith in Christ Jesus. The Bible bears witness to our Lord's life of obedience, His self-sacrifice to save us, and His resurrection to put the seal of certainty on all His words and works. The reading of the Bible brings Christ into our hearts and homes.

St. Paul encourages us further: "Let the Word of Christ dwell in you richly, teach and admonish one another in all wisdom, and sing psalms and hymns and spiritual songs with thankfulness in your hearts to God." There is profit and benefit when an individual reads the Bible. There can be a greater blessing when two, three, or more read it together and share their insights.

Bible reading should return to our homes to strengthen marriage and family life. In his poem "The Cotter's Saturday Night," Robert Burns relates that after "the cheerful supper" the father opens the Bible. Burns goes on: "The priest-like father reads the sacred page . . . then kneeling down to heaven's eternal King, the saint, the father, and the husband prays." Of course, wife, mother, and the children pray along.

Could we have more of this in our homes today? Could you perhaps start today to read the bible together with someone else?

Prayer Suggestion:

When your family reads the Bible together, pray that God may open His Word to you and bring Christ into your heart.

It Is Never a Comedown to Serve

Once, a magazine article dealt with former United States presidents—what they do, how they can continue to serve their country. One problem is: does it seem like a comedown when those who once held the highest office in the land hold some other kind of office? The article pointed out that ex-President John Quincy Adams served nine terms in the House of Representatives, while former President Andrew Johnson later became a senator.

Other people may find themselves in similar situations. Shall former top executives take lower positions in the company? Is it a comedown for retired or unemployed persons to do work not nearly as prestigious as their former work? Is it proper for former presidents of church groups to fill offices on a lower level, or shall they rest on their laurels, remain in splendid isolation, and not serve with their talents?

This involves no great problem for Christians whose main concern is to serve. They have before them the example of Jesus Christ, whose image of servanthood is stamped on them. They know that this Jesus, who came to serve and to give His life as a ransom for all, was the Son of God with divine honor and glory in heaven, on whom the angels waited. But He did not at all hesitate to become a true human being who washed the disciples' feet. He "emptied Himself, taking the form of a servant . . . And being found in human form He humbled Himself and became obedient unto death, even death on a cross."

Because He stepped down, He was also to step up, as St. Paul continues to say: "Therefore God has highly exalted Him." The way that Jesus went is a good way for us to go.

Prayer Suggestion:

Ask God, for Jesus' sake, to show you opportunities to serve with your talents, at whatever level.

Mutual Forgiveness: The Better Way

Some children's stories contain truths that adults might well ponder. One might say they are parables. Take, for instance, Eugene Field's description of the deadly duel between the gingham dog and the calico cat: "Employing every tooth and claw in the awfullest way you ever saw . . . they ate each other up."

In most of life's battles there are no victors, only victims. Mutual destruction would most likely be the outcome if two superpowers went at each other with nuclear weapons.

The "gingham dog and calico cat" theme applies also to personal feuds, to those smaller, everyday conflicts at home, in the office or workshop, in school, even in church. St. Paul tells the Galatians: "If you bite and devour one another, take heed that you are not consumed by one another."

How wise the saying of Jesus: "Agree with thine adversary quickly," or the words of St. Paul, "Do not let the sun go down on your anger." We keep peace in the family when we exercise mutual forgiveness and say our "I'm sorry!" before we go to sleep. Surely, in the course of the day misunderstandings can arise, angry words are spoken, feelings get hurt. This happens because opinions differ, wills clash, minds (if not bodies) collide. Such hurts can become festering wounds if left unattended.

The Christian faith has resources to help clear the air and preserve harmony. It is this, in the words of St. Paul: "Be kind to one another, tenderhearted, forgiving one another, as God in Christ forgave you." In love God has acted in giving us Christ and forgiving us in Him. Now we are enabled to forgive one another—a settlement much better than that of the gingham dog and calico cat who ate each other up.

Prayer Suggestion

Ask God to give you the right words as you seek to be reconciled with someone.

The Ideal of Service

The age of chivalry is past, but we are still intrigued by the tales of King Arthur and his knights of the round table holding forth with honor, virtue, loyalty, and romance at legendary Camelot. These stories, of French origin, were assembled and refined by Sir Thomas Malory in the 15th century. Modern drama has brought them back to life.

Why this appeal? Are we, in this age of realism and technology, still capable of harboring ideals? There are indications that this is so. We sense a longing for the return of qualities that make life worth living. Many young people today want to serve. They think there is more to life than making a buck, or making all the bucks. An ad in a modern, would-be sophisticated periodical shows a young man wearing an expensive tennis shirt, and the message that goes with the picture says: "He knows what he wants, and he wants it all." This is "me-first" selfishness. Most young people have enough of Camelot in them that they reject his idea of values.

Noble ideals are no accident. The willingness to serve is not automatic with human nature. It has its roots in a creed that transcends the self. Christianity is such a creed. Jesus Christ, the Founder, declared that He had not come to be served but to serve and to render the greatest service of all by giving His life as a ransom to set people free from sin. He assumed the title Servant—that Messianic figure of whom Isaiah the prophet said, "By His knowledge shall the Righteous One, My Servant, make many to be accounted righteous; He shall bear their iniquities."

Jesus calls us, not to be lords and ladies seated around His round table, but to be disciples with high ideals, to be servants, for He Himself is our Servant-King.

Prayer Suggestion:

Ask God to give you readiness to serve, rather than wanting to be served.

Alone but Not Lonesome

Many United States homes or households consist of one person. Living alone has become a life-style for quite a few people—for singles of various kinds: young adults, widows and widowers, the aging. Living alone doesn't necessarily imply contempt for marriage and family life. For a considerable number it is seemingly God's will that they live alone. Not all are equipped—and not all have the opportunity—for domestic life. So they live by themselves in one-person homes or apartments.

Those living alone are not lonesome if they keep up their activities and interests, their work, their social life with friends, and their membership in the church as the fellowship of believers. Although they have no children of their own, they can have a deep interest in children in need of their adult love.

Needless to say, a certain potential danger attends the single life—that of self-centeredness, or of withdrawal from community life. But it need not be so. The Christian religion equips a person for a fruitful life, whether married or unmarried. For one thing, no Christian is ever really alone, for he or she has the constant friendship and companionship of Jesus Christ. The Lord has promised, "I am with you always." The person redeemed by Jesus and sanctified by His Spirit is a member of the body of Christ, receiving all the benefits that go with that: forgiveness of sins, peace with God, a purpose in life, the promise of eternal life.

With these privileges go the opportunities to share the Gospel of God's love in Jesus. There are so many openings for Christian service that no one living alone can be lonesome. If nothing else, one can pick up the telephone and call someone who is housefast. There are opportunities to call on the sick in person, to use one's skills in many fields, to write thank-you notes and letters.

Alone, yes, but not alone. Jesus said, "The Father has not left Me alone, for I always do what is pleasing to Him." This is a good formula for anyone to follow.

Prayer Suggestion

Pray that God for Jesus' sake may use you to bring blessings into the lives of fellow people.

Jesus Cast Out Demons

A Scottish prayer dating from the Middle Ages reads, "From ghoulies and ghosties and long-leggety beasties and things that go bump in the night, Good Lord, deliver us!" The exorcism formula of the ancient church said this: "I command you, unclean spirit, to go out of this servant of Jesus Christ, in the name of the Father, the Son, and the Holy Spirit."

Not so long ago people would have called demonic possession a myth. Then came a time when interest in demons revived, as witness the many movies and TV programs based on the subject.

No doubt about it: there is a devil, and demons have possessed people, as the Bible accounts show. These were called *unclean* spirits. Now, there is already much uncleanness in the human heart, the fountain of "evil thoughts, murder, adultery, fornication, theft, false witness, slander," according to Jesus. Referring to this internal rubbish, Margaret Laurence has written in *The Fire-Dwellers*: "What a lot of heavy invisible garbage we live with!" Consider the mess a person is in when in addition to all this an unclean spirit takes up residence in him or her!

The liberating, healing ministry of Jesus included the casting out of demons, and He didn't have to go through a lengthy exorcism ritual to do so, for we read: "That evening they brought to Him many who were possessed by demons, and He cast out the spirits *with a word*." That shows the superior power of Christ. The unclean spirits Jesus expelled recognized Him as the Son of God who had come "to destroy the works of the devil." Through His death on the cross Jesus destroyed "him who has the power of death, that is, the devil."

Thanks to Jesus' victory, we are delivered from all fear, including the fear of the devil. He can have no power over us.

Prayer Suggestion

Pray that the Holy Spirit may keep you close to Christ, so that the devil may not lead you into doubt.

Is Yours a Marriage Made in Heaven?

Are marriages made in heaven? Many will say, "Of course not. Marriages, like other social contracts, are made on earth. They stem entirely from human contacts and rest on mutual agreement. Consequently when the two marriage partners no longer agree, they can terminate their relationship. Only people are involved; God has nothing to do with it."

Strange, isn't it, that this should be said by people who may otherwise believe in the intervention of God in their lives, who say history is "His story." They see God's hand in world events and the affairs of society. They may agree that God keeps a sparrow from falling, for that is what Jesus said. William Cullen Bryant said to the waterfowl that God "guides through the boundless sky thy certain flight." Should God not also be recognized as guiding so important a human relationship as marriage?

Joyce Kilmer's line has it that "only God can make a tree." Many would add that God also makes the fragile violets, the lilies of the field, the green meadows. But He has nothing to do with the making of a marriage?

God told Jeremiah that he was no accident: "Before I formed you in the womb I knew you, and before you were born I consecrated you; I appointed you a prophet to the nations." But God had no part in the making of the marriage out of which Jeremiah was born?

The Lord Jesus teaches otherwise. He holds that God is not only the Maker of heaven and earth but also the Maker of a marriage, and He adds, "What God has joined together, let not man put asunder." So speaks our Savior, who in love taught us and gave His life for us.

Prayer Suggestion

Pray that Jesus Christ may strengthen your life, your marriage, your family life by dwelling in your heart and home.

When a Child Represents Christ

Our Lord's "walking seminary" in which twelve students were enrolled sometimes became a lively discussion group. On one occasion Jesus asked His disciples, "What were you discussing on the way?" The question was greeted with an embarrassing silence, for they "had discussed with one another who was the greatest."

To teach His disciples a lesson in humility, Jesus placed a child in their midst. The child, far removed from pride, pretense, and wrong ambition, personified the kind of unfeigned faith and love that should mark every disciple of Jesus, young or old.

Because such a child personifies what a loving and loyal disciple should be like, our Lord went on to say, "Whoever receives one such child in My name receives Me, and whoever receives Me, receives not Me but Him who sent Me."

The person who has a childlike—not childish—faith is our Lord's delegate, or as they say in the motion picture industry, His stand-in. Such a person represents Christ; Christ is present in that individual. What this kind of a disciple speaks is like something spoken by Christ, for He declares, "He who hears You hears Me." Not only witnessing disciples but also those in need, like orphaned children, are Christ's substitutes. Jesus said if we did good to "one of the least of these My brethren, you did it to Me."

And Jesus Christ is in turn the delegate or representative of the Father, who sent Him to be the world's Savior. To be considerate of a child and to be willing to learn from him or her is to show love to the Son and the Father. Children are not ours to do with as we please; they are "little Christs" in our midst.

Prayer Suggestion

Pray that God may give you a childlike faith and in that faith the desire to honor Jesus Christ and all who represent Him.

Children Are God's Gifts

There has been trouble for children—those little people who some day will be big people. Their first problem is: are they allowed to be born? Some, if not aborted, are abused. This can be physical mistreatment, with visible results in their little bodies. Unseen but just as real are abuses affecting minds and spirits. The breakup of marriage and the home contributes to it, as does the parental attempt to smother children with material gifts but to withhold true, personal love.

How different is family life when children are appreciated for what they are: God's gifts! The psalmist declares that children "are an heritage from the Lord." To have children around the table is to have what God meant to be a blessing. I. J. Trunk, a Yiddish writer, speaks for people in general: To be "without offspring is like a tree that shall not bloom when a new springtime comes over the world."

Jesus said; "Let the children come to Me, do not hinder them; for to such belongs the kingdom of God." Our Lord extended the fullness of His love to children. He appreciated their humility, honesty, openness. Because they are good candidates for the kingdom of God, Christ did everything necessary to bring them into it. He died for them no less than for adolescents and adults. He wants them included when the young and old of all nations are made disciples through the teaching of the Gospel and its application in Holy Baptism.

The summer of adulthood, the autumn of retirement, the winter of old age will come soon enough in our lives. Let's appreciate the springtime that the children as God's gifts bring into our world!

Prayer Suggestion:

Pray that God may alert all parents to the responsibilities and privileges of rearing children.

Should the Rod Be Retired?

Harrow school, where since 1572 English lads, including Lord Byron and Winston Churchill, were educated, made an important policy change in the 1930s: it retired the rod, it dropped corporal punishment. The custodian shows visitors a birch rod and says, "It was last used in 1937, on a boy called Dunne."

The rod has been retired in many other schools and in homes during modern times—for worse or for better. For worse, when not only the rod but *all* discipline is discarded. And the results of a no-guidance, no-correction permissiveness are all too evident in our society. On the other hand, the dropping of a corporal punishment that was loveless, physically abusive, and emotionally damaging is for the better.

The writer of Proverbs does not have that kind of punishment in mind when he declares, "He who spares the rod hates his son," for he adds, "but he who loves him is diligent to discipline him." Discipline, of which there are many forms, is necessary. But it should be administered with love and understanding, as when a father, in Martin Luther's concept, holds the rod in one hand and the apple in the other.

The love that goes with child guidance and discipline is surely the kind that has its roots in the love of God in Christ. That was a reconciling, forgiving love. It was a love that looked to the total good of undeserving sinners—a love that moved God not to spare His own Son but to deliver Him up for us all. Such a love cannot but influence for good the attitude and action of parents toward their children.

It is not love to let children grow up like weeds. It is love to cultivate children as one would precious flowers.

Prayer Suggestion

Pray that God may keep you from disciplining anyone in blind anger. Ask for help to correct others in love.

A Change of Vocation

In this day and age of change in the world of work, it is necessary for many people to leave one vocation and enter another. This is sometimes a good thing.

Long ago two sets of brothers—Peter and Andrew, James and John—were fishermen, following their vocation on the waters of the Sea of Galilee. Jesus recruited them for a new vocation when He said, "Follow Me, and I will make you fishers of men."

After Christ's ascension and the outpouring of the Holy Spirit 10 days later, the apostles were full-time missionaries. Their vocation now was to be Christ's witnesses in all the world. They were to testify that salvation from sin and death is to be found only in the crucified and risen Lord. The Gospel was the net with which to catch people for Christ.

Some Christians in our time feel constrained to quit what they are doing in order to concentrate all their energies on missions. They become full-time fishers of people. Obviously it is not our Lord's will that all should do this.

Most of Christ's disciples today continue in their roles as business executives, mechanics, farmers, teachers, secretaries, and housewives. In so doing they fulfill the overall Christian vocation of being Christ's witnesses where they live and work. They are followers of Jesus, serving Him by serving other people and helping to build His kingdom from their present vantage points. They are "catching men"—and women and children—to be Christ's disciples and the people of God. You too are recruited to be a recruiter.

Prayer Suggestion

Ask the Holy Spirit to give you the courage to become a witnessing disciple of Jesus Christ right in your neighborhood.

Becoming Truly Alive

Pygmalion, king of ancient Crete, made an ivory image of a young woman, fell in love with it, and prayed to Aphrodite to make her alive so that he could marry her. G. B. Shaw used that legend as the basis of his play *Pygmalion,* on which the musical *My Fair Lady* rests. In it Prof. Henry Higgins takes Eliza Doolittle off the streets of London and makes a lady out of her.

What about such a theme? Can a person be made over into something new? In a way, yes, for that is the general idea behind education. However, an improved mind and character do not make for a new individual. Human powers in both teacher and learner are limited.

Only a spiritual power can make a person come alive. That is what St. Paul asserts: "If anyone is in Christ, he is a new creation"—not an improved or outwardly reformed person but an entirely new one, for the apostle adds: "The old has passed away, behold, the new has come." St. Paul should know; he himself went through such an experience. A hater of Christ and persecutor of Christians, he was converted and became the foremost advocate of Christianity in his time. That is what conversion or regeneration is all about—it is being born again, as Jesus said to Nicodemus: "Unless one is born anew . . . born of water and the Spirit, he cannot enter the kingdom of God."

All people are by nature dead in trespasses and sins. Through the Gospel, that is, the good news that Christ has redeemed them from the guilt, power, and penalty of sin, they are made spiritually alive. The Gospel of Christ can do that, for it is the power of the Holy Spirit unto salvation to all who believe it.

"Believe it"—that's all that is necessary to become a new creation in Christ. Believe it!

Prayer Suggestion

Pray that the Holy Spirit may make you over into the image of Jesus, your dearest Friend.

Tell a Vision

King Nebuchadnezzar of Babylon had a vision that, he believed, conveyed a divine message. What did it mean? Sending for Daniel, he told him, "Tell me the vision of my dream." Daniel explained what it meant. The king would be greatly humbled. He would dwell with the beasts of the field and eat grass like an ox. This, said Daniel, is what God meant to say through the vision.

Daniel was a man of great wisdom. In his youth he had been handpicked to receive special training. Young Daniel responded to his opportunity, becoming a man of great understanding and having the special gift of interpreting visions. When Nebuchadnezzar called for him, he was able to tell the vision.

The prophet Joel looked to Pentecost and the time after, saying, "Your young men shall see visions," and for that matter, tell God's visions. But many youths today go for another kind of "tell a vision," namely, TV. By the time an average student has graduated from high school he or she will have spent 14,000 hours in school, but 15,000 hours before the television set. They make TV less than a good thing for themselves when they let it keep them from self-development through learning.

Nothing so broadens a person, widens his horizons, and deepens his understanding than the Word, the means through which God communicates with us today. The Word of the Gospel imparts the highest knowledge, making us wise unto salvation through faith that is in Jesus Christ, the Savior. If you want to find this Word, turn to the Holy Scriptures. It gives you a new vision of life and a happiness you will want to share with others as you, like Daniel, tell a vision.

Prayer Suggestion

Ask God to lead you into all truth, especially the truth that Christ died for you to make you His own.

The Church Is a Ship

We find many ship stories in the Bible. We read about Noah's ark, about storms overtaking fishing boats on the Sea of Galilee, about St. Paul involved in a shipwreck. A ship is a means of transportation. It carries passengers to their destinations.

The Christian church is like a ship and in Christian art is often represented by a ship. The church consists of many members—people who through the ages make the voyage from this world to heaven. At the helm is Jesus Christ, who in one of the New Testament books is called the captain of salvation, because He gave His life in order to give life to His church. Because He is in charge, we can pray: "Jesus Savior, pilot me Over life's tempestuous sea."

As a ship is supplied with maps and charts, especially with a logbook, so the church has a book for the guidance of its members: the Bible. St. Paul says of this book, the Holy Scripture: "It instructs you for salvation through faith in Christ Jesus." And the psalmist tells us that we can never get lost on the sea of life if we take heed to the Word of God.

Many opinions and judgments have been expressed about the church. Some think of it as a ghost ship. Some try to describe Christians aboard this ship by borrowing the title of Katherine Anne Porter's book *Ship of Fools*. This is not new. Some people mocked Noah when he built his ark. St. Peter comes back to this ship built by Noah and declares that eight people were saved by it *from* the Flood water. So, he continues, God has provided a means whereby sinners are saved *by* the water—by the water of Baptism which the church administers.

Yes, the church is like a ship. It is good to be aboard!

Prayer Suggestion

When perplexed, ask the Savior Jesus Christ to give you guidance from the chart and compass of His Word.

Unity of the Faith

People don't always agree in areas where opinion prevails. Tastes differ in many things—in art, for example. Today many consider the Mona Lisa by Leonardo da Vinci, an outstanding painting. It was insured for $100,000,000 when it toured the United States. But the husband of Mona Lisa, one Francesco del Giocondo, didn't like the painting at all and refused to pay for it.

How is it with the Christian religion? Are its teachings just a matter of opinion and taste? Can a person page through the Bible and select only what he or she likes, as we do when we go through a cafeteria line? If so, then the humorist wasn't so far off base when he said: "There are so many changes in religion today that someone's thinking of putting out a Bible in loose-leaf."

Of course, everyone realizes that this would be impractical. Nor is it right. Christianity could not exist if people would read their own likes and dislikes into the statements of the Bible. St. Peter declares in his Second Epistle: "You must understand this, that no prophecy of Scripture is a matter of one's own interpretation, because no prophecy ever came by the impulse of man, but men moved by the Holy Spirit spoke from God."

Things are not as difficult as they may seem. All we need to do is to take the Word of God as it reads, without any prejudice or malice. What comes across is that all people are sinners and that Jesus Christ, by His dying on the cross and His rising again, is their Savior.

The Holy Spirit is at work in those who hear or read God's Word with an open mind and heart. From Him comes the unity of faith, and with it the persuasion, yes, conviction, that Christ is our dearest Friend. On this all Christendom agrees.

Prayer Suggestion

Pray that the Holy Spirit may reveal Christ to you as you study God's Word.

Physical and Spiritual Hunger

It has been estimated that every minute 28 people in the world die of hunger, of whom 21 are children. In the past five years more people have died of hunger than did people in all wars and revolutions in the past 150 years.

The problem is complex. More needs to be done than just giving food. Long-range planning is needed. The population explosion in countries already overcrowded is a factor. Another is better methods of food production and food distribution. All these problems need attention as we provide food. God tells us through the prophet Isaiah what He desires: "Is it not to share your bread with the hungry, and bring the homeless poor into your house; when you see the naked, to cover him, and not to hide yourself from your own flesh?" This puts helping the hungry on a personal basis.

Jesus re-echoed these words when He puts Himself into the picture of hungry and needy persons, saying to the righteous: "I was hungry and you gave Me food; I was thirsty, and you gave Me drink . . . As you did it to one of the least of these My brethren, you did it to Me."

People around us suffer from another kind of hunger and thirst—that of the soul. In human beings body and soul are so closely knit together that people suffer unless both the physical and spiritual hunger and thirst are satisfied. The psalmist exclaims: "As a hart longs for flowing streams, so longs my soul for Thee, O God." People cannot be truly happy unless they are right with God and live in fellowship with Him. Their hunger and thirst after righteousness is satisfied when through faith in Jesus Christ, who died to save them, they have peace with God. This peace they have because by faith Christ's righteousness is credited to them.

Prayer Suggestion

Pray that God opens your heart and hands to share your blessings with the needy.

The Bible, Our Reliable Guide

After an expedition through the Great Plains, which constituted the heartland of the Louisiana Purchase of 1803, Stephen Long reported: "In regard to this extensive section of the country, I do not hesitate in giving the opinion that it is almost wholly unfit for cultivation and, of course, uninhabitable by people depending upon agriculture for their subsistence." This area, however, turned out to be our breadbasket.

We have to face the fact that people, even experts, can give wrong opinions. Business leaders sometimes make errors in judgment. Doctors are not always correct in their diagnoses. Battles are lost because of a general's miscalculations.

It would be strange indeed if the field of religion were exempt. Some religious leaders have been embarrassed when they set a definite date for the Lord's return but nothing happened. Many people in our time have put blind faith in healers and cult leaders, only to be led like sheep to the slaughter. That was the case when hundreds of cultists in Guyana committed mass suicide in obedience to their leader.

St. John has good advice: "Beloved, do not believe every spirit, but test the spirits to see whether they are of God, for many false prophets have gone out into the world." The early Christians in the Macedonian city of Berea show us how to test the spirits: "They received the Word with all eagerness, examining the Scriptures daily to see if these things were so."

The Old and New Testament Scriptures, given by inspiration of God, are the basis for determining whether a proclaimed teaching may be accepted as true. These same Scriptures bear witness to Jesus Christ as the Son of God who came in the flesh to save us by His holy life, His atoning death, and His glorious resurrection.

Prayer Suggestion

Pray that God through His Holy Spirit may open to you the Scriptures and lead you to the saving Christ.

God Keeps an Eye on Us

After she had come to faith in Jesus, the gifted singer Ethel Waters loved to sing about how God was watching over her as He watches over the sparrows.

Jesus said, "Are not two sparrows sold for a penny? And not one of them will fall to the ground without your Father's will." In St. Luke's account Jesus indicated that a better deal could be made by buying in quantity: "Are not five sparrows sold for two pennies?"

Sparrows abounded in the vicinity of the temple and on the Mount of Olives—two places where Jesus and His disciples had often been. Like today, sparrows were not only of little value but also numerous. Yet they are God's creatures, and in His providence the heavenly Father keeps an eye on them. We are to be certain that God is watching over us, for He made us and in Christ redeemed us. God knows all about us, even the number of hairs on our heads.

Of course, sparrows, like people, have enemies. In his book *The Tin Drum* Gunter Grass describes a man who shot sparrows for pastime. The curious, seemingly contradictory thing about him was this: when he had completed his shooting, he would reach into his coat pocket for bird food and feed the survivors. The enemy who hunts people—the devil, that is—does not show kindness along with his cruelty. Therefore we need to pray that the heavenly Father would protect us from him. And God will certainly do that.

We know this is so, for in Jesus Christ God has already granted us the greatest of all gifts, as St. Paul points out: "He who did not spare His own Son but gave Him up for us all, will He not also give us all things with Him?"

He certainly will!

Prayer Suggestion

Ask God to strengthen your faith in His promise that He will protect and provide for you.

God Gives Us Things to Do

Alexander the Great in the fourth century before Christ was a great conqueror. The far-flung Persian empire fell to him, as did other lands. At age 32 he is said to have wept because there was nothing more to conquer.

There may be people today who have fulfilled all their ambitions and find nothing more to do, but their number is few. A farmer, having harvested his crop, has other things to do: fences to fix, buildings to paint, livestock to tend. A housewife's work is never done, and this is especially true if she has an outside job and a family to look after. In an office or workshop we always find things to do.

Having plenty to do is good medicine. Retired people are best off if they stay involved, not only in recreational or pastime activities but also in volunteer work in church and community projects. This puts purpose into life.

"Things to do" refers to activities beyond work done with our hands. It can refer to things we say—to good words. It can be writing and reading. It can be—*should* be, in fact—such spiritual acts as studying the Bible, praying and worshiping, working and witnessing for Christ as His disciples.

Jesus always had things to do: preaching, teaching, healing the sick, comforting and counseling on a one-to-one basis. He knew that soon the night would come when no one can work. So He made the opportunities of the day count.

The greatest thing Jesus did was to reconcile the whole world of sinners to God. He became our Substitute, obeyed God's law for us, died for us and rose again, that He might earn for us the righteousness in which we can be clothed by faith.

Prayer Suggestion

Ask God to show you things to do and give you the ability to do them.

Kings and Queens in God's Sight

When Prince Charles of England was four years old, it was reported that his parents were trying to bring him up as a normal boy. That resulted in his thinking for awhile that all children were princes and princesses, and that everyone's mother was a queen.

According to Holy Scripture all God's children are kings and queens. St. John the Divine dedicates his New Testament book, Revelation, "Unto Him that loved us, and washed us from our sins in His own blood, and hath made us kings and priests unto God and His Father" (KJV). This tells us how Jesus Christ, the King of kings and Lord of lords, made us kings and queens: He washed us from our sins with His blood and put on us the royal robe of His righteousness.

St. Peter tells his readers that they are a "royal priesthood," repeating what God had said to His Old Testament people through Moses: "You shall be to Me a kingdom of priests."

It is an honor, a distinction, a privilege to be royalty in God's sight. But this is no ground for pride, for an obligation is entailed. Rights in life are always accompanied by responsibilities; these are the two sides of a coin. It will not do for kings and queens to live scandalous lives. People want to look up to them. So it is with Christian royalty. These kings and queens are to be an example to others. What is more, they are a royal priesthood that serves, in the footsteps of our great High Priest and King, Jesus Christ, who came not to be served but to serve and to give His life a ransom for all.

As kings and queens, God's people are a credit to Him when they hallow His name, further His kingdom, and do His will on earth as angels do it in heaven.

Prayer Suggestion

Thank God for having called you to be a king or queen who serves Him and His people.

"Defend Me from Myself"

Michelangelo was a famous painter and sculptor, best known for his ceiling painting in the Sistine Chapel and his statues of David and Moses. He was also a poet, and as such expressed his inner feelings. In one of his poems, which was really a prayer, he stated, "Defend me from myself."

The Bible gives us portraits of people who were their own worst enemies. King Saul in the Old Testament might well have prayed, "Defend me from my own temper, depression, and jealousy." Another Saul—the one who became the apostle Paul might have prayer: "Lord, keep me from the false zeal that drives me to persecute Christians." Even after his conversion he had the problem of his alter ego, the dark side of his character, which caused him to exclaim: "I do not do the good I want, but the evil I do not want is what I do."

We are our own enemies when we work against our own best interests. It is as though a contrary will is built right into us. It is as though another voice within us—perhaps the voice of lust and greed and hate—outshouts the voice of conscience. Those who rob with a gun, or who as white-collar thieves juggle the ledgers to their own supposed advantage, know that they can get caught and be sentenced to jail. But they do it anyway. They are their own enemies; they cannot shift the blame on other people, on society, or on their environment.

So we pray with Michelangelo: "Defend me from myself. Keep me from being my own enemy. Instead let me be a true friend to myself by believing in Jesus, whose blood cleanses me from all sin, and by living according to the love of God proclaimed in the Gospel. For I know, Lord, that when I am in Your presence, I am safe."

Prayer Suggestion

Ask the Holy Spirit to overrule all evil impulses and fill you with love for God.

Jesus Knows Your Troubles

Talk about a man having troubles! In 1946 Arshile Gorky, an Armenian artist, had a fire that destroyed his studio and its contents. It was also that year that he learned he had cancer. One could understand why in 1947 he depicted his personal tragedy in a painting entitled "Agony." But there was more to come. In 1948 he broke his neck in an auto accident. The saddest event of all that year was his suicide.

Everybody experiences trouble, although not in the same measure. Rich people have available to them whatever money can buy. But money cannot buy everything. It cannot buy happiness in the home, health, inward peace, or escape from death.

The poor, too, have troubles: how to pay for food, clothing, the fuel used up in a cold winter, the education of their children. A man who struggled with these problems said, "The trouble with poverty is that it takes up so much of your time."

Rich, poor, and people in-between—the song applies to many among them: "Nobody knows the trouble I've seen." The man of the Bible who suffered so much, Job, said: "Man is born to trouble, as the sparks fly upward."

But there is One who knows, One who can turn things around: Jesus Christ. What a Friend we have in Him, for He bears all our sins and griefs. Our sins He bore long ago when, once for all, He as the Lamb of God went to the cross to set us free from them. All our griefs He continues to bear if we but believe in Him and ask His help. He invites us: "Come to Me, all who labor and are heavy laden, and I will give you rest." Take Him up on that promise!

Prayer Suggestion

Ask God to turn your troubles into experiences that glorify Him and benefit you.

From Fear to Faith

The Meramec Caverns in central Missouri, discovered in 1716 by Jacques Renault of Kaskaskia, Ill., were a shelter to early lead and iron miners. Blacks seeking freedom in the North used them as a station in the so-called "underground railroad."

Caves are mentioned in the Bible, usually as places of refuge. The prophet Elijah hid in a cave when wicked King Ahab sought to kill him. The Book of Hebrews in the New Testament tells us that persecuted believers like Elijah "wandered over deserts and mountains, and in dens and caves of the earth."

Nowadays it's back to the caves, or underground bomb shelters, if nuclear war threatens. Early man often lived in caves; must modern man return to caverns in order to survive? Surely we must hope, pray, and do what we can in order to prevent this. We must work for an honorable peace so that we can live above the ground and enjoy God's sunshine, sky, air, mountains, and trees.

What is more, in our attitude toward life as a whole, we need to overcome the cave mentality. Who because of fear—fear not only of bomb attacks but of everything else that threatens us—wants to make his or her permanent residence in caves? Who can really hide out from the world—from world events, progress, contacts with other people, and the opportunities to do good by crawling into holes?

So our statement of faith is not: "God is our Cave," but "God is our Refuge and Strength." Not to caverns but to the hills do we lift up the eyes of faith, for from above—from God—comes our help. From above came the Son of God, Jesus Christ, conceived by the Holy Spirit and born of the Virgin Mary, to be our Redeemer from sin and all the fears of life and death. This is our resolve: "My faith looks up to Thee, Thou Lamb of Calvary, Savior divine (*TLH*)."

Prayer Suggestion

Pray that God, through Word and Spirit, may strengthen your faith in Christ and give you courage for today's living.

Continuing the Work of Others

Two men named Moses have something in common. The first is Moses of the Bible, whom God appointed to lead His people out of Egypt into the Promised Land. Moses, however, could not complete the assignment since God would not permit him to enter the new land. It remained for Joshua to finish the work.

The other man is Moses Austin, who failed in his mining enterprise at Potosi, Mo. He then hoped to become a colonizer, settling 300 families in Texas. When he died, it fell to his son Stephen to complete the project—to Stephen F. Austin, hailed as the founder of the colony, the "Father of Texas."

Jesus said to His disciples: "I sent you to reap that for which you did not labor; others have labored, and you have entered into their labor." That came about when the apostles continued Christ's work. When they left the scene, they turned the work over to the next generation: Timothy, Titus, Mark, Luke, etc.

So it has always been. It happens today that certain individuals must carry on the work of predecessors. Children take over the farm or business of their parents. The original founders of the churches we see may no longer be alive, but their descendants carry on the church's mission.

See whether in your own life you can pick up the thread and complete the tapestry someone else has begun. Perhaps your parents left you what may be called an "unfinished symphony." You may be able to finish it. Perhaps others before you inaugurated special missions and works of mercy. They are no longer here to work at these projects, but you are here. You would honor them by carrying on their labors.

Jesus is no longer on earth to do His work of love. But you and I are here to be His hands, His feet, His mouth—we, whom He has redeemed to be His own and to serve Him. Let's do it!

Prayer Suggestion

Ask God to bless your effort as you carry on His work, as others before you have done.

Serving with Our Talents

A man of many talents was Harold Bell Wright. Gifted for his work as a minister in Pittsburg, Kansas, he was also a landscape painter and a writer. His 19 novels include *The Winning of Barbara Worth, The Calling of Dan Matthews,* and *The Shepherd of the Hills.*

Not everyone is blessed with that many talents, for God distributes His gifts to people "individually as He wills." It would be a dull world if every person had exactly the same talent in exactly the same amount. God creates variety when in His wisdom and love He apportions talents in differing kinds and measures.

What is more, by varying His gifts to us, God enables us to serve one another with our special abilities, this to the benefit of the whole group. A very good illustration of this is the human body, which consists of many members, each with its own function to the good of the whole body. A body is not all feet, or all hands, or all eyes. We as persons are variously endowed so that we can render mutual service. This applies not only to natural talents but also to the special gifts of the Spirit—gifts of teaching, comforting, edifying, healing wounded hearts, and the like.

While not everyone is as talented as was the aforementioned Harold Bell Wright, each has a talent or special knack of some kind: to be a musician, a skilled seamstress, a master mechanic. This fact undercuts jealousy, for while another may have a greater gift in one area, we can excel in our own specialty. This is for the good of all and to the glory of Jesus Christ, who redeemed us from sin that we might serve Him with our talents.

Prayer Suggestion

Pray for God's help in discovering and then developing your talents.

Jesus, More than a Superhero

Every country has its popular heroes—in sports, and also in everyday life and work: powerful steel-driving men, supermen in lumber camps of whom the legendary Paul Bunyan is a composite, railroad engineer Casey Jones of the Cannonball Express. We have also heroines: nurse Clara Barton, handicapped but courageous Helen Keller, woman suffragist Susan B. Anthony.

The Bible tells us of many Old Testament heroes and heroines of the faith. Their roll is called in Hebrews, chapter 11. Add to that list, people of the New Testament: the apostles, the seamstress Dorcas who sewed for the poor, the women who ministered to Christ, the young men who followed in the apostles' footsteps: Mark, Luke, Timothy, Titus. After them came brave Christians who were martyred for the faith.

We need heroes; our children especially need them. We have to be able to look up to certain people who set the pace—persons who exemplify the Christian virtues of faithfulness, honesty, love, compassion, selflessness. We need such personal examples in our age, which stresses: fulfill yourself, look to your own interests and let the rest of the world go by.

Beyond even the best human beings, we need to look to Jesus Christ. He is more than a superhero or superstar, as is shown by the titles He bears: Wonderful, Counselor, Mighty God, Prince of Peace, Captain of our salvation, Pioneer and Perfecter of our faith. In great love He laid down His life for us, and He now draws us to Himself through His Word and Spirit. Writes St. Peter: "Christ also suffered for you, leaving you an example that you should follow His steps." Jesus is the One whose amazing love "demands my soul, my life, my all!"

Prayer Suggestion

Pray for a faith that always looks up to Jesus, the Lamb of Calvary.

God's "Here I Am!"

Some troubled people think that God is playing "hide-and-go-seek" with them. They pray but get no answer, it appears. They seek His face, but God seems hidden, like the sun under a dark cloud.

God Himself admits to this, speaking through Isaiah the prophet; "For a brief moment I forsook you, but with great compassion I will gather you. In overflowing wrath for a moment I hid my face from you, but with everlasting love I will have compassion on you."

God's momentary withdrawal has to be recognized. It may be due to a number of things: we have offended Him with our disobedience; we have neglected prayer and worship; we have been too demanding in our prayers, prescribing the time, place, and manner of God's help. But such divine withdrawal is not abandonment; it is not permanent but temporary, to be followed by the experience of God's love and compassion. In Christ Jesus, through whom we sinners are reconciled, God is our heavenly Father. In His presence we are comfortable. He welcomes us, promising to hear our prayers.

For all who through faith in Jesus Christ are right with God, prayer is an open line to Him. Again, God says through Isaiah: "You shall call, and the Lord will answer; you shall cry, and He will say, 'Here I am!' " That doesn't sound like God playing "hide-and-go-seek." There is no mention here of a "busy signal" while we're trying to get through to God.

Let this be our resolve as it was the psalmist's: "Thou hast said, 'Seek ye My face.' My heart says to Thee, 'Thy face, Lord, do I seek.' "

Prayer Suggestion

Ask God for patience when His answer to your prayer seems delayed.

Mission in Reverse

In February of 1912 the mayor of Tokyo, Japan, sent 3,000 cherry trees to Washington, D.C., for planting along the Tidal Basin. The original cherry trees in Tokyo were chopped down and used for firewood during World War II. So in February of 1981, as a return favor, cuts from the Washington, D.C., cherry trees were sent to Tokyo for planting there.

This is like a mission in reverse. It happens that members of a daughter church help out the mother church that sent the original missionaries. Not long ago Christian converts from India, whose main concern was to minister to the poor, came to the United States to do a work of mercy in slum cities here. Dietrich Bonhoeffer said that Europe was living in the post-Christian age. If true, then it remains for younger churches elsewhere in the world to bring the Gospel back to where it came from in the first place.

In the Bible we read how the apostles, beginning on Pentecost, established the mother church of Christendom in Jerusalem. From there they went out as missionaries. We read also of a great need that struck early Christians in Jerusalem and that the young mission churches in Greece and Macedonia sent relief funds.

All of us, in our personal lives, can return favors—can do mission work in reverse, as it were. We can give love in return, and the place to begin is the home. Years ago our parents cared for us, guided us, provided for our needs of body and soul. There may come a time when we can, and should, requite our parents, that is, do for them in their weakness of old age what they once did for us. That is how to show gratitude to God and to our human benefactors.

"Be kind to one another, tenderhearted, forgiving one another, as God in Christ forgave you."

Prayer Suggestion

Ask God for the kind of love that delights in returning love.

Be Determined! Be Courageous!

A very determined and courageous young man is Carl Joseph, who won eight varsity letters at a Madison, Florida, high school despite the fact that he has but one leg.

Determination and courage—what assets they are in all of life! This is especially true of disabled people who find ways to work around their problem. They not only support themselves but also contribute to the good of society.

Determination and courage are important in one's religious life. Saul the Pharisee, for example, who became St. Paul the Apostle, had a physical ailment—a thorn in the flesh. But he accomplished infinitely much for his Lord. How? He tells the Corinthians that he *determined* not to know anyone among them except Christ Jesus and Him crucified. He was a man of great *courage* also, carrying on his work amid unbelievable odds as day in, day out he lived in peril of his life. On one occasion the enemies stoned him and dragged him out of town, supposing him to be dead. But Paul got up and went on to the next city to preach the Gospel.

Our Lord Jesus was a person of consummate determination and courage. He was determined to do the heavenly Father's work while it was day. When Peter tried to dissuade Him from going to Jerusalem to suffer and die as the Savior, Jesus rebuked him sharply, then continued the pilgrimage to begin His Passion.

What about us? Do we whine and complain? Faith in Christ can give us determination and courage to overcome our setbacks, disabilities, and obstacles. Let's think of that one-legged high school athlete in Florida who had to hop where we walk and run. If we can't proceed on two legs, then with God's help we'll do it on one.

Prayer Suggestion

Pray that God may give you the will and courage to surmount your obstacles.

The Promise of a New House

"This Old House" is the title of a once popular song.

When John Quincy Adams, age 81, was asked how he was, he replied, "Quite well, thank you! But the house in which I live is becoming a bit dilapidated."

The aging St. Peter spoke of his body as a temporary dwelling—as a tent that he must soon lay aside. St. Paul joins him in saying, "We know that if the earthly tent we live in is destroyed, we have a building from God, a house not made with hands, eternal in the heavens."

God has indeed prepared for His people a home for the soul in heaven, and there they safely dwell, clothed with immortality. When our Lord returns, He will reunite the believers souls with their resurrected, glorified bodies, as the apostle teaches, "The Lord Jesus Christ . . . will change our lowly body to be like His glorious body, by the power which enables Him even to subject all things to Himself."

Jesus Christ, having died to atone for the sins of the whole human race, rose again and became the Pioneer, Forerunner, and Firstfruit of all His departed followers, for they are participants of His resurrection and victory over the corruption of sin and death. As such they will appear in bodies that can be compared to completely renovated, remodeled houses.

On her 90th birthday a gracious lady, formerly the dean of women at a prominent university referred to herself as "an old jalopy," and added, "I'm looking forward to the day when I get to turn it in on a brand-new shiny model." That is the Christian's outlook!

Prayer Suggestion

Pray that God grant you strength of body, soul, and mind.

Missing Persons

In the fall of 1872 the cargo ship Mary Celeste, en route from New York to Gibraltar, was found drifting off the Azores. No crew member was aboard. The prepared meal in the galley was un-eaten; in fact, the cooking range was still warm. What happened to the men? Nobody knows.

Missing persons! These are not only the MIAs, the soldiers missing in action. They are civilians, too: teenagers running away from home, children kidnapped, husbands or wives deserting their families, persons meeting with foul play. People's disappearance, like that of the men on the ship, can occur under mysterious circumstances. We don't know what happened to them.

The Bible speaks of a missing man fully accounted for. It was the godly man Enoch, of whom it is said: "Enoch walked with God; and he was not, for God took him." The Epistle to the Hebrews explains that he was taken up into heaven "so that he should not see death." The same explanation holds for another missing person: the prophet Elijah, who was taken up into heaven. The first two sons ever born, Cain and Abel, were missing per-sons—Abel, because his brother killed him, and Cain, because he went out of the presence of the Lord and of his parents—and became a wanderer on the face of the earth.

Thank God, another missing person showed up again: the prodigal son, who repented and came home again. Joyfully the father exclaimed to the other son: "This your brother was dead, and is alive; he was lost, and is found."

What about missing persons today—those who have run away from home and have gone out of the presence of the Lord? A homecoming is possible. Let them confess: "We have sinned against heaven and before our family members." Jesus died, so that such sins can also be forgiven. The heavenly Father is waiting to receive them with open arms.

Prayer Suggestion

Pray that an erring sinner known to you may be regained for Christ.

Coming to Christ Just as We Are

A renowned artist returned to his hometown to paint a familiar street scene where he once lived. In the picture he wanted to include a true-to-life man—the ragged, unkempt street sweeper. Told that he would be in the picture, the man returned the next day all dressed up, washed, and wearing a respectable suit. The artist had to send him away, for he had wanted to paint him as he appeared every day, not as he looked when all spruced up.

Charlotte Elliott has given us the hymn "Just as I Am, Without One Plea." One of the stanzas reads: "Just as I am, though tossed about, With many a conflict, many a doubt, Fightings and fears within, without, O Lamb of God, I come, I come."

Those who come to Jesus just as they are, confess thereby that they are in need of the Savior. They are hiding nothing, they are not pretending to be what they are not. The street sweeper who spruced himself up to get into the picture would not have appeared as his true self; the artist could not accept him as authentic.

A truly remarkable statement of the Holy Scripture is that God "justifies [declares righteous] the ungodly." He does not wait until they have cleaned up their lives or dressed themselves up in the robes of their own pretended righteousness. Christ died for all people while all people were yet sinners. Satisfaction was rendered for all their shortcomings, trespasses, and debts. God says to all who hear or read His Word: "Come as you are—wretched, pitiable, poor, blind, and naked. Don't bother to cover up your deficiencies with pretenses—with pretty, Sunday-go-to-meeting clothes. Come, trusting in Jesus Christ, and I will lay on you the robe of Christ's perfect righteousness. Then you will be a best-dressed person."

What should our response be? "O Lamb of God, I come, I come."

Prayer Suggestion

Pray for courage to come to Jesus without pretense, just as you are.

When Friends Become Foes

During the battle of Chancellorsville General "Stonewall" Jackson lost not only his left arm but also his life. Three days after the amputation he contracted pneumonia and died. What hurt most of all was that he was shot by a Confederate picket who in the twilight mistook him for a Union general.

Quite often people destroy those who are on their side, intentionally or unintentionally. We tend to hurt those whom we love—or should love. Many become the victims of violent attacks by individuals known to them, by those in their own home. Jesus said that a person's foes are quite often those of his own household. Not rank outsiders but his own brothers sold Joseph into slavery in Egypt. In our Lord's parable, the heart of a loving father was not wounded by a stranger, servant, or neighbor but by his own son—the prodigal son. And according to the book of Job, who was it that said to the sufferer: "Curse God and die," thus hinting at suicide? It was Job's own wife.

The Confederate sharpshooter who fatally wounded his own general did so by mistake, but "Stonewall" Jackson was just as dead as though shot by an enemy sniper. What is called for is utmost caution on our part so that we don't wound those near and dear to us, that we don't "slay with the tongue."

Jesus Himself had the sad experience of being betrayed by Judas Iscariot, a member of His own group, as the psalm had declared: "My bosom friend in whom I trusted, who ate of My bread, has lifted his heel against Me."

It was painful to Jesus when one of His own, Peter, denied Him and when all the disciples forsook Him and fled. But He did not cease loving them, and this love seeks to embrace us, too, as St. Paul teaches: "God shows His love for us in that while we were yet sinners, Christ died for us."

Prayer Suggestion

Pray that you may forgive others as God in Christ forgave you.

You Haven't Seen Anything Yet

This line occurs in Walt Disney's movie *Dumbo*: "I think I will have seen everything when I see an elephant fly."

Wonderful things do occur. We see jumbo jets, much bigger than elephants, fly. Not only is our technological world full of wonders, but so is nature, where the "impossible" happens every day. Design engineers say that a plane built along the lines of a bumblebee would never get off the ground. But here is God's bumblebee, and it flies!

God has another kingdom in which He performs even greater wonders. These are, as the refrain of a Christmas carol has it, the "wonders of His love." What a wonder that God extended His love to people who did not at all deserve it! Indeed, "While we were enemies we were reconciled to God by the death of His Son." What a wonder that this Savior now rules in the hearts of people, so that through them His blessings are extended as far as the curse of sin is found.

It would be a wonder to see a dead person become alive: the daughter of Jairus, the youth of Nain, Lazarus, and Jesus Himself on Easter morning. But is it not just as wonderful to see people spiritually dead—dead in trespasses and sins—become spiritually alive, to serve the living God and to love where formerly they hated?

Take the case of John Newton, whose hymns we sing. The tablet at his resting place reads: "John Newton, clerk, once an infidel and libertine, a servant of slavers in Africa, was by the rich mercy of our Lord and Savior Jesus Christ preserved, restored, pardoned, and appointed to preach the faith he had long labored to destroy."

No, to see an elephant fly wouldn't be the greatest wonder. A much greater one occurs when a sinner is born anew and becomes a Christian.

Prayer Suggestion

Pray for someone who needs to come face to face with Jesus, the Savior.

Being Wise in Our Generation

The newspaper told about a student who was expelled from a medical school. Instead of accepting the decision, he stole official stationery from the dean's office, wrote himself a glowing recommendation, and was admitted into another medical school. Deceitful? Yes, but also clever.

Jesus spoke in a parable about a clever steward, or estate manager, who, about to be fired, reduced the indebtedness of the owner's tenants, gained their goodwill, and eventually cashed in on the favors by moving in with them.

Jesus draws the lesson: "The children of this world are in their generation wiser than the children of light." The Lord is not condoning dishonesty, or sinful cleverness, or crooked business dealings. He is saying that we should learn from these people how to use our heads, how to be wise and resourceful—of course, in an honest manner. In another saying Jesus put wisdom and honesty together when He declared: "Be wise as serpents, and innocent as doves."

The "wisdom literature" of the Bible—Proverbs, Ecclesiastes, etc.—is full of hints on wise and proper procedure. The sayings of Jesus reflect such wisdom, as when He compared those who hear and keep His Word to a wise man who built his house on a rock foundation.

The greatest of all wisdom is stressed by St. Paul when he wrote that the Holy Scriptures "make us wise unto salvation through faith which is in Christ Jesus." To know and believe that Jesus Christ, God's Son, died for our sins and rose again from the dead—this is the wisdom of faith. It brings peace with God; it gives a perspective from which to view all of life—from here to eternity.

Prayer Suggestion

Ask God to give you wisdom in dealing with life's problems

Have You Greeted Someone Today?

Overlooking the river at Savannah, Ga., is a bronze statue of Florence Martus, whose distinction it was that she greeted every passing ship—by day, waving a handkerchief, and by night with a lantern.

What is so special about being a greeter? Words and deeds of welcome add the human touch, especially where strangers are involved. A greeting can break the ice, so that the warmth of human feeling takes the place of coldness and loneliness. In our sequestered world, with fearful people living in sealed-up, burglar-proof houses, neighborly greetings are much in place. A friendly "hello" to visitors at church, to fellow workers and seat companions in air travel can open the door to edifying experiences.

Early Christians, considering themselves as brothers and sisters in Christ, exchanged greetings. Quite often St. Paul was the bearer of such exchanges. In his first letter to the Corinthians he states: "The churches of Asia send greetings. Aquila and Priscilla, together with the church in their house, send you hearty greetings in the Lord. All the brethren send greetings. Greet one another with a holy kiss."

"Greetings in the Lord!" It was the Lord Jesus who made Christian fellowship possible. He, the eternal Son of God, could have kept His distance from the fallen human race. But He didn't do that. He became one of us, died for us, and rose again. How wonderful His Easter greeting to the cowering disciples—His shalom: "Peace be with you!" His words actually convey peace with God. Now we have an Easter greeting suitable for every day of the year: "He is risen!" Yes, He is risen and lives, and we have risen with Him!

Prayer Suggestion

Pray that Christ's love to you may prompt you to speak words of love to others.

Taking Risks

People who enjoy themselves at Lake Tahoe on the California-Nevada border may not be aware of a great tragedy enacted in nearby Donner Pass on Halloween in 1846. Families going west in a wagon train led by Captain George Donner were caught in an 8-day blizzard. Of a party of 89 persons, 42 perished. Had they listened to good advice, they would not have attempted the trip into the Sierras so late in the year. They thought they could beat the snow.

The world is full of people who imagine they can beat the odds, people who take foolish risks. So often they come to grief. So it was with the prodigal son in Christ's parable, who thought the glamor and bright lights out there in the world were for real. He came back home in rags. What folly for Christ's disciple, Judas, to think he could get away with stealing from the disciples' treasury! To Peter our Lord said, in effect: "Don't chance it! Don't be so foolish as to think that you can by your own strength withstand the temptations of this night." But Peter wouldn't listen. He thought he could make it through the narrow pass, but the blizzard of enemy attacks caught up with him.

Of course, we sometimes have to take risks, and we cannot always rely on the advice of others. But before undertaking any kind of venture, it is good to think things over carefully, to consider the pro's and con's, to learn as much as we can from knowledgeable people, and above all, to take it to the Lord in prayer, asking His guidance.

There is great wisdom in the Bible—in Proverbs and Ecclesiastes, for example. We do well to heed it. But the greatest wisdom is to be wise unto salvation through faith in Jesus Christ, who lived, obeyed the Law, suffered, died, and rose again to make us one with God. There is no risk involved—only safety—in accepting this wisdom.

Prayer Suggestion

Pray that the Lord may guide you as you make important decisions in life.

Waiting to Grow

Walter H. Aiken's song, "Waiting to Grow," anticipates the wonders of nature's awakening in the spring: "Think what a host of queer little seeds, Of flowers and mosses and ferns and weeds Are under the leaves and the ice and the snow Waiting, waiting, waiting to grow."

There is seed in Christians waiting to grow—the seed of God's Word, as Jesus teaches in the parable of the sower. "The seed is the Word of God," He declares. St. Peter reminds Christians that they "have been born anew, not of perishable seed but of imperishable, through the living and abiding Word of God."

To be born anew means that the Holy Spirit through the Gospel as a powerful seed has brought us to faith in Jesus Christ, who was offered up as the Lamb of God for the sin of the world. A great change has taken place, for we are given new hearts. But the new life is not to be static or stunted, for St. Paul writes, "We are to grow up in every way into Him who is the Head, into Christ." St. Peter adds, "Grow in the grace and knowledge of our Lord and Savior Jesus Christ."

The spiritual seed is in all who hear and accept the Word of God. It wants to germinate and grow, so that we bear more and more fruit. So let it be the end of winter in our lives. Let the ice and snow of the coldness of our hearts melt under the warm sunshine of God's love in Christ. Let the flowers of a new, beautiful life appear. Let the trees in our inner being blossom and bear fruit in terms of Christian service. God has implanted the seed of the Word in His people. It is waiting, waiting, waiting to grow. It wants to grow in your heart and life.

Prayer Suggestion

Ask that through the Word the Holy Spirit may increase your faith and bring about a greater yield of His fruits in you.

The Brightest Day

The spiritual "Swing Low, Sweet Chariot" reflects the account of the prophet Elijah's rapture into heaven in a fiery chariot after he and Elisha had crossed the Jordan. But it is not only a yearning for heaven that the song expresses in its "carry me home" refrain. It speaks also of the joy and happiness in this life that comes from believing in Jesus. The lines say:

> The brightest day that ever I saw . . .
> When Jesus washed my sins away.

Already in this life we have a foretaste of eternal life when Jesus Christ comes into our hearts. The same Jesus whom we expect to see face to face in heaven dwells in us now through the Gospel we believe and apply. Already now we have the promise of forgiveness, peace with God, and everlasting life. The Good Shepherd Jesus says regarding His sheep: "I give them eternal life." Note the present tense. Again, He declares in His prayer to the Father: "This is eternal life, that they know Thee the only true God, and Jesus Christ whom Thou hast sent."

This is not to say that there is nothing more awaiting us in the life to come, but it is to say that also this present life in a troubled world knows bright days—days of hope, days of delight as we associate with fellow Christians, days of contentment as things fall into place. And the brightest day? Surely the day when we came to know Jesus as our Savior from sin. It is written, "The blood of Jesus His Son cleanses us from all sin." And: "To Him who loves us and has freed us from our sins by His blood ... to Him be glory."

The unknown writer of the spiritual says it all: "The brightest day that ever I saw . . . When Jesus washed my sins away."

Prayer Suggestion

Thank the Lord Jesus Christ for coming into your life and daily assuring you that you are at peace with God.

The Bridge of Hope

In historic Chester, England, visitors can see an old footbridge over which condemned felons were led from prison to the Chapel of Little John for their last prayers. It is called, understandably enough, the Bridge of Sighs.

From time to time there will be such a bridge in everybody's life, also for law-abiding people. In the lives of some the "bridge of sighs" becomes all too real. From the Golden Gate Bridge many have jumped to their death. Once the *New York Times*, estimating that some 35,000 persons commit suicide every year, added: "Those who succeed are a tiny fraction of the despairing among us."

If sin had not come into the world, there would be no sighs, no sorrow, nor hopelessness. Consequently if we are to have a better outlook on life, we need to recognize what lies at the root of despair and to turn to God for help.

God has made provision for the bridge of grief to become the bridge of relief. In fact, one could say that His own Son is that Bridge—the Span across the great gulf between a holy God and sinful people. St. Paul writes, "There is one Mediator between God and men, the Man Christ Jesus, who gave Himself as a ransom for all." In our stead Jesus bore all our sins and griefs so that we might have peace, hope, and joy.

Now if sigh we must, it is the sigh of relief and redemption. Problems we will continue to have, and burdens we will still have to bear, but through Christ we have access to the heavenly Father. The hymn lines say, "Prayer is the burden of a sigh, The falling of a tear, The upward glancing of an eye, When none but God is near (*TLH*)." Make use of this "prayer bridge," for it leads to the heart of God!

Prayer Suggestion

Pray that God may show you the way to go when difficulties and important decisions confront you.

The Jesus Book

A humorist has said, with a great deal of truth: "There are so many changes in religion today that a publisher is thinking of putting out a Bible in loose-leaf."

Now, it doesn't matter to God in what format we publish and read His Word, whether in a scroll, as manuscripts stitched together called a codex, a bound book, or even on microfilm. If anyone would like an interleaved Bible so that he or she could insert study notes opposite the text, God might even say, "That's a very practical idea!"

But the idea of a loose-leaf that the humorist was speaking of meant something else, namely, that one could take out pages of text he didn't like and insert revisions more in keeping with today's thinking. A Bible made that flexible and variable would no longer be of any use. No two people could agree on what goes out and what goes in. Such a Bible would have lost its divine authority. Lost would be every "Thus says the Lord" and "Thus promises the Lord."

With that also Jesus Christ would be lost. Our Lord said that the Holy Scriptures testify of Him. They bear witness that the Son of God became truly human so that He might surrender His life for the salvation of all people. "The blood of Jesus, His Son, cleanses us from all sin," writes St. John. If certain pages of a loose-leaf Bible were to be removed, the page saying this would be the first many people would remove. Who would want that kind of a Bible?

The sign for Bible in the language of the deaf is the combined sign for Jesus and for a book. How apt! That is exactly what the Bible is—the Jesus Book.

Prayer Suggestion

Speak a prayer of thanks to God for having revealed the Savior Jesus Christ to you in the Scripture.

Pass It On!

We owe a great debt of gratitude to God for having brought our forebears to the new world. And we are greatly indebted to our pioneering ancestors for leaving us a legacy of loyalty to God and to the country they helped found. Such loyalty was especially strong in those who came to these shores to seek religious freedom.

In his hymn "O God, Beneath Thy Guiding Hand" Leonard Bacon pays tribute to "our exiled fathers" (and mothers) who crossed the sea and who "with prayer and psalm worshiped" God. They brought along more than their few personal possessions; they came with a great treasure of intangibles, as the hymn says: "Laws, freedom, truth, and faith in God Came with those exiles o'er the waves; And where their pilgrim feet have trod, The God they trusted guards their graves."

What is important for us as the beneficiaries of these blessings is that we pass on this heritage to our children and children's children. People in ancient Greece, like people today, were fond of relay races—races in which runners carried torches, each one covering a distance and then passing it on to his waiting partner. As the exchange was about to take place, people in the stadium shouted, "Let him who has the torch pass it on."

That is what we tell one another as we think of the torch of truth we hold in our hands: Pass on the Gospel of Jesus Christ! Go into all the world and proclaim to people what our Christian parents—and their parents and grandparents before them—have entrusted to us. Of course, we cannot all be traveling missionaries, so we do what the hymn says, "If you cannot speak like angels, If you cannot preach like Paul, You can tell the love of Jesus: You can say He died for all."

In doing this, the faith that our fathers and mothers have passed on to us will be the faith of our children.

Prayer Suggestion

Give thanks to God for having enriched you with the Christian faith. Ask Him to help you pass it on to others.

Hard Times, Soft Hearts

Undoubtedly many people could identify with expressions in Stephen C. Foster's song "Hard Times, Come Again No More"— expressions like "sup with sorrow," the "sigh of the weary," hunger "lingering about the cabin door." The song says, by way of making the fortunate ones aware of the poor: "While we seek mirth and beauty and music, light and gay There are frail forms fainting at the door."

The scene is reminiscent of Jesus' parable of a rich man, who feasted sumptuously every day, and poor and sick Lazarus at his door, who hoped for crumbs and leftovers.

For Lazarus, after a while, there were no more hard times, because he died and angels carried his soul to heaven. How different life would have been for him if his hard times had been eased by compassionate hearts and helping hands!

St. James describes what happens when in hard times people of need meet hard hearts: "a brother or sister is ill-clad and in lack of daily food, and one of you says to them, 'Go in peace, be warmed and filled,' without giving them the things needed for the body."

But how different when hard times prompt Christian love, as Jesus said: "I was hungry and you gave Me food, I was thirsty and you gave Me drink, I was a stranger and you welcomed Me, I was naked and you clothed Me, I was sick and you visited Me, I was in prison and you came to Me." Indeed, hard times, but soft hearts!

How can it be otherwise? Jesus gave His life for us. As St. Paul writes, "You know the grace of our Lord Jesus Christ, that though He was rich, yet for your sake He became poor, so that by His poverty you might become rich."

Christian love—that is the best defense against hard times!

Prayer Suggestion

Pray that hard times may not come, but if they do come, that God may prompt you and others to share.

The Way to Peace

People visiting the ancient castle in Edinburgh, Scotland, can from the ramparts look down on a beautiful scene below. There was a time when the area was covered with the water of a loch for the protection of the castle. But after Scotland and England formed one government in 1707, there was to be no more war. So the loch was drained and the land converted into the beautiful Princes Street Gardens.

One is reminded of what the prophet said, "They shall beat their swords into plowshares, and their spears into pruning hooks." Of course, since the time Isaiah said this, there have been many wars: holy and unholy wars, civil wars, wars of oppression and revolution. What kind of peace did Isaiah have in mind?

He wished to say that the people's warfare with God was ended. He foretold the coming of the Messiah as the Prince of Peace. Upon Him was to be the chastisement that made us whole, and with His stripes we are healed, as Isaiah writes in the 53rd chapter of his book.

When Christ the Lord was born in Bethlehem, the angels, appropriately enough, sang of "peace on earth, good will toward men." Truly in Him is our peace, for He has removed the separating walls between people and God, between people and people. Indeed, "God was in Christ reconciling the world to Himself." Jesus the Savior tells us, "Peace I leave with you, peace I give to you; not as the world gives do I give to you."

When in Christ we have peace with God, we will work toward peace on earth. We will drain the water from moats and turn the land into flower gardens. We will beat our swords into plowshares, and our spears into pruning hooks.

Prayer Suggestion

Ask the heavenly Father to grant you peace in the knowledge that in Christ all your sins are forgiven and you are His dear child.

Bad Beginnings, Good Endings

In the university city of Oxford, England, there were at times bad relations between townspeople and students. During a crisis in 1209 A.D., when feelings ran so high that local citizens wanted to lynch some students, a group of scholars fled to the city of Cambridge and there became the nucleus of Cambridge University. Some minuses here led to a plus for England: another great university.

With the slaying of Stephen the Martyr a persecution was touched off in Jerusalem, resulting in what was really a blessing: Christians fled to other cities, like Damascus, taking their faith with them and forming the nuclei for more churches.

In one's personal or family life, as well, it is not unusual for a feud to have good outcomes. The bad feelings of Jacob's sons toward their brother Joseph caused them to sell him to Egypt as a slave, where God made him a prime minister and chief food administrator during a seven-year famine. All had a happy ending, as Joseph phrased it: "You meant it evil against me; but God meant it for good, to bring it about that many people should be kept alive."

Very likely, you could cite instances in your own life that show how God over rules people's evil intentions or ill will, and makes them serve your best interests. So it is never a good idea to avenge oneself on evildoers. We let God have the last word.

He who stands head and shoulders above Joseph as one who was hated, sold as a slave for 30 pieces of silver, and nailed to the cross, but who came back from the dead to make good come out of evil was Jesus Christ. His enemies meant to do Him in, but God had other plans. Through His dying and rising again He became our Savior. This is not to say that evildoers did a good thing and are excused. It is to say that God, in control of people's lives, ordains that all things work together for good to those who love Him.

Prayer Suggestion

Pray that God may control your life, letting His will be done for your ultimate good.

Christ's No to Narcotics

Drugs are a gift of God and have their proper use. Who would want to do away with digitalis for heart disease, insulin for diabetes, antibiotics for infection, and anesthetics in surgery? The problem is, however, that drugs are shamefully abused.

Most of the drugs available today were unknown in Jesus' time. There was, however, a poisonous, bitter herb which in Hebrew was called *rosh* and which is translated as gall, hemlock, and wormwood. It had the power to deaden feelings. A stupifying drink of wine mingled with gall was offered to Jesus at His crucifixion. But He refused to drink it. He said no to narcotics.

Our Lord went to Calvary to suffer and die for the sins of the whole human race. Since this was His purpose, it would not do for Him to escape pain by taking an intoxicant mixed with a narcotic.

We are thankful that Jesus said no to the drugged drink, for now no doubt is cast on Him as as the "Man of sorrows and [one] acquainted with grief." Now there is only certainty that "He has borne our griefs and carried our sorrows," that "He was wounded for our transgressions" and "was bruised for our iniquities," as Isaiah had foretold.

We stand with Jesus when we refuse to take drugs unless so prescribed by our physician. To know that through Jesus Christ we are at peace with God—that is the best tranquilizer there is. The peace our Lord promised to give comes from faith in the Gospel, not in the bottle, not in a vial of pills. Do you have this peace?

Prayer Suggestion

Ask God to keep you from harmful drugs and to let you find peace in Jesus Christ, your Redeemer.

Be a Friend to Yourself

Who is your worst enemy? The tax collector? The law officer?
Your business rival? The chances are that the one causing you
the most grief is someone much closer to you. Look into the mirror
and you'll see who is probably your worst foe. This is so in the
area of health, as Dr. Karl Menninger's book *Man Against Himself*
indicates. Overeating, overworking, worrying—all contribute to
one's distress.

A nation can be its own worst enemy. Its downfall is more
apt to come from inner moral collapse than from an invading
army.

The Bible declares that one who associates with thieves hates
his own soul. It characterizes people, giving us examples of people
who stumbled by their own fault. Christ's disciples are always
mirrors reflecting human nature. Peter was his own worst enemy
when, despite Jesus' warning, he trusted in himself and at a critical
time denied his Lord. An even worse example of self-enmity is
Judas Iscariot, the betrayer—not only of Jesus but of his own best
interests when money became his god.

Working against oneself all started when Adam and Eve in
the Garden brought about their downfall through willful disobedience. But God was gracious in sending His Son as their—and
our—Savior. Jesus Christ, the Second Adam, brought us life by
giving His life as an offering of reconciliation with God. Now we
can sing "What a Friend we have in Jesus, All our sins and griefs
to bear!"

When we follow Him, keep His Word, love God above all
things and our neighbors as ourselves, we are no longer our own
enemies but our own best friends, for what is to God's glory and
our neighbor's welfare is always to our own best interests.

Prayer Suggestion

Pray that God may redirect your thoughts and energies toward
helping others—and yourself.

Faith, Yes! Fanaticism, No!

People who visit Salem, Mass., and other New England places are reminded that the same Puritans who founded those great colleges—Harvard, for instance, in 1636—were also the ones who executed innocent people for witchcraft—20 in Salem alone, in 1692.

God wants us to have zeal for His work and Word, but not misguided zeal. Crusaders and those who work for "causes" should remember that. St. Paul said of certain people: "They have a zeal for God, but it is not enlightened"—not in keeping with knowledge. He himself was an example of that before his conversion, when "as to zeal [he was] a persecutor of the church."

Faith, yes! Fanaticism, no! One can compare the two to fire. How wonderful fire is when it is kept under control, warming a room or cooking food. But how frightful is fire when it gets out of hand. It can burn down your home or destroy a whole city.

Zeal under control is not the same as lukewarmness, which God doesn't want, either. When there is no zeal, people are neither hot nor cold in their Christianity. That makes for indifference, for an "I don't care" attitude.

Faith with the kind of zeal God wants comes about when the Holy Spirit through the Gospel leads us to Jesus Christ, who died to save us and rose again. Given a new heart, we will be, in Paul's words to Titus, a purified people "who are zealous for good deeds."

Prayer Suggestion

Pray that the Holy Spirit may give you greater faith, along with love, warmth, and zeal for all that is good.

Cursing Cramps One's Style

Cursing, profanity, obscenity, vulgarity of speech, four-letter words—whatever we call it—is creeping more and more into movies and TV programs. Some people regard this as "adult," as a sign of maturity, as evidence that we, having overcome our Puritanism, have come of age.

Referring to the growing use of profanity in the entertainment media and elsewhere, Janet Maslin wrote in the *New York Times*: "A man who swears a lot is generally just a lout," and "Obscenities chart the limits of a character's imagination." In other words, they show how cramped a person's style is. He or she is more a moron than a mature person. With a limited vocabulary his or her character is badly flawed.

The words we use are not our business alone but always involve the next person—the listener—and affect him or her for better or for worse. St. Paul writes, "Let no evil talk come out of your mouths, but only such as is good for edifying, as fits the occasion, that it may impart grace to those who hear!" Elsewhere the apostle urges that our speech "always be gracious, seasoned with salt." That says that our speech may indeed have a flavor—be strong and colorful and imaginative—but within the limits of moral and social propriety.

Words show not only who we are but *whose* we are: the children of our heavenly Father. He took us as we were, steeped in sin, and gave us a new heart, cleansed us with the blood of Jesus His Son, and put a new language into our mouths. In Christ we are a new creation, with clean minds and clean mouths.

Prayer Suggestion

Ask God for strength not to profane His holy name but to let all your words glorify Him and edify other people.

It's the Contents That Counts

In his book *Something's Going On Here* Bob Benson states, "We are vessels, wrote Paul. But whether we resemble fine crystal or inexpensive jars isn't the issue—only our contents counts."

What St. Paul wrote is this: "We have this treasure in earthen vessels, to show that the transcendent power belongs to God and not to us." The treasure in Jesus' words is the pearl of great price, the treasure laid up in heaven. It is the Gospel of the forgiveness of sins and of peace with God through the redeeming merit of Jesus Christ. This treasure was committed to despite his human frailty and poor health. He sees an advantage in this, for now all accomplishments of the Gospel must be credited to God and not to him. Elsewhere he has said the power of God's grace is made perfect in his weakness.

Indeed, we are vessels. The divine Potter, however, has not made us all alike. By His grace some are highly talented, of noble character, and we can say of them thay they resemble fine crystal. Others are more like inexpensive jars—like empty jelly jars that some of you may use in your home as drinking glasses. These, too, in God's sight are quality people, for the Gospel in them makes them so. The point is: intrinsically, the value does not lie in us personally but in what the Word of God has accomplished in us and through us.

Benson states, "Only the contents counts." Those contents are the Gospel of Christ, which we cherish, our faith in it, and our love because of it. So, whatever kind of vessel you are, you are precious and useful because Christ dwells in you. You are somebody.

Prayer Suggestion

Pray that through the Gospel, Christ may enable you to serve Him with the gifts He has given you.

Letting God Be God

"You shall not make for yourself a graven image," God says. In ancient Egypt, Pharaoh Ramses II had more than 1,000 statues made of himself. Of the six statues in his wife's temple, four were of himself. What arrogance for a human being to pose as God and have people worship him!

Today people have pictures taken of themselves, or perhaps even a bust or a statue made, but not for idolatry. They are apt to practice idolatry in other ways. They may say, "Moral law or no moral law, I do as I please; I do my own thing." This is making oneself into a god. It is taking love away from God and lavishing it on the ego—on self-aggrandizement.

For this, people in our technologically advanced society are paying the price, for with the inordinate self-centeredness goes a penalty. A sickness of the spirit is not only revealed but also worsened when people are preoccupied with themselves. For this sickness they vainly seek all kinds of cures in the many cult movements, in promises of self-fulfillment, in analyses of their inner selves.

We need to take ourselves off the high pedestals and put God back into place as Number One. Away with all these graven and ungraven self-images by which people demean and dehumanize themselves by playing God!

Jesus enables us to do this. He is the Physician of the soul, spirit, and mind—and in many instances, of the body also. He gave His life on the old rugged cross to make our lives new.

Prayer Suggestion

Ask that Jesus Christ come increasingly into your life with His love, wisdom, and joy.

On Eagles' Wings

One of the endangered species is the eagle—the magnificent bird that has been the symbol of the U.S.A. since 1782. One of the reasons why eagles are in danger of extinction is that the pesticides they eat so soften the egg shells that they are easily broken during incubation. Thus the eagle cannot renew his species.

The Bible speaks of another kind eagle renewal. In Psalm 103 we read that God "satisfies you with good as long as you live so that your youth is renewed like the eagle's." The reference is to the annual period when eagles molt and shed their feathers. It is a time of rejuvenation. With their new feathers they can spread their wings in a six or seven foot span and soar with renewed strength.

So it is with people who are renewed in God's grace, as Isaiah writes, "They who wait for the Lord shall renew their strength, they shall mount up with wings like eagles." What a wonderful comparison! We are enabled to bounce back from mental depressions, ailments, and periods of spiritual gloom. We can make a comeback and again spread the wings of faith and fly. We may be down at times, but we are not out—not when we daily walk with God, live in Christ, and abide in the fellowship of the Holy Spirit. In God the Father we have a kind Maker and Provider. In God the Son "we have redemption through His blood, the forgiveness of our sins, according to the riches of His grace." In the Holy Spirit we have a Counselor, and Comforter.

When the blues bother us, we can say with the psalmist: "why are you cast down, O my soul . . . Hope in God." With hope based on a sure faith, we can fly again.

Prayer Suggestion

Counteract your dejection by prayerfully counting your blessings and thanking God for each one of them.

The Way to Get Even

In 1911 the famous painting by Leonardo da Vinci, the Mona Lisa, was stolen from the Louvre in France. Two years later it was found in an attic in Florence. The man who had taken it said he did it in order to get even with Napoleon for looting so many of Italy's art treasures during the war.

Today people still try to get even. What in the lives of little tots is tit for tat becomes an eye for an eye and a tooth for a tooth in many adult lives. It is a mistake to take the law into one's own hands, for there are legal ways for restitution to be made in our lives as citizens. It is not good to let thieves get by with stealing or murderers with killing, for then there will be more of this.

It is another matter in person-to-person relationships. Here we are dealing with personal and private affairs—things that ordinarily do not come under the purview of the legal authorities, things like "he insulted me before my friends," or "she said this about me which isn't true." Then the temptation is great to repay in like coin: an insult for an insult, a lie for a lie.

There is a better way to get even, that is, to even things off. It is the way of love and forgiveness. But that is hard, because it cuts against the grain of human nature. It requires big persons, in fact, persons who are born again and have become new creations in Christ. It takes people who know and believe that for the sake of Jesus Christ, through whose redeeming work they are right with God, all their wrongdoings and wrongsayings and wrongthoughts are forgiven. Now I can and will forgive my neighbor, my brother, my sister. That is really getting even! That is setting things straight in God's sight, with the neighbor, and in your own heart.

Prayer Suggestion

Ask that God again take you in spirit to the foot of Calvary's cross and show you at what great cost you have been forgiven.

Names, Not Numbers

A judge in the Hennepin County District Court in Minnesota has refused the request of a man to have his name legally changed to a number—number 1069. The judge stated that such a change would be dehumanizing.

Names are important. God has revealed Himself to us by name, not by number. His name is Yahweh, the Lord, the Almighty, God Most High, or, with reference to the Trinity, Father, Son, and Holy Spirit. God's name is not just a word tacked on, but it is God Himself as He has revealed Himself. The psalmist declares, "According to Thy name, O God, so is Thy praise unto the ends of the earth; Thy right hand is full of righteousness." And Jeremiah: "This is the name by which He will be called: "The Lord [Yahweh] is our righteousness." What meaning Jesus puts into the divine name when He calls God His and our Father. God's name describes God as He is.

We too have names—last names passed down from generation to generation, and first names selected by our parents. God honors such names and calls us by them. What God said to His people as a whole He says individually to each member: "I have called you by your name, you are Mine." It is not numbers but names that God enters into the book of life.

When Christ, the Son of God, was born, He was properly called Jesus, which means Savior, for He would save His people from their sins. He lived up to His name. Into that name we were baptized and thus made participants or partners of every promise of God. In thankfulness we bow our knees at the name of Jesus Christ.

What's in a name? All that we are and hope to be, all that God means to us and we mean to Him—that is what lies in the name.

Prayer Suggestion

Ask God to help you hold fast to the name of Jesus Christ, the Savior, for then your name will be written in the book of life.

Prayer Opens Doors

Sometimes in life it seems that every door is closed to us—the door of opportunity, the door of hope, even the door to further progress of the Lord's Word and work. Missionaries experience this feeling. Certainly St. Paul and his coworkers felt boxed in when they were "forbidden by the Holy Spirit to speak the Word in Asia" (Acts 16:6)

But prayer changes things. When one door is closed, God opens another. In answer to prayer St. Paul could enter other mission fields. While in Ephesus he wrote, "A wide door for effective work has been opened to me."

Prayer opens the door to the fulfillment of every Christian's mission in life. When in our various vocations in life we ask for God's guidance, He will direct our footsteps on the right road. Every believer can testify on the basis of experience: God "leads me in paths of righteousness for His name's sake."

When people seemingly give no answer to our knocking, when doors are sealed, when the handles are on the inside with no one there to turn them, take it to the Lord in prayer. We have this promise, "He [God] who did not spare His own Son but gave Him up for us all, will He not also give us all things with Him?"

God has already honored and enriched us with His greatest gift: His own Son, Jesus Christ, our Lord and Savior. He gave Him that by His death on Calvary's cross He might redeem us from the slavery of sin to be God's free children. If God has done this much, surely He will in answer to prayer give the lesser gifts also. For this we have His word: "Call upon Me in the day of trouble: I will deliver you, and you shall glorify Me."

Prayer Suggestion

Ask that God for the sake of Jesus Christ may show you the way out of difficulties by giving you wisdom and the courage to act on it.

Bypassing Boredom

Much of what people do or don't do is related to boredom. It may go by other names—tedium, ennui, dullness, the blahs—but its nature is the same: a physical, mental, and emotional weariness due to life's drab routines and its recurring sameness.

This mood or state of mind is not new. In 1890 Henrik Ibsen wrote a play that theater groups still produce: *Hedda Gabler.* It is the story of a woman trapped in a situation that offered no outlets, only inner struggles and self-doubts. We hear her say, "I often think I have a talent for only one thing in life: boring myself to death." Boredom drives some people to alcohol and other drugs.

We can devise no single, sure-fire formula for bypassing boredom to fit everyone, for our lives differ. We can, however, pick up hints from others. That's why the study of biographies can be so helpful. Look at some lives pictured in the Bible. St. Paul, so often in prison, overcame the boredom of being behind bars by writing letters, conversing with his jailers, speaking to God in prayer, making plans for his next mission trips. Can you imagine Dorcas of Joppa (nowadays Tel-Aviv) being bored while she sewed coats and garments for the poor? Timothy could not have been bored if he did only half the things St. Paul suggested to him: use the gifts that were in him, give attendance to reading, teach, visit people, witness to the faith.

These are, of course examples from the Bible, and that has significance. These were people who believed and lived the Christian faith. They stood close to Jesus, wanting their lives to count for Him because He had given His life for them. This motivation is available also to us today, and we can say: Bye, bye, blues! Farewell, boredom!

Prayer Suggestion

Pray God that you may find meaning in life by serving.

At Home with God

In 1904 a wealthy industrialist from Kansas City, Mo., bought 2,500 acres of land in the Ozark hill country of Missouri. Hoping to make his home there, he engaged stonemasons from Scotland to build him a castlelike mansion of 60 rooms. But he never got to live there, since he lost his life in a street accident in 1906. Today the building stands in ruins.

All that people can build is temporal; only God and His works are eternal. That's why the psalmist declares, "Blessed are all who take refuge in Him." God is our dwelling place in all generations. We sing, "Our God, our Help in ages past, Our Hope for years to come, Our Shelter from the stormy blast, And our eternal Home."

We know what God has done to make Himself our Refuge, our eternal Home. In love He sent His Son into the world that by His suffering, dying, and rising again He might save us and found a kingdom, His saving church, of which He makes us members. Christ loved the church and gave Himself for it. In Psalm 2 the heavenly Father speaks of the King whom He has set on Zion, His holy hill. This is the Messiah, whom He addresses in these words, "You are My Son, today I have begotten You." And to us God says that we should "kiss the Son," that is love Him, believe in Him, serve Him.

Jesus of Nazareth is this King, this Messiah. Of Him at His baptism—and later at the Transfiguration—the Father said, "This is My beloved Son, with whom I am well pleased." Him the Father was pleased to raise from the dead in public testimony of His eternal lordship. St. Paul writes, "He is the Head of the body, the church . . . For in Him all the fullness of God was pleased to dwell." Blessed are all who take refuge in Him!

Prayer Suggestion

Pray that the Holy Spirit may assure You that in Jesus Christ God has accepted you into His family and that He will fulfill all your needs.

High Visibility

From the glassed-in skywalks of two tall buildings in Boston one can see the sprawling metropolitan area. One particular day a sign in the skywalks said, "Visibility 80 Miles."

From the vantage point of Mount Nebo Moses enjoyed high visibility, for God showed him "all the land" that Israel was about to enter. Because he had disobeyed God's command, Moses could not set foot in the Promised Land. But God let him see it from a mountaintop.

We don't always have a clear outlook on life. We are earth-bound creatures, and we often have a worm's-eye view of life. We live in narrow and confined valleys, in back alleys. Sometimes our daily tasks shut us in. The clouds of daily cares set low ceilings; the mists of misfortune deprive us of visibility. Then it is time to head for the mountains to recapture vision.

The psalmist said, "I will lift up my eyes to the hills, from where my help comes. My help comes from the Lord, who made heaven and earth." When the journey of faith takes us up to a mountaintop with God, the murky picture begins to clear up. We begin to see how things work together for our good. We learn anew who we are, why we are here, and where we are going.

From the top of Mount Calvary we observe how the love of God was at work in the crucifixion of Jesus Christ to effect our salvation. We see that love extending far into the world, far into our lives, as though one were standing on top of a tall skyscraper and seeing how everything fits together. What a beautiful sight that is!

Prayer Suggestion

Pray for the long-range visions of a faith that sees beyond the immediate obstacles to the glorious goal ahead.

Christ Is the Bridge

One cold night late in 1977 over a hundred motorists were trapped for nine hours on a Mississippi River bridge near St. Louis. A collision involving several trucks was the cause. The people spent a very uncomfortable night. Ordinarily a bridge fulfills its function of bringing people across a river or stream. Sometimes this is not the case.

It is not so with Jesus Christ, who is the Bridge between us and God. He is the only Way to the heavenly Father, the one Mediator between God and people—always true, trustworthy, reliable. St. Paul states of Christ: He "gave Himself a ransom for all." He did not offer gold or silver, or anything else of material worth, to redeem the human race from the slavery of sin. He offered the highest good: His own life. Then He rose from the dead, thereby establishing Himself before the world as God's Son, who had performed a sufficient sacrifice for the redemption of all people. Yes, Christ is the perfect Bridge!

How foolish for a person to say he doesn't need Christ as the Bridge, and how futile to try to be his own bridge to God on the strength of his works or merits. The "do good—be good" bridge of self-righteousness does not lead to heaven. People who try it are like the motorists on that bridge near St. Louis: helplessly stalled, freezing in the cold, finding no rest.

Christ is the right Bridge, and all who come to Him by faith and believe in Him as their Savior are crossing over from the guilt of sin to the forgiveness of sin, from the fear of God to the love of God. Holy Scripture is full of road signs to lead you to Christ, the Bridge. Read it and follow the signs.

Prayer Suggestion

Ask for the Holy Spirit's guidance so that you may be drawn closer to Christ and through Him be daily renewed.

The Light That Doesn't Fail

In the novel *The Light That Failed* Rudyard Kipling tells the story of an artist who is gradually losing his sight. Only a person who has experienced this can understand what it means to lose so precious a gift of God.

It was on a Sabbath day that Jesus dealt with a man who had no sight to lose: he was born blind. Our Lord kindled the light of his eyes for the first time—a work of love properly performed on the Sabbath, despite the protests of the Pharisees. As for those who are spiritually blind—and all people are that by nature—Jesus said, "I came into this world that those who do not see may see."

As long as our Savior was in the world, He was "the Light of the world." He was the Light that didn't fail, for He opened people's eyes to the fact of their sinfulness; He enlightened them as to the way of salvation. He declared Himself to be the Way, the only way to peace and life with the heavenly Father, for He gave His life a ransom for all.

"*As long as* I am in the world, I am the Light of the world," said Jesus. But what happens now that He is no longer in the world in His visible presence? Has darkness taken over? Not at all, for His Word still shines. What is more, His people, bearing the light of the Gospel, are in the world. He tells them, "You are the light of the world," and St. Paul adds, "You shine as lights in the world"—in a crooked and perverse world.

Are we letting Christ's light shine through the forests and thickets of this world?

Prayer Suggestion

Pray that God may enlighten you through His Word, enabling you to lead others to the light in Christ Jesus.

Good, but Not Good Enough

Several years ago the Columbia Broadcasting System had to eliminate from a popular serial the representation of poor persons because the network was receiving too many CARE packages for these fictitious characters.

This is one of the many good features about people in general: they will respond to appeals for help, especially if the need can be visualized in terms of flesh-and-blood persons who are suffering. Love and compassion are human virtues that make life more livable in a world that is often cold and cruel. They should be recognized as good and laudable qualities, and children should be taught, mostly by parental example, to practice love for the neighbor, particularly the neighbor in need anywhere in the world.

Helping fellow human beings, if the effort is not to be tainted with selfishness, should be prompted, in St. Paul's words, by "love that issues from a pure heart and a good conscience and sincere faith." Unless works of love answer to this description, they are not good enough, and God can have no pleasure in them.

Listen to these words of the apostle on genuine love flowing from genuine faith: "If I speak in the tongues of men and of angels, but have not love, I am a noisy gong or a clanging cymbal. . . . If I give away all I have, and if I deliver my body to be burned, but have not love, I gain nothing."

Do you love Jesus Christ, who first loved you and gave Himself into death for you? "Yes," you say, "I truly love Him and am sincerely appreciative for what He has done for me." If you love Him, you will love His people also. It is as simple as that.

Prayer Suggestion

Ask God to lengthen, deepen, and widen your love to the Savior Jesus Christ, so that you may more fervently love human beings for whom He died.

God's Graffiti

On some houses in Chester, England, one can read statements of faith written in large enough letters so that they can be read from the street—statements like: "The Lord's providence is mine inheritance," or "In the Lord is my strength." While God has not commanded us to adorn the outer walls of our homes with such declarations, they do afford relief from the prominent, often garish, commercial signs affixed to city buildings.

Regrettably the walls of many homes bear another kind of implied inscription: the graffiti of sin—of lovelessness, selfishness, conformity to the world.

What counts in identifying a home as Christian is not what is written on the outside but what goes on in the inside—what goes on in the hearts of the people who occupy the house. Joshua of old said what should go on: "As for me and my house, we will serve the Lord."

Serving God comes in response to faith in Jesus Christ as the One who redeemed all people by His death and resurrection. The nurture of the Christian faith cannot be stressed enough. St. Paul told the trembling jailer of Philippi: "Believe in the Lord Jesus, and you will be saved, you and your household."

How wonderful when the home is God's little church, where parents and children gather around the family altar for worship! There the family members love and serve the Lord Jesus, and in love serve one another, as St. Paul writes, "Be kind to one another, tenderhearted, forgiving one another, as God in Christ forgave you."

Spiritual shabbiness inside a home is far worse than paint pealing off on the exterior walls. So let it in effect be written and carried out: "As for me and my house, we will serve the Lord."

Prayer Suggestion

Pray for God's help to make your home a place where faith in Christ prevails and adorns the house inwardly and outwardly.

Trifles and Treasures

These words of Jesus have sometimes puzzled people: "If your right eye causes you to sin, pluck it out . . . If your right hand causes you to sin, cut it off." Naturally, Jesus does not want us to understand this literally, as though He instructed us to mutilate our bodies for the sake of some spiritual gain. We dare not abuse the God-given members of our bodies.

Our Lord's intent goes much beyond physical surgery. He is pointing out the wisdom of removing from our lives whatever is harmful, lest we forfeit the one thing needful in time and in eternity: peace with God through our Lord Jesus Christ.

The rich man in Jesus' parable lived for the sake of the luxuries his wealth could provide. In the end he lost it all, including heaven. It would have been much better to do a little amputating, that is, separating his heart from his wealth and using his goods to minister to the poor to the glory of God. His true wealth ought to have been the abundance of what God offered him: the forgiveness of sins that Jesus Christ had come to procure for all people. Then he would have been rich in God.

The quest of earthly treasure and pleasure can mean compromises and the sacrifice of integrity, good character, the Christian faith. It can result in the loss of eternal life. Is it not better to let go the lesser things, so that we can retain the greater? This is simple, elementary arithmetic, and much in the Christian religion is based on just such simple, clear thinking. Jesus asks the simple question, but what a penetrating one: What shall it profit a person if he or she gains the whole world but in so doing loses spiritual values, yes his or her own soul?

Prayer Suggestion

Pray that God may give you the wisdom to separate the chaff from the wheat in your life—the trivia from the treasures of grace and forgiveness you have in Jesus Christ.

God's Shining Lights

The wrapper on a new light bulb says that it will give off 1,190 lumens of light and that it will shine for about 750 hours.

God's people are lights, as Jesus said, "You are the light of the world." St. Paul tells Christians to "shine as lights in the world," which he describes as "a crooked and perverse generation." St. Peter adds that God has called His people "out of darkness into His marvelous light." The darkness out of which they have come is sin, ignorance, superstition. The light in which they now live and which they reflect is the Good News that God loves them for the sake of Jesus Christ, that He has forgiven them all their sins, that by His Holy Spirit, He "turns them on" and enables them to let their light shine to God's glory and the good of the whole human family, to brighten the corner where they are.

But how much light does God want us to give off? No exact measurement can be made of that. The amount of light given off and the degree of brilliance with which it is done varies from person to person, in keeping with talents given, opportunities available, and the intensity of God-given faith. But this is sure: all members of God's family shine—the missionary who teaches and personifies the Gospel in primitive lands, the man and woman doing their daily work faithfully, the aged and the sick bearing their burdens with cheerfulness. They all give off light. What spiritual candle power!

And for how long should they shine? That is easily answered: as long as God gives them life. That may be 750 hours, the life expectancy of the average light bulb, or ten times that long, or 75 years. Christ is the Light, and to His glory we shine.

Prayer Suggestion

Ask the Holy Spirit to enlighten you, so that, knowing Jesus Christ as your Savior, you will radiate and reflect the wonderful love of God.

Jesus Makes the Difference

Why do people like or dislike the city or community where they live? Quite often it doesn't depend on the climate, or nice buildings, or amusement parks, but on whether they have friends there. In Caroline Keppel's song about a lover, "Robin Adair," it is asked, "What's this dull town to me? . . . where's all the joy and mirth that made this town a heaven on earth?" The answer is right there: "Robin's not near." People make the difference.

The presence of Jesus in our lives is the great plus, no matter where we live. He brings light and joy into the home, as a hymn stanza says, "Oh, blest the house, whate'er befall, Where Jesus Christ is all in all! For, if He were not dwelling there, How dark and poor and void it were!"

The room was dark and gloomy where the disciples were assembled after the crucifixion and burial of Jesus. Peter, the usually impetuous one, was there, and so was John, the disciple whom Jesus loved, and yet the place was cheerless. Then the resurrected Lord appeared, and how brightening His presence was! He brought hope, peace, and the forgiveness earned for them on the cross. John writes in his Gospel, in what may be one of the great understatements of the Bible: "Then the disciples were glad when they saw the Lord." They were jubilant!

What is heaven like? The Bible speaks of it in picturesque language: a heavenly city of pearly gates and streets of gold. But that is not what makes heaven a place where we want to be. We want to be there because Jesus, our dearest Friend, is there. In His company we find joy here in life, and the fullness of joy with Him in eternal life.

Prayer Suggestion

Pray that Jesus by His presence may brighten your life and make you one of His shining lights.

Jesus Gives Full Coverage

An interesting, if unpleasant, story lies behind the naming of Piccadilly Circus, a concourse once said to be the center of London if not of the whole British empire. At an earlier time a house of ill repute was allegedly located in the area, where sins were committed, or as people said, "little sins"—peccadillos in Spanish. From that supposedly came the name of the place: Piccadilly.

How is it with wrongdoing—is there such a thing as a little sin? Some theologians have distinguished between *venial* sins, or those everyday failings of which Christians readily repent, and *mortal* sins, which kill faith. A similar distinction would be involuntary and voluntary sins.

The trouble with such distinctions is that people may draw wrong conclusions, as though venial or involuntary sins were allowable, just so we avoid the gross sins. If we did that, however, we would be tempted to consider ourselves impeccable, and that is sinful pride.

In God's sight any transgression of His holy will is a sin, whether venial or mortal, involuntary or voluntary. God rules evenhandedly in regard to both *quality* and *quantity*. St. James writes, "Whoever keeps the whole Law but fails in one point has become guilty of all." One crack or break ruins the whole mirror. Let the distributor in a car be out of order and the whole vehicle comes to a standstill.

Now as for salvation from sin: Jesus died not only for the big sins but also for the little ones without distinction, for St. John declares, "The blood of Jesus His Son cleanses us from *all* sin." Also our peccadillos get us into trouble with God, and we need to avoid them. But this is also true: Jesus gives us full coverage of *all* sins.

Prayer Suggestion

Pray that for Jesus' sake God would forgive you all sins, also those of which you are not aware.

God's "Not Guilty" Verdict

Some persons bear the burden of guilt, if not their own then someone else's. A French writer has stated that Americans "want to be blamed for everything wrong in the world." They feel they must make restitution.

Sometimes conscience reaches back, wanting to assume the guilt of ancestors. An instance of this is the responsibility that Nathaniel Hawthorne apparently felt for the wrongdoing of his Puritan forefathers who in Salem, Mass., condemned witches to death. He writes in *The Scarlet Letter*, his novel on sin and guilt: "I hereby take shame upon myself for their sakes."

Of course, if a present-day generation repeats the wrongs of ancestors, it is equally at fault, not for other peoples' sins but for their own. In the Bible, the prophet Ezekiel makes this plain. He speaks against the then current proverb that the children's teeth are set on edge because their parents ate sour grapes. He teaches that people who repent are not held accountable for the sins of previous generations.

The Bible holds that no one can redeem his brother, his sister, his father, his mother, nor anyone else by trying to assume their guilt and shame. But what a mere human being was unable to do, Jesus Christ, true God and true man, did in behalf of us all. He gathered up all the sins of the world and bore their penalty on Calvary's cross. Now God's verdict concerning all who believe in Christ is "Not guilty!" In light of God's own pronouncement, it is unnecessary, even wrong, to try to bear one's own or other peoples' wrongs. God's own Word put this song on our lips: "I lay my sins on Jesus, The spotless Lamb of God; He bears them all and frees us From the accursed load."

Prayer Suggestion

Pray for a stronger faith in God's own promise that for Jesus' sake you are forgiven.

Beginning Our Work with Prayer

In the graveyard at Old Mines, Mo., the town where the Frenchman Philip Renault began to mine lead as early as 1726, one finds human interest items, such as this headstone inscription: "Henry B. Murphy, died February 28, 1859, from injuries received from the explosion of the steamer *Princess*."

Some occupations, like working in the mines, are hazardous. Jesus once spoke of 18 persons, probably workmen, on whom the tower of Siloam fell and killed them. No occupation is absolutely safe. Even the shepherd of Jesus' day had enemies threatening him: wolves, thieves and robbers.

Some say: Get out of high-risk jobs! But if all did that, who would mine our coal, fly our planes, serve as policemen? But we can be careful, anticipating potential dangers and taking precautions accordingly. Further, it helps to reduce accidents when we learn our jobs thoroughly and get enough rest at night.

But most of all, it helps when we begin our work with prayer. We can say: "Lord Jesus, let the holy angels be with me today, guarding me in all my ways. Keep me from falling into any kind of danger, either by my own neglect or from other causes. Keep me aware of the safety of my fellow workers. Remove from my heart and mind all distraction, and conflicts I bring with me from home. Give me inner peace, knowing that through Your redeeming merit I am at peace with God. Enable me to do my best at work, bringing to my tasks not only courage but also due caution. I put myself into Your hands, Lord Jesus!"

It certainly makes a difference when by prayer we put things into perspective. It makes for safety.

Prayer Suggestion

Pray that God may keep you alert to potential dangers at work and at home.

Freedom for Something

World War II was over for a long time, but for 29 years Hiroo Onoda, a lieutenant in the Japanese army, hid out in the jungles of the Philippines. Why didn't he come forward so that he might be taken back to his homeland? Conditioned to military obedience, he said he had been waiting for orders to return to Japan.

Today most people are different. Far from waiting for orders, they consider themselves free spirits who recognize no authority in home, school, at work, or in their vocation as citizens of the land.

No one values his or her freedom higher than a Christian, that is, the freedom from the slavery of the "thou shalt" and "thou shalt not" of the Law as prerequisites of salvation. Christians are free from the fear of punishment for being unable to keep God's law perfectly. How were they freed? St. Paul tells the Galatians: "Christ redeemed us from the curse of the law—for it is written, 'Cursed be everyone who hangs on a tree.' " Christ went to the cross to settle all the demands of God's law. Now we are free. As Gospel believers we refuse to be legalists who make salvation, fully or in part, depend on doing the works of the Law.

Christians interpret their freedom *from* something as freedom *for* something: to love God and serve one another. The New Testament records many instances of converts using their freedom in this way. Women like Dorcas and Lydia were free to serve. Onesimus, the run away slave, was free to return to his master, and Philemon, who owned him, received him as a brother.

Are you chained to the vice of self-service, or are you free to be Christ's servant?

Prayer Suggestion

Give thanks to Jesus Christ for freeing you from sin, asking Him to help you stand firm in freedom under the Gospel.

Government and God

The Declaration of Independence signers were not anarchists nor atheists. They declared for government and for God.

As for government, they were not bedeviled with the anarchistic ideas that "government," "law and order," "civil obedience," "armed forces," and "police" were bad words. Their concern was not *whether* there should be government, but *whose* government they should recognize. In the Declaration of Independence, which was signed on July 4, 1776, the founding fathers faulted the ruler abroad for misgovernment and the abuse of power. In their document they cite reasons for breaking with an overseas government and for declaring their loyalty to "the United States of America, in General Congress assembled." Yes, the signers were for good government.

They were also for God. They appeal to Him in their document some four times, referring to Him as God, Creator, Supreme Judge of the World, and Divine Providence.

Similarly many people today stand for government and for God. As to the former, they agree with the sentiments of Stephen A. Douglas as inscribed on his tomb in Chicago: "Tell my children to obey the laws and to uphold the Constitution." The God they serve is not some vague national deity but the One who has revealed Himself in Jesus Christ as the God of love. This God they serve because His Son, our Lord Jesus Christ, "came not to be served but to serve, and to give His life a ransom for many." Because they are for God, they are also for government, His institution.

Prayer Suggestion

Pray for all who are in authority, that through them God may grant us peace, justice, and good order.

Freedom for Something

Independence Day, July 4, 1776, marked the signing of the Declaration of Independence. In this document a baker's dozen of colonies in America declared their freedom from a tyrannical government abroad.

Independent nationhood implies not only a freedom from something but also a freedom for something—freedom to determine its own affairs, freedom for all citizens to make a decent living, educate their children, pursue happiness, and worship God according to the dictates of their own consciences. Our forefathers over 200 years ago deemed this kind of freedom worth fighting for.

In their misguided zeal some citizens march and demonstrate for a freedom that is more license than liberty: freedom for filthy speech, free sex, pornography, and other so-called freedoms passing for civil rights. These "causes" are caricatures—hollow mockeries—of the freedom on which the United States of America stands. It bears repeating that the "civil rights" coin has another side that is clearly stamped "civil responsibility."

The freedom-for-something theme invites the American people to draw on inner motivation to fulfill their functions. For many that inner motivation stems from their gratitude to Jesus Christ for turning slavery under the Law to freedom under the Gospel. He fulfilled the Law, suffering also the consequences of humankind's disobedience. The watchword now is, according to St. Paul: "For freedom Christ has set us free; stand fast therefore, and do not submit again to a yoke of slavery."

Prayer Suggestion

Ask God to guide this nation in the right use of freedom and keep it from every abuse of freedom.

What Remains to Be Done

Ah, Wilderness, the only one of Eugene O'Neill's plays that has a happy ending, tells about the July 4, 1906, weekend events of the Millers, a New England family.

On another July 4, this one in 1776, "Ah, Wilderness" could well have described the infant country that was to develop into the United States of America. The original thirteen colonies lay along the Atlantic seaboard. Not much was known of the land lying beyond the Appalachian Mountains. The Louisiana Purchase had not yet added the vast territory between the Mississippi River and the Rocky Mountains. All that was known was that this was a wilderness.

The signers of the Declaration of Independence, while they could not have foreseen all the pleasant and unpleasant events of this country's history, were given to high political ideals. In the words of Abraham Lincoln's Gettysburg Address, they "brought forth upon this continent a new nation, conceived in liberty and dedicated to the proposition that all men are created equal."

This was, to be sure, a good beginning. What remains to be done is to translate the high ideals into realities, so that not only a privileged few but all citizens can enjoy the inalienable rights of life, liberty, and the pursuit of happiness. Unless this occurs, this nation, unlike O'Neill's play, will have an unhappy ending.

We can only look to the God of all grace, to the Father of our Savior Jesus Christ and our Father, to help us fulfill the principles on which our nation stands.

Prayer Suggestion

Thank God for His shower of blessing on this land, praying also that He lead us to use them rightly.

A Song of Loyalty

David begins Psalm 101 with this resolve: "I will sing of loyalty and justice; to Thee, O Lord, I will sing." He then elaborates on loyalty, justice, and righteousness—virtues that give strength to a nation, and civic qualities that need emphasis at all times.

Where is a good place for right citizenship to begin? Surely the home for it represents community life in miniature. A nation is only as strong as its homes, and homes are only as strong as the moral character of the people in them. Therefore it is important as David goes on to say: "I will walk with integrity of heart within my house."

Moral integrity carries over from homes to schools and to places of employment. The psalmist resolves, "Perverseness of heart shall be far from me; I will know nothing of evil." At work it is important what we do with our hands and head, but of even greater importance is what we are at heart.

Moving on to a still larger circle, David is determined to practice good citizenship toward all the people of the land: "I will look with favor on the faithful in the land, that they may dwell with me." We are a nation of many millions of inhabitants. All these fellow citizens have the same rights we desire for ourselves. Can people say they are loyal to their country when they refuse to let others live with them?

Loyalty to God goes hand in hand with loyalty to the neighbor. Jesus Christ the Savior of humanity, stated it very clearly, "Render therefore to Caesar the things that are Caesar's, and to God the things that are God's."

Prayer Suggestion

Thank God for the blessing we enjoy in this land, especially for freedom of worship.

The Business of Politics

Almost every other year, we have the opportunity to put one of our civic privileges and responsibilities into practice: the opportunity to vote.

On election day, good citizens should not only vote, but vote according to their informed convictions and best knowledge. Paul Simon of Illinois has written, "Voting means not only going to the polling booth and making an 'X' for the candidates whose names sound good; it means casting an intelligent, informed vote."

To be intelligent, informed voters, citizens use the intervening time to study the issues, evalute the candidates' speeches, and discuss public affairs with others.

Politics is the citizen's business, also after—and especially after—the scandals summed up under the title "Watergate." We cannot withdraw into our shells under the pretext that politics is dirty business. If it is dirty in spots, that is all the more reason for citizens to clean it up. An effective broom or cleaning mop at our disposal is the ballot. Another way is to write constructive letters to those who represent us in government.

To be good citizens is a large, encompassing order, but we can be equal to it. Christ calls us to be the salt of the earth and the light of the world. Our Savior from sin, having made us a new creation in Him, gives us strength for all of our tasks.

Prayer Suggestion

Pray that God may open your eyes to the privileges and duties of citizenship.

Passing On What We Have Received

When Leonard Jerome, the once wealthy American businessman and maternal grandfather of England's Winston Churchill, lay on his deathbed, he said to his family, and these were his last words: "I have given you all I have. Pass it on." The report goes on to say that he left his family mostly debts.

Only Jesus can say that He bequeathed us something truly precious for time and for eternity. No, He didn't leave us material wealth: real estate, gold, silver, dollars, or diamonds. He gave us something far better, saying: "Peace I leave with you; My peace I give to you; not as the world gives do I give to you." This peace is reconciliation between God and the sinful human race, and Jesus gained it for us when He gave His life. He declared that He, the Son of Man, had come to serve and to give His life a ransom for sinners.

Redemption is our Lord's legacy. But for what has He redeemed us? He has given us not only eternal life in the future, but also spiritual life in the present. To what end shall we use it? Winston Churchill, the grandson of the aforementioned Mr. Jerome, also spoke on his deathbed. His last words were: "Life is a journey well worth making." This is especially true if in our journey through life we confess faith in the Savior Jesus Christ and put this faith into practice by doing good, not in order to be saved, but because we are saved.

When we use our lives to glorify God and love our neighbors, we pass on what we have received. In Christ we have peace—peace with God, peace with one another, peace with ourselves. We share this peace when we lead other people to Christ, the Prince of Peace.

Prayer Suggestion

Ask God for a willing and able spirit to share the love God has given you in Christ.

The Joyful Outlook on Life

For some people, even for those perfectly healthy and in possession of needful things, life is dreary, like a cloudy day.

On the other hand, it is often the heavily burdened person who is thankful, hopeful, joyful. Much suffering has not deprived him or her of the treasure of happiness. A man who spent a great deal of time in prison and faced death on many occasions was St. Paul. He could live with seeming contradictions; he could be, in his own words, "sorrowful, but always rejoicing."

Pessimism looks at the dark side of things. Instead of seeing a glass as half full, it is to pessimistic people half empty. Nothing is ever half won; it is always half lost. They cannot find delight in wild flowers, for they see them as weeds. How refreshing it was when a well-known entertainer, Jerry Lewis, said after his double-bypass heart operation in a Las Vegas hospital: "The sage brush is beginning to look like orchids."

The Christian's joyful outlook on life is not fantasy, is not blue-sky optimism, but realism. It has a real foundation. It can exist when dark clouds blot out the sun, for it does not depend on changeable weather, nor on fickle human emotions, nor on here-today-gone-tomorrow success. It rests not on human beings but on Jesus Christ, who for us and for our salvation passed through the dark night of suffering and death to rise again on Easter morning. The Holy Spirit He sends us is the author of our faith in the Savior and of all its fruits. As St. Paul has written: "The fruit of the Spirit is love, joy, peace . . ."

Look out your window. What do you see? A glass half empty or half full? A field of weeds or of wheat? Sage brush or orchids?

Prayer Suggestion

Ask God to help you find or keep the joy Jesus has promised you.

In God's Who's Who

Just about everyone knows that on the fateful night of April 18, 1775, Paul Revere rode from Boston toward Lexington and Concord to warn the people of the approach of enemy troops. What many people don't know is that on the same night another rider was on a similar mission. He was William Dawes, a forgotten man.

Among Bible people, you sometimes find one man overshadowing another. Peter is better known than Andrew his brother. John lived to a very ripe old age and is known to us for writing a gospel, three epistles, and the book of Revelation, but his brother James, martyred as early as A.D. 44, is scarcely known to us. We know about Thomas—his doubts, his return to faith. His name indicates that he was a twin, but of his twin brother or sister nothing is known.

There are today people who like the rider William Dawes are overshadowed by the more celebrated Paul Reveres. It doesn't really matter, not if what they do is to the glory of God and the good of their fellow human beings. Suffice it that God knows. He will lay His own kind of blessing on all unsung heroes and heroines who without acclaim do their job faithfully as mothers and homemakers, as fathers and breadwinners, as workers everywhere who know that they serve God in their vocations.

Jesus Christ came not to be served but to serve and to give His life a ransom for all. "The world knew Him not," writes John. But that did not keep our Lord from dying on a cross to redeem the world. In doing so He left us an example that we should follow in His steps. Those who do, have their names in the book of life, in God's Who's Who.

Prayer Suggestion

Ask God to show you opportunities of service and give you the ability to fulfill them.

Don't Give Up!

One day a submarine exploded in a Scotland harbor, and many men were wounded. One badly hurt man said to the medical attendants, "No good working with me. I'm through. Help the others." Nevertheless he was rushed to a hospital in Glasgow, where he recovered. He entered a happy marriage, had a family, and after a useful life retired in a peaceful village. It was a good thing that the first-aid men didn't give up on him.

No one can really say for sure that a situation is hopeless. Many patients, one pronounced incurable, have recovered. Many vexing problems in the home, thought to be insurmountable, have been solved and marriages saved. A failing business enterprise may enter a new cycle and be saved from bankruptcy.

With God nothing is impossible. Into His hands we can confidently entrust our affairs, no matter how difficult they are. God not only knows their outcome but also has the power and gracious will to turn the outcome to our good. With His help we can approach our problems with new hope. Did not God solve the greatest human problem of all—sin? He sent His Son Jesus Christ among us that, by walking the way of the cross, He might set our feet on the road to eternal life.

"Don't give up the ship!" said wounded Captain Lawrence as he was being carried from his post in a War of 1812 sea battle. In less dramatic situations you may be tempted to give up, to throw in the towel, to abandon trust in God. Don't do it! With the psalmist say to your soul, "Hope in God; for I shall again praise Him, who is my help and my God."

Prayer Suggestion

Ask God for the confidence to live day by day in His love, letting tomorrow take care of its problems.

Between Two Dangers

When St. Paul was on his way to Rome for a hearing before Ceasar, he passed through the straits of Messina, a dangerous passage. On the Italian side was a projecting rock called Scilla, while on the opposite side, on the coast of Sicily, was Charybdis, a treacherous whirlpool. Mariners had all they could do to steer a course between the two.

Human life is full of dilemmas, of dangers on both sides. As one expression has it, we find ourselves between the devil and the deep blue sea. Parents face the danger of either neglecting their children, or of being overprotective. Neither is in the child's best interest. As Christians we want to avoid loving the sinful world, and we have to avoid the other extreme, too, that of fleeing the world like hermits. Over against those who err, we face the danger of overreacting in judgment, or the opposite danger of not reacting at all, of being indifferent. Both show a lack of love.

What can we do when trapped between two dangers? We have to give the situation careful thought, consult with others, pray to God for guidance, and then exercise good judgment, that is, a judgment informed by God's Word.

It is helpful to ask: What would Jesus do if He were in my place? Jesus Himself had many choices to make, as when in the Garden of Gethsemane He had to choose between saving His own life and saving the lives of the countless people He had come to redeem. He chose the latter, though it meant His death. For the joy that was set before Him He endured the cross and won through to victory. He knows what it means to face dilemmas, and He will help those who in prayer ask His guidance.

Prayer Suggestion

Ask God for the wisdom and courage to proceed safely when dangers abound on both sides.

Straightening Out the Picture

While Jesse James and the Ford brothers were discussing their next holdup in a St. Joseph, Mo., house—so the story goes—James noticed that the wall picture "God Bless This House" was hanging crooked. As he got up to straighten it, he was allegedly shot to death by Bob Ford.

What Jesse James needed (and many others today need) is a straightened-out life. It matters not how people acquire what is not theirs: by robbery, by theft, by cheating—they are crooks walking a crooked mile. It matters not what the sin is—hurt to the neighbor, sexual immorality, gossip or slander—people who commit it are out of line with God's moral law. Their lives are full of dangerous S-curves.

Sin is crookedness, and for that there is only one corrective: faith and life in Jesus Christ. The Son of God came into this world, which St. Paul describes as "a crooked and perverse generation," to straighten things for everyone. It was for this that He died and rose again. The work that the Savior was to do was foretold by Isaiah in picturesque way: "Every valley shall be exalted, and every mountain and hill shall be made low; and the crooked shall be made straight, and the rough places plain."

Christ can turn things around in your life. He wants to come to you with many blessings—with His forgiving love, with a new set of values, with a clear sense of direction. He wants to straighten out the dangerous S-curves in your life; He wants to straighten out the picture.

Prayer Suggestion

Ask Jesus Christ to work in your heart and home to make life pleasant, beautiful, and straight.

In Step with the Heavenly Father

Some people reenact the sins of their parents, as when they abuse their children because their parents did this to them.

Sometimes it is the other way around: parents reenact the sins of their children. In 1801 Philip Hamilton engaged in a duel, which was against the law, and lost his life. Three years later his father, Alexander Hamilton, likewise disobeyed this law. In the same wooded spot at Weehawken, New Jersey, he dueled with Aaron Burr and lost his life. He learned nothing from his son's experience.

There is no reason to imitate or perpetuate anyone's sin— neither for the children to repeat their parent's sin, nor the parents their children's. Every person is individually accountable to God. Every person receives guidance from God on how to live.

That is a wonderful thing, for He in whose footsteps we walk is our heavenly Father. He is the one whose thoughts we think, whose example we follow, whose love we imitate, for we are His family. St. Paul tells the Galatians: "You are all the children of God by faith in Christ Jesus. For as many of you as have been baptized into Christ have put on Christ."

Here lies the secret of the ability to live like the heavenly Father: Christ has redeemed us from sin, set us free, and through Holy Baptism takes us into fellowship with Him, giving us the power to lead an upright life in accordance with our heavenly Father's Word.

So in the so-called Hamilton families of today, let not the son defy the law and let not the father follow the example of his son. Let all members of the family be in step with the Father in heaven!

Prayer Suggestion

Thank God for parents who walk with God and whose teaching and example children can safely follow.

Have a Heart!

In *The Wizard of Oz*, it is a great moment in the life of the Tin Man when he finds a heart. He becomes human.

It is a turning point in all peoples' lives when God gives them a new heart. Such a spiritual heart transplant takes place when the Holy Spirit through the Gospel makes Christians of them. They then give themselves to Jesus Christ, who gave all—His own life—for them.

The world needs people who have a heart, who are loving, compassionate, merciful. So often it seems that people have become robots, mechanical beings going thoughtlessly and heartlessly through their daily routines. A robot or computer can be programmed to do many things—to operate intricate mechanisms, to store up valuable facts, to cough them up on demand. He can be said to have a brain, but alas, he has no heart. Human beings shouldn't be like that.

We have a heart when we let justice be tempered with mercy, when we go the second mile with someone at work who has difficulty meeting expectations. We have heart when in emergency situations we share our bread with the hungry, clothe the naked, provide shelter to the homeless, then help such victims to plan a more stable future and give them an opportunity to get on their feet, so to speak.

Some people consider having a heart as a sign of weakness, of being soft. Instead, to have a heart bespeaks courage; it is a sign of strength. To give deprived people a chance, to see a problem through to a solution, to be a person who cares—that requires heart.

The quality of life is greatly improved when we show heartfelt love.

Prayer Suggestion

Ask God for Jesus' sake to give you a clean, new heart, and to renew a right spirit in you.

The Healers

Many wounds were made when, in the Crimean War, Lord Cardigan led what is known in story and song as "the charge of the Light Brigade." Three fourths of the men were lost. All the while another kind of heroism was performed, although it was not considered a spectacular feat: Florence Nightingale was the first army nurse to go into combat zones to help the wounded.

Some things people do are considered more glamorous than others. Deeds of great daring appeal to the imagination, although they do not always change the course of history. At the same time other people are quietly working away at the task of improving the lot of humanity. They may rate scant attention, but as helpers and healers they are the true benefactors of the human race.

Before Christ ascended into heaven He appointed twelve to make disciples of all nations. Many thought that their mission would come to nothing. But it wasn't long before the critics changed their ridicule into a complaint—a complaint that was really a compliment—when they said in Thessalonika: "These men . . . have turned the world upside down." That was made possible because the apostles and all their helpers had not gone out to do violence, to start bloody revolutions, to strike wounds, but to heal—to heal the hearts of people with the Gospel of Jesus Christ.

The early Christians could turn the world upside down because in Christ God had already turned it around. He so loved all people everywhere in the world that He gave His only Son, Jesus Christ, to be wounded for their transgressions, so that by His stripes they might be healed. All who go out to tell this Good News are healers.

Prayer Suggestion

Ask God to help you reach out to others with words of the Gospel and deeds of love.

Unsung Heroes and Heroines

The town of Amherst, Mass., was the birthplace of the poet Emily Dickinson (1830–86). After her death 1,776 unpublished poems were found in the drawer of her writing desk. It indicates that her contemporaries and neighbors were not too appreciative of her work.

Jesus said that a prophet is apt to have honor everywhere else but in his own country. The same is true of persons in other vocations. Sometimes it remains for later generations to discover their talented and painstaking labors. It may be true also of you. You have worked hard, given of yourself, put forth great effort for a worthy cause and you get hardly a thank-you.

We cannot let nonrecognition bother us. We must not lament when we, like the comedian Dangerfield, "get no respect." Our good deeds stand on their own merits. Let it suffice that God knows. Even when we rest from our labors, our deeds still follow us. Along with our names, our efforts are written in the book of life, and they cannot be erased.

The poet John Keats, who died at age 25, wanted this written on his tombstone: "Here lies one whose name was writ in water." We are mortal, and the memory of our fellow human beings may be short, but God remembers. He knew us before we were born, loved us, and redeemed us through His Son Jesus Christ that we might serve Him. As Isaiah puts it, God has engraven us on the palms of His hands.

In her time and place Emily Dickenson enjoyed scant recognition, but she kept on with her excellent work. So let it be with us.

Prayer Suggestion

Pray that God may sustain you in your zeal even when your work is not appreciated.

Proper Self-Image

In Joseph Kesserling's play *Arsenic and Old Lace* an actor playing the role of Teddy Brewster thinks he is Teddy Roosevelt. He runs up and down the stairway pretending that he is leading a cavalry charge up San Juan hill. He imagines that the Panama Canal runs through the basement of his home.

It is one thing to pretend—children often do that at play—and another to be deceived. In their delusions people often get fiction mixed up with fact. It happens in many areas of life—in business, when a bad deal is mistaken for a good one; in the home, when someone in the dark reaches into the medicine cabinet and takes the wrong pills; in travel, when one turns left instead of right.

It is especially bad when delusions are perpetrated in the name of religion. Some leaders of religious cults make promises they cannot fulfill. Some deceive their followers into believing that they are what they are not—or that they are not what they are. To tell people, for example, that they are without sin and have in them the potential of moral perfection is to cast them in false roles. Thus many a Teddy Brewster is led to think he is Teddy Roosevelt.

There is no mistaken identity, no false self-image, no deceptive roleplaying, no delusion in these words of St. Paul: "You [God] made alive, when you were dead through . . . trespasses and sins . . . God, who is rich in mercy, out of the great love with which He loved us . . . made us alive together with Christ, for "in Christ we have redemption through His blood, the forgiveness of our trespasses."

Now we don't have to pretend to be what we are not, for God has given us our true identity. In Christ we are His children and heirs of eternal life.

Prayer Suggestion

Ask the Holy Spirit to clear your heart and mind of all delusions and to lead you into all truth.

What an Exchange of Roles!

As a student in Magdeburg, Germany, Martin Luther was shocked at seeing a man, who was a member of a religious order, carrying a sack and begging in the streets. Because of the discipline to which he subjected himself, he was a thin, wasted figure— nothing more than "animated bones," as someone said. What was remarkable about this man was that he had been Prince William of Anhalt, a German state. He voluntarily exchanged his luxurious life as a nobleman for a miserable existence.

Although we may not approve of what this man did, we can refer to his self-denial as somewhat descriptive of someone else's far greater exchange of roles in our behalf. St. Paul speaks of this in Philippians, chapter 2, where he declares that Jesus Christ, who was God's true Son and thus "in the form of God" and equal with the Father, took the form of a servant, not only to serve but to become obedient unto death, even death on a cross.

When you read about Jesus in the Gospels—how He was rejected, despised, hated, spat upon, crowned with thorns, and nailed to a cross—you get an inkling of what it meant for the Son of God, the King of the angels, to leave the glory of heaven in order to become our Savior here on earth. Christ's self-chosen humiliation and poverty was far greater than that of Prince William of Anhalt. The latter probably did it trying to earn his salvation. Jesus did it out of love to us, for we cannot save ourselves.

How do we benefit? St. Paul tells us in Second Corinthians 8: "You know the grace of our Lord Jesus Christ, that though He was rich, yet for your sake He became poor, so that by His poverty you might become rich"—rich in forgiveness and peace with God!

Prayer Suggestion

Say a prayer of thanksgiving to Christ for what He did in your behalf.

Guide and Guidebook for Life

People who travel need maps, guidebooks, and tourist literature. A book that has served travelers well by pointing out where to go and what to see is known as *Baedeker*. It is a guidebook that was first issued by Karl Baedeker in 1839, and it has in our time been reissued by the author's grandson. The book is accurate and reliable. All of life is a journey, taking us to many places, some interesting and exciting, and some not. Life's journey is marked by uncertainty, by questions like these: Is this the road to go in order to reach my goal? Is this the way to take in order to avoid moral perils and pitfalls, and to live a life pleasing to God?

We are blessed in having a travel guide: Jesus Christ. He declares Himself to be the Way, the Truth, the Life, promising that all who follow Him will not walk in darkness but will enjoy the light of life. He proclaimed Himself as the only Way to the Father in heaven, as the only bridge and road to eternal life.

But you may ask: Did Jesus not ascend into heaven? How can we follow a Guide who is no longer here on earth? Indeed, we can follow Him, for we have a divine Guidebook, the Holy Scripture. It brings us the teachings of Jesus and what the prophets and apostles taught concerning salvation in Him. "The Sacred Writings," says St. Paul, "are able to instruct you for salvation through faith in Christ Jesus."

Jesus Himself declares that the Scripture testifies of Him. It testifies that He, the Son of God born of the Virgin Mary, gave His life a ransom for all. It invites, "Believe in the Lord Jesus, and you will be saved."

There is no need to wander through life without a sense of direction. We have in Christ a reliable Guide, and the Bible as our guidebook.

Prayer Suggestions

Ask the Holy Spirit to guide you into all truth by leading you to Jesus, your Guide, Guardian, and Friend.

God's Welcome to All

In Maxim's Restaurant in Paris there is a table, No. 16, which is sometimes occupied, sometimes not. It is permanently reserved for celebrities. Undoubtedly the proprietor has difficulty at times in determining who is and who is not a prominent person.

There is no test of human merit or worthiness one must pass in order to qualify for God's favor. "Thou preparest a table before me," wrote David in his shepherd psalm, the 23rd. Before he became king, David was a plain, ordinary shepherd boy, and even then he knew that he was recipient of the goodness of God. The meek, the humble, the weary, the ordinary folk—the non-celebrites—are invited to eat and be satisfied. This is God's invitation through Isaiah: "Come, buy and eat! Come, buy wine and milk without money and without price."

In response to such an invitation Charlotte Elliott resolved, in a hymn we all love to sing: "Just as I am, without one plea But that Thy blood was shed for me And that Thou bidd'st me come to Thee, O Lamb of God, I come, I come."

Someone has said: "You don't have to be in *Who's Who* to know what's what." It is often to common people that God reveals true wisdom. Jesus thanked the heavenly Father for making great truths known to babes, that is, to people who don't let pride and prejudice and pretention get in the way of understanding. St. Paul tells the Corinthians: "God chose what is low and despised in the world . . . so that no human being might boast in His sight."

The One whom God sent to save the human race from the folly of sin was not a great philosopher, a mighty king, or a recognized celebrity. He was Jesus of Nazareth, who calls Himself meek and lowly in heart, then invites us: "Come to Me, all who labor and are heavy laden, and I will give you rest."

Prayer Suggestion

Simply say now: "Lord, I come to You with all my failings, because I know You will receive me."

211

You May Be Close!

Sometimes we are closer to what we seek than we realize. After a blinding blizzard, victims have been found, frozen to death, only a few feet from their homes. Once an empty car was found near the Missouri River, and on the seat lay a copy of the book *The Christian's Secret of a Happy Life.* The owner of the car was found in the river, a victim of suicide. Perhaps he was much closer to finding peace and meaning in life than what he knew.

To a scribe who had given a wise answer Jesus said, "You are not far from the kingdom of God." He was not yet a follower of Christ—he was not yet in Christ's kingdom—but he was close.

When St. Paul, having made a defense of the Gospel he preached, asked King Agrippa whether he believed, the king replied: "Almost thou persuadest me to be a Christian." Also he may have been close to finding his salvation in Christ.

So it may be in our lives. Here we are with problems that seem insoluble. But who knows? An extra inch, another forward step, another ten minutes of patience—what a difference they can make! That burden you are carrying, can you bear it yet a few more feet? Perhaps you are close to your goal, closer to help and relief than you think. Can you wait a little while longer for a wayward son or daughter to come home, or for a letter from him or her?

In your relation to God, you have frequently and fervently prayed for light, but darkness seems to continue around you. Sometimes it is the darkest right before the dawn. So hang in there! God encourages us to be patient, to wait on Him. Think how patient He was with us. To this day God has not given up on us. He wants us to be His children through faith in Jesus Christ, who died and rose again to save us. He wants you to be close to Him.

Prayer Suggestion

Pray that God may give you the patience to wait for His timing.

Who Are We Really?

In Sigmund Romberg's operetta *The Desert Song*, battles are fought between French troops and a tribe of northern Africans. The French governor's son, Pierre, is secretly sympathetic with the natives. So he puts on a mask and aids them as the unidentified Red Shadow. All the while Margot, his sweetheart, finds herself in the strange position of despising him as the governor's son but loving him as the Red Shadow.

On the stage of everyday life people often wear masks and play contradictory parts. It is interesting to note that the word "hypocrite" originally meant a mimic, an actor who on the stage pretends to be somebody else.

There was such a pretender in the circle of Christ's disciples: Judas Iscariot, who skillfully disguised his absence of faith from the other disciples. More and more he revealed his true self, as when he spoke the lines: "Why was this ointment not sold for three hundred denarii and given to the poor?" He objected to Mary's gift to Jesus, not because he loved the poor but because he loved money and stole from the treasury of Christ's disciples.

It is important to ask: Who am I really? Do I play roles to deceive people? Am I what I pretend to be? Do I pretend to be what I am not? Am I like the aforementioned Red Shadow—or like a modern Zorro—who puts on a mask and plays a deceptive role?

Our Lord desires us to be disciples who have unfeigned, genuine faith in Him and who serve Him and His brothers and sisters with a love consistent with such a faith. For it was not as a stage actor, but as one loving us sincerely that Jesus Christ went to the cross to make us His people.

Prayer Suggestion

Ask the Holy Spirit to work in you the fruit of Christian sincerity after the image of Christ's sincere love.

Christ, Friend and Brother

Heinrich and Thomas Mann had much in common. They were brothers, and both were authors. Yet they were not close. As boys they shared a bedroom but seldom played together. It is said that for a whole year they didn't speak to each other.

In some families brothers and sisters, also parents and children, are cold and distant in their feelings. Sibling rivalry can contribute to this. Some families are divided because of the way the inheritance has been divided.

When this happens, we can better understand what the Biblical writer tells us in Proverbs: "There is a friend that sticks closer than a brother." Such a friend may give the ultimate sacrifice, as many men have done in battle for their buddies. Jesus said, "Greater love has no man than this, that a man lay down his life for his friends."

Jesus is our Friend—with a capital "F"—because this is precisely what He did. He gave His life on the cross so that we might have forgiveness of sins and peace with God. He is indeed the great Friend, for He died not only for His friends but also for His enemies—for all people, in other words. St. Paul declares, "While we were enemies we were reconciled to God by the death of His Son."

But in Christ we have more than a Friend; we have also a Brother. The aforementioned Heinrich and Thomas Mann lacked a sense of brotherhood and so had to turn to other persons for close friendships. In Jesus Christ we have a Friend and a Brother in the same person. He is our Brother because He and we have the same heavenly Father. How wonderful for us that He is not ashamed to call us His brothers and sisters! Close to Him, we are close also to one another.

Prayer Suggestion

Ask the Holy Spirit to draw you closer into the family of faith.

When Is It Time to Pray?

Every year there are many boating deaths and injuries in the United States.

Ever since human beings took to the water for pleasure or business, accidents and deaths by drowning have occurred. The prophet Jonah, cast overboard, would surely have drowned had not God intervened. The story of a shipwreck in the Book of Acts, which involved St. Paul during his voyage to Rome, is a classic in its description of heroic seamanship during a storm.

Perhaps the best-known sea story in the Bible is that of Jesus fast asleep in the boat during a storm on the Sea of Galilee. The disciples, some of them experienced boatmen, did their utmost to keep the ship afloat. When sensing the danger of a shipwreck they aroused Jesus and said, "Save us, we are perishing."

We don't have to wait until things get worse before we pray. During a severe storm on the Mississippi River, Huckleberry Finn and Jim, the runaway slave, were caught on their raft. "Aren't you going to pray?" Jim asks. To this Huck replies: "It isn't bad enough yet."

We don't want to become a statistic in life's storms. So we exercise skill and care. What is more, we pray. "Pray constantly," St Paul tells the Thessalonians—also in good times and when the weather is fair. The disciples prayed not only during the tempest but at other times as well, for so Jesus had taught them. He also *enabled* them and us to pray directly to the Father when by His atoning self-sacrifice He took away our offenses, made peace between us and God, and opened the door of prayer.

When is it time to pray? You know the answer: All the time!

Prayer Suggestions

Ask Jesus, the Captain of our salvation, to pilot you, guide you, and steer a safe course for you on life's tempestuous sea.

Christ's Sustaining Arms

The familiar domesticated fowl—chickens—were known in ancient times. They are shown on Egyptian monuments and are mentioned in the Bible. The third watch of the night was called cockcrowing. To Peter our Lord said, "Before the rooster crows tonight you will say three times that you do not know Me." At another time Jesus referred to a mother hen gathering her chicks under her wings and protecting them.

He went on to say to Jerusalem, in a sense as the parent of children: "How many times I wanted to put My arms around all your people . . . but you would not let Me." Her leaders, playing it cozy with the Romans, failed to provide the spiritual nourishment and guidance the people needed. What was worse, they killed the prophets and stoned God's messengers. And when the Messiah came in the person of Jesus of Nazareth, He was sent to the cross by them.

Now enthroned in Jerusalem above, which St. Paul calls the "mother of us all," Jesus cares for His church. His heart goes out to all its members, especially to the young. He pleads with parents to guide and guard the children God has entrusted to them. Through His Word He gathers young and old about Him to nurture them into a fellowship so that He may use their arms to sustain the weak.

We are grateful that the exalted Christ even now puts His arms around us all, "just as a hen gathers her chicks under her wings." What is more, having strengthened us, He uses our arms to support our brothers and sisters as they bear heavy burdens. Christ has no other arms but ours.

Prayer Suggestion

Pray that the Lord may sustain you with His love and enable you to lend support to others.

The Herd That Heard

Who are the sheep that are led beside still waters, find pasture, and are guarded and protected? They are the ones that listen to their shepherd and follow him. It is "the herd that heard."

Such are the people who constitute the flock of Jesus Christ, the Good Shepherd. They recognize His voice as He speaks in His Word. They are well provided for. Forgiveness, assurance of salvation, peace with God, a life made meaningful—all these blessings Christ procured for them when He laid down His life. The psalmist David sums it up: "Goodness and mercy shall follow me all the days of my life, and I shall dwell in the house of the Lord forever."

Some, of course, don't want to belong to "the herd that heard." They insist on doing their own thing. They leave verdant valleys, thinking they can climb mountains although they are not mountain sheep; they fall and break legs. They regard it more exciting to follow religious hirelings, even the thinly disguised thieves and robbers. They don't think that the devil is the big, bad wolf after all. So they take off on their own and soon lose their way. They would be easy prey if the Good Shepherd did not go after them and bring them back.

And lest we think that we are not that foolish, we consider St. Peter's words to us, "You were like sheep that had lost their way, but now you have been brought back to follow the Shepherd and Keeper of your souls."

Words from The Whiffenpoof Song say: "We're poor little lambs who have lost our way . . . We're little black sheep who have gone astray." That is hardly news, but this is the Good News, in Jesus' words: "The Good Shepherd gives His life for the sheep."

Prayer Suggestion

Pray that the Holy Spirit may open your inner ears to hear the voice of the Good Shepherd.

A Choice to Be Made

In his American classic *The House of the Seven Gables* Nathaniel Hawthorne tells how greed can bring misery on a family through many generations. He pictures one character as bearing the image of Mammon, the god of materialism. Mammon represents not money but the love of money.

In John Milton's *Paradise Lost*, Mammon is presented as an evil angel. Filled with greed, he is forever admiring the gold with which the streets of heaven are supposedly paved, and of God's glory it wants to see nothing. For this he was expelled from heaven.

As Mammon in the above story could not love both God and gold, neither can human beings. Jesus declares, "No one can serve two masters; for either he will hate the one and love the other, or else he will be devoted to the one and despise the other. You cannot serve God and Mammon."

Mammon calls many shots today. It rejoices when people acquire money and goods dishonestly, when profits mean everything and poverty means nothing, when the black, flowing gold, oil sits on the throne, when people build their houses of seven or more gables by unrighteousness and their rooms by wrong.

However, Jesus is a much better choice than Mammon, for all the good is on the side of our Savior. He gives life—the life in God that extends from here to eternity. The forgiveness and peace He obtained for us is spiritual wealth far exceeding any worldly treasure. It is not lessened by inflation, excessive interest rates, skyrocketing consumer price index. It is safe. So we seek first God's kingdom and receive many other things as a bonus.

Prayer Suggestion

Pray that the Holy Spirit may increase in you the love of Christ and make you rich in Him.

Reversing the Flow of Life

An earthquake that rocked the New Madrid, Missouri, area in 1812 was said to have for awhile reversed the flow of the Mississippi River.

Are there events that can so drastically affect people as to cause the streams of their lives to flow backwards? Or to alter their course? In her life's story, significantly entitled *Changing*, the Norwegian actress Liv Ullman declares, "The void that Papa's death left in me became a kind of a cavity, into which later experiences were to be laid."

Not only tragic events but also wrong thoughts can reverse the flow of one's life. This fact is demonstrated in people described for us in the Bible. When Adam and Eve in Paradise resolved to disobey God, their lives—and those of all their descendants—were radically changed.

We have in Jesus' parable of the successful farmer the owner's decision to build larger barns so that he could store up all his grain for his own selfish use—this, instead of letting his riches flow out from him to help the poor.

Or think how misdirected was the life of one Saul the Pharisee, who persecuted Christians! But by the grace of God his life was channeled into the opposite direction, so that he who once hated Jesus Christ became His friend and great spokesman. St. Paul came to realize that Christ loved him and died for him.

This is what is meant by being born again—not necessarily a great personal upheavel like an earthquake; it can be like the quiet origin of the Mississippi River beginning with little springs at Lake Itaska in northern Minnesota.

The reversed life, like that of St. Paul, is a stream of refreshing water touching the lives of many people.

Prayer Suggestion

Ask for God's help to make your life a refreshing stream flowing out to others.

Let the Compliment Stand

Sometimes we take away with one hand what we give with the other. The former TV personality Art Linkletter, after he had delivered a school lecture on drug abuse, got this note from a boy: "You are the best speaker I ever heard." But then in a P.S. note he spoiled it by adding: "You are the only speaker I ever heard."

In His Word God speaks well of people who believe in His Son, calling them His children. He says through St. Paul: "In Christ Jesus you are all sons [and daughters] of God through faith. For as many of you as were baptized into Christ have put on Christ." Having said that, God doesn't turn around and take away that title by calling us brats.

This spills over into our relationships with one another as brothers and sisters in Christ. St. Paul urges us: "Love one another with brotherly [and sisterly] affection; outdo one another in showing honor." We show love by speaking words of commendation and approval when someone has done something good. As we are "kind to one another, tenderhearted, forgiving one another as God in Christ forgave" us, we go a step farther and compliment one another for a job well done.

We do that, of course, but sometimes tend to take away the commendation by adding criticisms, thus spoiling the whole effect. Imagine a man saying to his wife: "You prepared a fine meal this evening, but the potatoes lacked salt, the steak was overdone, and the gravy was lumpy." Or what happens to a wife's intended compliment: "You are the best husband a wife could have!" when she starts to enumerate his faults?

Constructive criticism has its place. But let us not voice it in such a way and at such a time as to destroy that rare utterance: a compliment!

Prayer Suggestion

Ask the Holy Spirit to help you speak words of encouragement to members of your family.

"Get Me to Christ on Time"

"Get Me to the Church on Time" is a lively song in the musical *My Fair Lady*. It has overtones of the importance of timeliness.

On July 31, 1976, a cloudburst in the Rocky Mountains in Colorado caused a roaring torrent of water to come down the canyon of the Big Thompson River. Property damage ran into the millions. Far more serious was the fact that over a hundred lives were lost. For various reasons the flash-flood warning from the National Weather Service came two hours too late.

It is a tragedy, also in people's spiritual lives, when certain actions come too late. St. Paul tells us not to let the sun set on our anger but to be reconciled at once. Death can intervene, and then it is too late.

Above all we want people to be reconciled with God now—now, before it is too late. That's why we do mission work. A missionary tells about a mother in India who was willing to have her children instructed in the Christian faith. But she added: "For me you are too late."

We are grateful to God that the Gospel of salvation in Jesus Christ comes to many people in time and gives them peace. We not only appreciate but also support ministry and mission so that many millions can hear the Word of God in time and be saved. But we have to be concerned about many others for whom the message comes too late. God wants all people to hear the offer of forgiveness and grace and to heed it while there is still time. He has said through St. Paul, "Behold, now is the acceptable time; behold, now is the day of salvation." Do heed God's message! It will bless you.

Prayer Suggestion

Pray that the Gospel of Jesus Christ may reach people in time, so that they may escape divine judgment for sin and reach the high ground of life in the love of God.

Understanding Our Traditions

Sometimes people don't know why they do certain things. Take the case of a holy man in India who kept a cat with him when he meditated and prayed. He did it for the simple reason that mice scurrying around him disturbed him. Other people didn't know the reason, so they concluded that one couldn't rightly meditate and pray unless a cat was present.

There are many religious customs passed on from previous generations. In many instances we continue them without knowing the reason, origin, or purpose. What is the meaning of "Amen" in our prayers? Why do we celebrate Christmas and exchange gifts? Why is Good Friday observed? What does the symbol IHS stand for? Why do we make the sign of the cross? Why do we attend Holy Communion?

Some customs or traditions, which once may have had an edifying use, are retained long after the usefulness is over—or worse, when they are given wrong meanings, stand in the way of the Gospel, or keep us from understanding the message of God's Word. Then they become false substitutes for vital religion.

Jesus had to confront such a situation, telling His contemporaries: "You teach for doctrine the commandments of men." Man-made religion passed on from generation to generation becomes a hindrance to personal commitments to Jesus. It is what St. Peter has in mind when he reminds his readers that they are ransomed from sin-encrusted traditions, as well as from the power of sin as such, indeed not with gold or silver "but with the precious blood of Christ, like that of a lamb without blemish or spot."

Some traditions are good, giving continuity and balance to our unsteady lives. We should know what they mean, and retain them if they are good and helpful.

Prayer Suggestion

Pray that the Holy Spirit lead you into all truth, also concerning traditions we have inherited.

The River of Divine Grace

The Hindus regard the Ganges River as sacred because they believe it came down from heaven. They believe its water has healing power.

A river well known to Bible readers is the Jordan. In it Naaman of Syria dipped himself seven times and, by a special act of God, was cured of his leprosy.

In Jesus' day, John the Baptist called people to repentance and baptized them in the Jordan.

Jesus was baptized in this river, not for Himself—for He was without sin—but that He might fulfill for us all righteousness. Later our Lord instituted a permanent baptism, telling His disciples to evangelize among all nations and baptize people in the name of the triune God. Jesus said "baptize"; He doesn't require that it be done in a river. Ordinary water, thanks to the power of God's Word and Spirit joined with it, has the power of washing away sin. Jesus died on the cross to put this power into Baptism.

A river—the Jordan, the Nile, the Mississippi—is a picture of God's abundant grace, as the psalmist declares, "Thou givest them drink from the river of Thy delights." Again, "There is a river whose streams make glad the city of God."

When you cross a river during your trips, or you sit on a river bank to fish or just to meditate, consider how the river of God's grace has been flowing into your life, enriching you with many blessings: your family and friends, health, a place and purpose in life, peace with God. And always there is more, as St. John tells us, "From Christ's fullness have we all received, grace for grace." In fact, in St. Paul's words: Where sin abounded, grace did much more abound."

Prayer Suggestion

Pray that God, for Jesus' sake, may continue to let His grace flow into your life.

Using All Our Resources

A boy was trying to move a heavy stone. He pushed, he pulled, he tried everything. His father, coming by that way, asked, "Son, have you used all your resources?" The boy replied, "Sure I have. Can't you see how hard I'm working." To which the father said, "But you haven't asked me yet."

This little vignette from daily life is repeated in peoples' spiritual lives. Here we are, working hard to move a rock, solve a problem, get a job done. We are applying our know-how—all our wisdom and strength. We go to other people for advice and assistance. We may go to the library to get books on the subject. And yet we haven't used all the resources at our disposal. We haven't taken our problem to the Lord in prayer. We haven't plugged in to God, the Source of all power.

God has promised to help us, whatever our task, our trouble, our trying situation. He declared to St. Paul: "My grace is sufficient for you, for My power is made perfect in weakness." Ours is a God of great wisdom and power, of love and compassion. With Him nothing is impossible. Available to Him—and to us through Him—are vast resources, for the solution of our problems.

What a pity when we don't avail ourselves of these resources, by asking for God's help! Here is His invitation to us all: "Call upon Me in the day of trouble; I will deliver you, and you shall glorify Me." Always this declaration is in effect: "He who did not spare His own Son—His own Son Jesus Christ—but gave Him up for us all, will He not also give us all things with Him?" We can rest assured that He will. We can cast all our care on Him, for He cares for us.

Prayer Suggestion

Pray that God, for the sake of Jesus, would send you help in the difficult circumstances of life.

How Tall Are You?

You can state your height in terms of feet and inches. One man, said to be "the tallest man in the world," was 8 feet, 2 inches tall.

As persons having also a mind and soul, we have dimensions other than physical height. The boy Jesus grew in all dimensions: mental, physical, spiritual, and social. For He "increased in wisdom and in stature, and in favor with God and man."

To this day it is the concern of parents that their children have balanced growth, that they might be, in Tennyson's words, "a tower that stood foursquare to all the winds that blew." After we have reached physical maturity, room remains for other growth: mental, social, spiritual.

The question "How Tall Are You?" can be asked of our spiritual height. The apostles asked it of their hearers and readers. St. Peter wanted the converts to nurture themselves with the pure spiritual milk of the Word, that "by it you may grow up to salvation." Note the emphasis on maturing, on growing up. And in the Letter to the Hebrews the author urges us to feed our souls with the "solid food" of the Word that is appropriate for adult faith.

How? St. Paul urges that we study the Holy Scripture for growth in faith and training in righteousness, "that the man of God [the Christian person, that is] may be completed, equipped for every good work."

Holy Scripture is the proper source and tool, for it bears witness to Jesus Christ, who was crucified for our sins and was raised to make us spiritually tall people. Faith in Christ adds inches to our stature.

Prayer Suggestion

Pray that God, through the Gospel, enable you to stand tall in your faith in Jesus Christ, the Savior.

Jesus Took Our Place

Alongside the rink where hockey is played is a penalty box, or "sin bin," where players who have broken a rule must sit out for several minutes. Recently the goalie of a National Hockey League team was penalized for a minor infraction. But the goalie was needed at his key position and could not serve. So one of the other players was designated to serve the penalty for him.

In the hockey game of life many sins are committed, and all offenders ought to be assigned to the penalty box. But like that goalie, they can't assume the penalty for their sins. So someone else is named to take their palce in the "sin bin." That Substitute for sinners is Jesus Christ. This the Bible clearly teaches. In the Old Testament Isaiah writes: "He [the Messiah] was wounded for our transgressions; He was bruised for our iniquities; upon Him was the chastisement that made us whole, and with His stripes we are healed."

Did Jesus go into the "sin bin"for us, the offenders against God's holy law? Listen to the words of St. Paul: "God made Him to be sin for us who knew no sin, that we might be made the righteousness of God in Him." Again, St. John: "Christ is the expiation for our sins, and not for ours only but also for the sins of the whole world."

Several points have to be kept in mind. 1. In hockey the substitute for the offender could not be just anyone, not a spectator, for instance, but has to be one of the players. So He who takes our place in God's penalty box has to be one of us, a human being—not an angel. 2. Those who carelessly sin, thinking that there is always one to suffer for them are forfeiting their forgiveness. 3. God never assesses a double penalty for a sin. Because Jesus was penalized, we who believe in Him are forgiven; we go free. Thank God for that.

Prayer Suggestion

Pray that your forgiveness in Jesus may give you a new lease on life, to live for him.

Unopened Mail

During World War 11 the scientist Albert Einstein wrote a letter to the President, urging that the nuclear bomb not be used. After the President's death, the letter was found unopened. What if the letter had been read? Would it have made a difference in the outcome of things?

You and I would be disturbed to find letters from friends or relatives that through neglect or oversight, we had never opened. And we wouldn't like it if people on the receiving end of our letters hadn't thought enough of them—and of us—to open and read the mail.

This very thing, however, happens all too often in our spiritual lives: we leave God's special-delivery letters to us unopened, unread, unapplied. What letters are these? The divinely inspired messages gathered into a book called the Bible—the 66 letters (we call them "books" of the Bible) that make up the contents of the Old and New Testaments. Some of these messages are actually in the form of letters, or epistles, written by the apostles as they were moved by God the Holy Spirit.

God's letters to us contain good news, in short, this news: "God so loved the world [all people, that is], that He gave His only Son [gave His only Son Jesus Christ into death in our behalf], that whoever believes in Him should not perish but have eternal life."

A young man or young woman at college will eagerly open letters from home, not only to be assured of their parents' love and concern but also to take possession of checks or money orders the letters may contain. Shouldn't we do the same with the letters from our heavenly Father in order to receive His gifts?

Prayer Suggestion

Give thanks for God's letters to you in the Bible, then read them.

Our Will in Keeping with God's Will

We know when there is a collision. On the morning of July 9, 1918, two trains collided near Nashville, one a local and the other an express carrying soldiers. The result was 171 injured and 101 killed.

There were fatalities when another kind of collision occurred: when the will of Adam collided with the will of God in the Garden of Eden. God had said, "Don't—don't eat the fruit of the tree of knowledge of good and evil." Adam said, "I will." Death resulted from the collision of the two wills—death to the whole human race, as St. Paul has written: "Sin came into the world through one man, and death through sin."

Thanks to the second Adam, Jesus Christ, sin and death were overcome. He submitted to the will of God, not only in being obedient but also in paying the price of sin by His death. This is now the new equation, as assured by our Lord's resurrection: "The wages of sin is death, but the free gift of God is eternal life in Christ Jesus our Lord."

Of course, when people insist on going contrary to God's will, there will be more "train wrecks," more collisions, with the casualties running high. But for Christians, whose will gladly and willingly coincides with God's, the wreckage is removed and the tracks are cleared for continuing the journey of faith. Now no hang-ups, no collisions mar the pilgrimage of life that leads to eternal life. Passengers in the train of faith can say with the psalmist: "I delight to do Thy will, O my God: Thy law is within my heart."

Prayer Suggestion

Ask God for the renewal of your heart, mind and will.

This Dragon Is for Real

When the Chinese celebrate their new year, they include in their fun festivities a make-believe dragon, sometimes 60 feet long. The dragons in old-time fairy tales were likewise figments of the imagination.

There is, however, a real dragon—not an ugly, visible creature or fire-breathing monster, but an invisible spirit controlling many other evil spirits. This is the devil. The book of Revelation in the Bible speaks of his expulsion from heaven: "The great dragon was thrown down, that ancient serpent, who is called the Devil and Satan, the deceiver of the whole world—he was thrown down to the earth, and his angels were thrown down with him."

The devil is for real. Nothing pleases him more than when he deceives people into believing that he doesn't exist. It pleases him to no end when people turn from the true God, forsake the faith, give themselves over to immorality, and join cults including Satan worship.

For the devil, as the Bible—and John Milton on the basis of the Bible—brings out, the heavenly paradise was lost. But for us it is not lost, for Jesus Christ regained it. He, the Son of God, became a human being "that through death he might destroy him who has the power of death, that is, the devil, and deliver all those who through fear of death were subject to lifelong bondage." Jesus, the woman's Seed, crushed the serpent's head, broke his power, unmasked his deceit, and reopened paradise.

Oh, yes, the devil is still at large and working overtime, but he cannot accuse us, for we are righteous in God's sight through faith in Jesus. He can tempt us, but he cannot control us, for we belong to another Lord; we belong to Christ.

Prayer Suggestion

Pray that the Holy Spirit will help you overcome the Evil Spirit's temptations.

From Seats to Streets

Mission Inn at Riverside, Calif., has on display a large, sturdy chair that is said to have historical significance. Its claim to fame is that the 350-pound president, William Howard Taft once sat in it.

Sitting in chairs is a favorite pastime for many people, although too much of it keeps them from accomplishing anything. Sitting on thrones is another ambition cherished by many, for it bespeaks honor and power.

It is true of some of Christ's followers that they want to sit. The mother of James and John came to Jesus with the request: "Command that these two sons of mine may sit, one at Your right hand and one at Your left in Your kingdom." It was a request Jesus could not grant, for He didn't want then—and doesn't want now—His disciples to be overlords. He wants them to be servants, for that was what He was. He said, "The Son of Man came not to be served but to serve, and to give His life as a ransom for many"—as the price for everyone's redemption.

Indeed, there is a time for everything, also a time to sit, to meditate, to listen. There was such a time for Mary of Bethany, who sat at Jesus' feet to hear His Word. Her sister Martha, busy in the kitchen, should have done the same.

Today at stated times we sit in our churches to worship, to hear the Word of God. It is not a waste of time, not if we go from seats to streets, there to do God's work in the world.

Someone has likened Christ's people to soldiers who are to be found in two places: fort and field. In church we meet to be briefed through the Gospel for the work God wants us to do. But we don't remain sitting in our fortress but venture out into our various fields, as the hymn line declares, to "practice all that we believe."

Prayer Suggestions

Pray that God make His will known to you and give you the desire to do it.

Mountain Climbing

Scaling mountains involves danger, especially for amateurs who take foolish chances. Once a man good at playing the guitar but inexperienced in mountain climbing, took a 1,500 foot plunge from the top of Mount Whitney in California because he thought he could save time by sliding down instead of making the safer step-by-step descent. He was fortunate to survive, although he suffered fractures, bruises, and a gash over his eye that required over 100 stiches.

In all of life, we have mountains to climb: not only inviting challenges but also such obstacles as reverses in business, sickness, separation from loved ones, family divisions, poverty. In scaling these mountains we avoid taking ill-advised chances and rash actions. Instead we supply ourselves with the right equipment: prayer and the Word of God.

Think of the mountain climbing St. Paul had to do in order to cope with and overcome his obstacles: arduous travels, perils on land and sea, open hostility to the Gospel, stoning, beating, and his own failing health. But he made it to the top. He reached his goal of proclaiming Christ throughout the Roman Empire, even Rome itself. He knew that a crown of righteousness was reserved for him in heaven as a token of victory.

You and I likewise climb mountains. We walk in the footsteps of our Lord Jesus Christ, who ascended Mount Calvary to redeem us from sin and gain for us a life lasting from here to eternity. United with Him by faith, we have the courage and strength to climb every mountain of adversity, and we also exercise caution in order to avoid falling. In faith we lift up our eyes to Jesus, the Lamb of Calvary, who leads us—safely and surely.

Prayer Suggestion

Ask God for Jesus's sake to give you the willingness and strength to grow in Christian living and to help the church grow.

The Joyful Road

It was a heartbreaking journey the Cherokee Indians had to make when in the winter of 1838 the U. S. Army led them from their traditional homeland in North Carolina to Indian Territory, later called Oklahoma. Many died along the way. The journey was rightly called the "Trail of Tears."

Not everyone must make so hard a journey, but for all people come times of trial and trouble. Into everyone's life some rain must fall.

The important thing then is how we react, how we respond. In the Bible we read that Job suffered untold grief, but his wife, instead of comforting him, suggested that he curse God and die. Many suicides today stem from the inability of the victims to cope with life's setbacks. Many crawl into their inner selves and slip into a catatonic state. In our complicated society we have a high incidence of mental illness, much of it resulting from the stunning blows of live's reverses. We know, too, that some turn to alcohol and other drugs.

There is a better way to react, a way to turn the trail of tears into a road of happiness and joy in Jesus Christ. When the jailer of Philippi, having been kept from suicide, asked what he should do, St. Paul told him, "Believe on the Lord Jesus Christ and you will be saved." He tells us the same: believe that Jesus died to wipe away your sins, believe that He rose from the dead to give you new life, believe that He is your Friend bearing all your sins and griefs, believe that you can come to Him in prayer and be relieved of your burdens.

Yes, He can turn your trail of tears into a journey of joy, for here is His promise: "Your sorrow will turn into joy ... and no one will take your joy from you."

Prayer Suggestion

Pray that the Holy Spirit may enter your heart and bring you the gift of joy.

God's Trees of Righteousness

In Israel, near the entrance to Yad V'Shem, is a garden named "The Avenue of the Righteous." It consists of 700 trees planted in honor of those who risked their lives to save people from the Holocaust. This is a fitting tribute, and the fact that trees were chosen as symbols of such people is also most appropriate.

The prophet Isaiah called God's people "the trees of righteousness." The righteous are like trees that bring forth their fruit in their season. The righteous are genuine, honest, sincere—without falsity, deceit, or hypocrisy. By their fruits—by their words and works—it is known what they are inside, in their heart of hearts. They don't speak with forked tongues, neither are their fruits or deeds like gilded nuts hanging on Christmas trees.

The righteous are compassionate. In Isaiah's words, they share their bread with the hungry, bring in the homeless poor, cover the naked with clothes. On Judgment Day the Lord Jesus will say to people who are designated "the righteous": "I was hungry and you gave Me food, I was thirsty and you gave Me drink, I was a stranger and you welcomed Me, I was naked and you clothed Me, I was sick and you visited Me, I was in prison and you came to Me." Later He explained: "What you did to the least of these My brethren, you did unto Me."

The righteous do such good works not in order to be saved but *because* they are saved. How are they saved? St. Paul replies, "By grace you have been saved through faith—faith in Christ, who died to save us and gain for us the perfect righteousness that God accepts. Now we are the trees of righteousness in God's garden.

Prayer Suggestion

Pray that the Holy Spirit may make you a tree yielding much beautiful fruit.

Be Yourself

Overlooking the waterfont of Copenhagen, Denmark, is the bronze statue of a little mermaid who, according to Hans Christian Andersen's fairy tale, wanted to become human. It was an impossible wish. Despite the claim of certain theories, no creature can turn itself into another one, for the Creator has ordained that all creatures reproduce themselves after their own kind.

Just as a mermaid, if such a being existed, could not become a person, so human beings can't turn themselves into angels or become other human beings. There are people who, not liking themselves or having ulterior motives, act as if they were other persons. We may call them hypocrites, that is, actors who on the stage of life pretend to be somebody else.

It is impossible to change ourselves into other people; so we shouldn't even try. "Be yourself!" we often say, and that is good advice, especially when that "yourself" is the renewed self that finds fulfillment in being what God wants you to be. The person whom the Holy Spirit has brought to faith in Jesus Christ as the One who died to save us all and rose again is indeed a new creation. However, he or she is still the same person: a person whose natural talents, are no longer used to selfish ends but together with the spiritual gifts the Holy Spirit imparts, are used to God's glory and the well-being of others.

So let Christians be what they are: God's children who find pleasure in serving their heavenly Father. They can't be carbon copies or clones of other people. They are persons with their own identities, each one, as it were, custom-made and individually fashioned by God. Yes, be what you are!

Prayer Suggestions

Pray that the Lord may help you become the kind of person He wants you to be, a person renewed in Christ's image.

Loving the Neighbor

A man, Charles Neider by name, has written a book on *Travels in the Antarctic*, in which he extols the beauty of the South Pole region, stating that no murder has ever been committed in Antarctica. The reason is that no people live there.

Murder is almost as old as the human race. Cain, the first person ever to be born, was also the first murderer. Out of jealousy he slew his brother Abel, to the great grief of his parents, Adam and Eve.

Rare is the day in our big cities when no homicide is committed. Quite often killings occur over trivial matters—over a few dollars and cents. Petty jealousies and irritations in marriage can develop into hatred and anger, and these can lead to murder committed in the heat of passion. An expert on crimes holds that "the roots of criminology do not lie in bad housing, unemployment, or ghetto life." The roots lie in human nature corrupted by sin, as Jesus declared: "Out of the heart come evil thoughts, murder, adultery, etc."

St. John writes: "Anyone who hates his brother is a murderer." Before this he has written: "We know that we have passed out of death into life, because we love the brethren." There lies the solution. Gun control might help, but it doesn't get to the root of the problem. We love our fellow human beings because we know that God so loved the whole human race that He gave Jesus Christ, His only Son, as the Savior. Because we love God, we can love the neighbor also and do him or her no harm but only good.

Prayer Suggestion

Pray that God the Holy Spirit may fill your heart with love that seeks the neighbor's well-being in life.

Work That Is Never Done

In the year A.D. 1248 the first stone was laid for the magnificent Gothic cathedral in Cologne. Since that time, the work of repairing, replacing, and adding something new has continued. Said Anton Meid, the chief stone mason: "We will never be finished. In a way that's part of the beauty of the work. We just become part of the cathedral."

As it is with the cathedral as a visible symbol of Christendom, so it is with individual Christians and with Christ's church as a whole: the work is never done; we have to keep building. At no point can we say, "I have it made, now I am a perfect Christian." Instead we must all say with St. Paul: "Not that I have already attained [my likeness to Christ] or am already perfect, but I press on to make it my own, because Christ Jesus has made me His own." Here he stresses also the motive for growing, maturing, continuing to build up our personal Christianity: Christ by the shedding of His blood has made us His own, so that we might serve Him and grow daily in His likeness.

Not only individual Christians but also the entire Christian church, the communion of saints, is like an unfinished symphony, a cathedral that is never totally completed, but requires continual work—our support, our prayers, our service, our personal witness—so that the company of Christ's people may grow.

Not until our Lord returns in glory to complete His kingdom and carry His church with Him into heaven can we lay aside the trowel, that is, the Gospel as our building tool. So we keep on with our work as the years pass by.

Prayer Suggestion

Ask God for Jesus's sake to give you the willingness and strength to grow in Christian living and to help the church grow.

What's Right with Me?

Someone asked during a televised interview: "What question do people most often ask you? Is it about sex? About money? About drugs?" "No," replied Ann Landers, whose newspaper column is widely read: "The question most often asked is 'What's wrong with me?' "

This question occurs to people everywhere: at home, in school, at work, in a doctor's office. It prompts them to worry, to look into mirrors, to turn to alcohol and other drugs.

The Word of God has something to say on the subject of what's wrong with people. Much of it is said in church. When President Calvin Coolidge was asked what his minister had preached about, he allegedly replied with his usual brevity: "About sin." "But," said the other, "what did he say about sin?" "He was against it," said the President. Sin—the transgression of God's holy will, wrongdoing according to moral and spiritual standards, neglect of the good—that's what's wrong with you and me and everybody, and God is *against* it.

But God is also *for* something. He is for setting things right. He is for turning sinners around. To that end He sent His Son into the world to undo sin by obeying God's will perfectly and by assuming the guilt and death sentence of all people's sin, as St. Paul states: "God made Him to be sin for us who knew no sin, that we might be made the righteousness of God in Him."

Through faith in Christ we are right with God. We are declared holy. We are made the children of God and brothers and sisters to one another. We know we are loved, and that enables us to love fellow human beings. We have peace with God, with others, with ourselves. That's what is right about us.

Prayer Suggestion

Ask God to help you think of yourself as a person whom God loves and who in turn loves others.

The Better Way

Two beggars, one lame and the other blind, were supposedly caught up in a procession. They were told that the relics of St. Martin, which were thought to have healing power, were being carried through the street. Now the beggers depended on lameness and blindness to make a living. If they were healed, they would lose their livelihood. So the lame man jumped on the shoulders of the blind man and steered him away from the procession and any possibility of healing.

Sometimes people get so accustomed to their ailments and somehow find them so rewarding that they refuse to get rid of them. Some enjoy being sick, for then they get attention. Some run away from work because they don't want to lose their place on welfare roles. Others spurn friendship, for they suspect that to have and to keep a friend, one must *be* a friend, and that price they don't want to pay.

The Bible records many instances of people preferring the lesser to the greater, evil to good. Jesus spoke of people who had their wires crossed in this way when He said He often wanted to gather them together, as a hen gathers her chicks, but they would not. He offered love, forgiveness, peace, healing, but they would rather continue in sin's misery.

Today God still wants to be a loving Father to all, giving rain and sunshine from heaven, giving especially His Son, Jesus Christ, as Savior, Friend, Brother, Counselor. But some would rather have another god—the mammon of materialism, the little tin deities of wealth and pleasure and pride. So the lame ones jump on the backs of blind runners to escape healing, and continue in their disabilities. How foolish! There is a better way—the way that leads to God through Jesus Christ.

Prayer Suggestion

Pray that God may open your eyes to the great treasures He wants to exchange for your trinkets.

God May Have a Better Plan

People's well-intentioned, best-laid plans sometimes miscarry because of factors they can't control. At Christmastime a Lynn, Mass., manufacturer arranged for 1,500 one-dollar bills to be thrown from an airplane to people waiting on the ground. It didn't work; a wind arose to carry all the bills out to sea.

For many others, more noble and worthwhile plans have gone awry. In the Old Testament Jacob must have had ambitious plans of his own for his gifted, favorite son, Joseph. But the brothers sold him to Egypt, where as prime minister he kept many people alive during the famine, including the patriarch Jacob and his family. It is clear that God had intervened. In the New Testament we read that Paul and Barnabas planned to do mission work in Asia Minor, but, we are told, "the Spirit of Jesus did not allow them." In a vision God let these missionaries know that He wanted them to work in Macedonia. In response to this call they entered the continent of Europe, a most fruitful field.

Undoubtedly we have all experienced how our plans had to be changed, and we were disappointed. It could well be that God intervened; He had something better in mind. Many people have passed through all kinds of failures, only to find them to be stepping-stones to success. Many have learned to pray, as did Jesus, "Not my will, but Thine be done." They have experienced how right the hymn line is: "What God ordains is always good." They feel fortunate and richly blessed that through a change in their plans they were drawn closer to the Savior Jesus Christ, who died for them that they might live for Him. They stay responsive to His will, which they know is prompted by His love for them.

Prayer Suggestion

Pray that God may reveal His plans for you, giving you the willingness and strength to follow them.

Making Spiritual Progress

Sometimes progress in one area is offset by disadvantages in another, so that for every forward step, we take one or two backward.

According to traffic studies made in New York City, horse-drawn vehicles about a hundred years ago could travel at an average speed of 10 1/2 miles an hour in that city. Today there are so many cars in that area that they can clock only 3 miles an hour.

God desires that we make spiritual progress in our lives—not just change, but improvement. In place of standing still or backsliding, let there be true inner growth. While it is God-pleasing for us to be firmly established in our church life, we have to be alert to the possibility that, in the absence of forward motion, such establishment can mean arrested spirituality—being fixed in immature faith and undesirable habits.

It is said that a certain church deacon, as well he might be, was very fond of these words of Isaiah: "If you will not believe, surely you shall not be established." One day when his wagon became thoroughly stuck in the mud so that it could not move forward or backward, a neighbor came along and said, "Deacon, I am sure that you believe, but I can also see that you are well established." To be established in such a way prevents growth and progress.

God has made every provision for our progress in faith and life. He gave us His Word—the milk of the Word, as St Peter tells us, that we "may grow up to salvation," that is—grow in our love for Christ, who in love gave His life for us. We can help one another grow, as St. Paul writes, "Speaking the truth in love, we are to grow up in every way into Him who is the Head, into Christ."

This is true spiritual progress.

Prayer Suggestion

Pray that the Holy Spirit through the Word may cause you to grow in faith and all its fruits.

The Gift of Memory

At a meeting held in support of a historical society the speaker said, "Let us not be like mules, who know nothing about their antecedents and have no hope for progeny."

One of the Creator's great gifts to human beings is the power of memory—the remarkable faculty of the mind to recall, the ability to bring the past into the present for the purpose of gaining a better perspective for the future. To recall the past is not the same as living in the past. Memory aids us in living a balanced life in the present, and in preparing intelligently for the future.

In the Bible, God's people are continually encouraged to remember the past—how God delivered them from bondage in Egypt, led them safely through the Red Sea, and settled them in the Promised Land. From God's acts in the past we can draw confidence for our todays and tomorrows. Said the psalmist: "I remember the days of old, I meditate on all that Thou hast done."

Sometimes, impulsive, impatient young folks think that wisdom was born with them and that they can instantly create what past generations labored long to produce. People who think that way should study history, particularly the history recorded and interpreted in the Sacred Scriptures.

We thank God for the gift of memory. Because young Timothy had memory, St. Paul could tell him to continue in what he had learned, reminding him how from childhood he had learned the Holy Scriptures, through which he was made wise to salvation through faith in Christ Jesus. In another place, St. Paul said: "Remember Jesus Christ, risen from the dead, descended from David, as preached in my gospel."

Yes, do remember!

Prayer Suggestion

Thank God for the gift of memory, asking Him to bring the truth of His Word to your remembrance.

Getting Rid of Haunting Ghosts

Blithe Spirit, a play by Noel Coward, is a farce about a British novelist and his wife who are haunted by his first wife's ghost.

We don't believe there are ghosts of the departed who come back to bother the living, but there are other, nonghostly things that can happen, and do. Call them the not-so-blithe spirits, if you will—the memory of neglected opportunities, the pangs of an accusing conscience, the regrets over false choices, distracting questions about things that might have been—the chickens of past misdeeds that come home to roost. These so called ghosts of the past may come to haunt you at the most inopportune times, like when you want to get some sleep, or when you are on vacation and had expected to enjoy yourself.

There is no magical formula for exorcizing these demons of depression, but there is certainly something we can do to send them on their way. We can get rid of these unwelcome guests by setting our thoughts in order according to the Word of God. We can do this in prayer form as we say to God: "Dear Lord, I confess that I have done many sinful and foolish things, but I regret them. I want to straighten things out with those whom I have hurt. So I ask You to forgive my sins and cover them with the shed blood of Jesus Christ, who died for sinners just like me. I rely on Your promise that in Your sight bygones are bygones."

So away all haunting memories! You can bother me no more, for here is the Word of God: "Though your sins are like scarlet, they shall be as white as snow." And: "Who shall bring any charge against God's elect? It is God who justifies. Who is to condemn? It is Christ Jesus, who died, yes, who was raised from the dead, who is at the right hand of God, who intercedes for us."

Peace of mind awaits all who come to Jesus with their burdens, He will give them rest.

Prayer Suggestion

Pray that God may fill your heart with His love and forgiveness in Jesus Christ.

Self-Healing or Christ's Healing?

"Physician, heal yourself!" is an old saying. Doctors of medicine are like other people: they have ailments, they are mortal. The personal physician of the surrealist painter Salvador Dali called on his patient, and while he was doing this, he had a heart attack himself and died.

We are not always above the advice we give to others, nor subject to the treatment we recommend to them. Hence the saying, whether we are doctors or not: "Physician, heal yourself!" applies to us. We need to stay well and be healed by the same means we prescribe for the people about whom we care. This is true of parents especially. Not only the children but also the fathers and mothers need rest, exercise, and the right foods. Those who teach need to practice what they teach.

The truism "Physician, heal yourself!" does not apply, however, to the spiritual dilemma in which we all find ourselves. There is no do-it-yourself salvation. Augustus M. Toplady, the writer of "Rock of Ages," declares in well-known words: "Not the labors of my hands Can fulfill Thy law's demands; Could my zeal no respite know, Could my tears forever flow, All for sin could not atone; Thou must save, and Thou alone." This is but a paraphrase of the words of St. Paul: "By grace you have been saved through faith; and this is not your own doing; it is the gift of God."

So instead of "Physician, heal yourself!" we say, "Jesus, my good Physician, heal me." And He will heal, for He has the right remedy. He knows the right treatment. He took upon Himself the entire sickness of our sins and carried the burden to Calvary's cross. We are relieved, we are cleansed, we are healed.

Prayer Suggestion

Thank God in words like these: "I thank You that my soul was healed by what Your Word revealed."

You Are God's Genuine Art Work

During the 1890s the artist Homer Winslow painted "The Signal of Distress," a picture showing sailors fighting a storm. Recently it was sold for $1,700,000. The value of a painting depends to a large extent on whether it is a genuine work of a famous artist—Picasso, Van Gogh, or Winslow.

In our relation to God, it is not only important *who* we are but also *whose* we are. Every person is a genuine piece of art because the Creator is known to be God. Psalm 100 declares: "Know that the Lord is God! It is He that made us, and we are His." The King James Version translates: "It is He that hath made us and not we ourselves."

In other words, we are not self-made people, not pieces of art we ourselves designed and executed. We are genuine art and most valuable, because *God* is our Creator. And what a wonderful job He did! The psalmist exclaims: "I will praise Thee, for I am fearfully and wonderfully made!" Also intricately and efficiently made! We have eyes to see, ears to hear, a brain to think, feet to walk, hands to do delicate work, enabling us to become artists ourselves.

We are precious in God's sight not only because we are His authentic workmanship. St. Paul reminds the Corinthians that they were bought with a price—a very high price and one exceeding the value of all the gold and silver in the world—the blood of Jesus Christ. So let them not sell themselves short, or sell themselves back into the slavery of sin from which they were brought free. Let them not turn their body, which is the temple of the Holy Spirit, into a cheap instrument for sinning. And let them not by careless behavior cause a weak brother or sister, "for whom Christ died," to fall.

God has put a price tag of supreme value on every human being.

Prayer Suggestion

Pray that God may keep you mindful of your worth in His sight and that you may appreciate the worth of others also.

God knows All Languages

What language does God speak—Hebrew, Greek, German, English? Clarence Day, who tells about his childhood in *Life with Father*, describes his feeling when he opened a French Bible for the first time. He says, "Aside from a few odd words in Hebrew, I took it for granted that God had never spoken anything but the most dignified English." Very likely the stately English of the King James Version gave him that idea.

God does speak. To Moses in the burning-bush incident, God might have spoken in Hebrew or in Egyptian; Moses knew both languages. To other persons in Biblical and pre-Biblical times God may have spoken in Hebrew Aramaic or in Greek, depending on whatever language(s) those persons spoke and understood.

As far as the written Word, the Scripture, is concerned, the Holy Spirit availed Himself of the languages these inspired writers spoke and wrote: The Old Testament in Hebrew and Aramaic, the New in Greek.

The fact is that the all-knowing God knows, speaks, and understands all languages even the charismatic tongues.

This means much to us. Whether the Gospel, that is, the Good News that God so loved the world that He gave His only Son, Jesus Christ, as Savior, is proclaimed or published in English, in French, in Chinese, or in Russian, it has the same power to bring people to faith in Christ.

Further, since God knows all languages, we can pray to Him in any tongue. Yes, we can pray silently, without any spoken words at all, for God reads the thoughts of our hearts and minds.

Prayer Suggestion

Praise God and state your petitions in your own words; God understands.

245

Are You Overweight?

In a Missouri state park in the Ozarks foothills is a narrow passage between two huge granite boulders. It is aptly nicknamed "Fat Man's Squeeze."

There are other situations in life where being overweight can become a hindrance. One pundit refers to obese persons as creating a pressing problem in a bus. Another has conjectured, undoubtedly falsely, that a former queen of England referred to herself as "we" because there was so much of her. Apart from inconveniences of obesity, one has to consider the health aspect of it. Many people do that and consequently go on diets.

One can be overweight also in a spiritual sense. When God's people became indifferent to His Word and sought their fill with earthly riches and pleasures, God said to them through the prophets that their hearts were fat. The people had become lazy and were no longer in good spiritual condition. They got that way because they failed to exercise their faith in worship and God-pleasing good works. Their interest centered in themselves as they sought self-fulfillment in personal luxury and ease.

Jesus was aware of the problem—how people could become so fat in heart and spirit that they could no longer enter through the passage that leads to eternal life. He said, "Enter by the narrow gate."

At another time He said that some people had so encumbered themselves with riches that it would be easier for a camel to squeeze through the eye of a needle than for them to enter God's kingdom.

So we trim down, desiring to serve our Lord with the kind of self-sacrifice that He performed to perfection when He gave His life to make us His own.

Prayer Suggestion

Ask the Holy Spirit to help you get rid of the excess weight of sin that you may run—and win—the race of life.

246

Asked to Serve? Do It!

When Ralph Waldo Emerson, a renowned author and lecturer, left Boston to settle in Concord, he was willing to render humble services to the then semirural community. One of several offices he held was that of hogreeve, whose duty it was to impound stray hogs.

We ought not consider it beneath our dignity to serve with whatever talents we have. It would, of course, be depreciation of God-given talents if someone capable of being mayor of the city were a dogcatcher. But if this someone is not eligible to be mayor, then lower positions are not to be despised. A dogcatcher works for the common good.

Are you needed for a community service such as driving a school bus or clerking in a local election? Go. Do you have a chance to clean the house and yard of a sick person in your neighborhood? Do it. Do you know of elderly people who would come to church if someone picked them up? Offer to do so.

The Bible cites many examples of humble service. Dorcas of Joppa sewed garments for the poor. God's prophet, Amos, was a herdsman and fruit picker. St. Paul worked as a tentmaker to support himself while preaching the Gospel. Most of all, we think of Jesus Christ, who became a Servant in behalf of us all, symbolizing His Saviorhood role by washing the disciples' feet. As the Servant He became obedient to the point of death, even death on a cross, to redeem all sinners. To all whom He has thus befriended, our Lord declares, "Follow Me." The response of the redeemed is this: "Then all that you would have me do Shall such glad service be for you That angels wish to do it too. Christ Cruicified, I come."

Prayer Suggestion

Pray that God may open your eyes to the need for service, and a willing heart to render it.

Forgiveness Is the Key

In George M. Cohan's play *Seven Keys to Baldpate* a fiction writer needs a quiet place where he can undisturbed turn out a 10,000-word story in 24 hours. Since it is winter, he thinks that surely Baldpate, a summer resort, would be such a place, so he obtains a key to it. He soon learns, from the steady procession of people coming there, that other keys to Baldpate are extant.

To Peter Jesus said after the apostle had confessed his faith in Him as "the Christ, the Son of the living God": "You are Peter, and on this rock I will build My church . . . I will give you (singular) the keys, of the kingdom of heaven, and whatever you bind on earth shall be bound in heaven, and whatever you will loose on earth shall be loosed in heaven."

But Peter was not the only one who was given keys to Christ's kingdom. Our Lord gave the office of the key's also to the other apostles, saying: "If you (plural) forgive the sins of any, they are forgiven; if you retain the sins of any, they are retained." What is more, the power to forgive and thus open heaven is by our Lord given to all Christians, even if only two or three are gathered together as His church. Jesus says to all Christians in Matthew 18: "Whatever you bind on earth shall be bound in heaven, and whatever you loose on earth shall be loosed in heaven."

Forgiveness is the key that not just one person has but that Christ has given to all Christians. "Forgive one another, as God in Christ forgave you," St. Paul tells the Ephesians. And not only is forgiveness the key that opens heaven but the one that throughout life opens doors to happiness, fellowship, and friendship. There is not just one key—not just seven keys either—to the Baldpate of divine grace, but there are as many as there are Christians in Christ's church.

Prayer Suggestion

Ask God to guide you in using the key of forgiveness in Christ to open the rusty door of someone's sin-encrusted heart.

Is Life Worthwhile?

Some people do not consider life worth living. An estimated 35,000 persons commit suicide in the United States annually. And who is to know how many have thought about it, or have tried it and failed? States the *New York Times:* "Those who succeed are a tiny fraction of the despairing among us."

The last words Winston Churchill spoke before sinking into his final coma were: "Life is a journey well worth making." The life of this English statesman was exceedingly important for millions of people during the dark days of World War II. But one does not have to be famous or rich or honored before his or her life is worthwhile.

What makes anyone's life a journey well worth making is the fact that life is a gift from God. He gave it to us to use and to enjoy so long as He entrusts it to us. It is eminently worth while if it enriches the lives of others by words of encouragement and deeds of love, however small they may seem. There is a place—and there is a need—for everyone who can contribute to the common good: the elderly by words of wisdom, the handicapped by their example of courage, the so-called failures in life's enterprises by renewing their efforts to succeed.

Is your life worthwhile? It has to be, not only because God the Creator gave it to you but also because He redeemed it from sin's destruction through His Son, Jesus Christ, who laid down His life in our behalf. The Holy Spirit has given you a new life, and with it imparted to you the power to love even as you have been loved. Love puts a new price tag on your life.

Prayer Suggestion

Ask God to give you the strength and vision to live your life to His glory by helping people in need.

Christ's Kind of Mind

Teachers of old distinguished four types of mind: one like a *sponge*—it sucks up everything; one like a *funnel*—it lets everything run through; one like a *strainer*—it lets the wine drain away but keeps the dregs; one like a *winnow*—from which one blows away the bran but keeps the flour.

What kind of mind ought we to have according to the Bible? Certainly one that does not soak up everything indiscriminately, for we are to test everything; certainly not a mind that lets the truth come in one ear and go out the other, rather one that retains God's Word; certainly a mind that can distinguish good from evil, keeping what is good; certainly a mind that lets itself be nourished by the Bread of life, shunning the chaff of spiritual "fast foods" and "junk snacks" so readily offered in the name of religion.

What kind of mind, heart, or character should we have? A retentive one, as Jesus said: "Blessed are they that hear the Word of God and keep it"; certainly one that is responsive to the voice of conscience; a mind that knows compassion and love and then acts on it; certainly a mind of humble service, as St. Paul writes: "Have this mind among yourselves, which is yours in Christ Jesus, who . . . emptied Himself, taking the form of a servant, and being born in the likeness of men. And being found in human form He humbled Himself and became obedient unto death, even death on a cross."

Jesus came to be the Servant in our behalf. That is what He had on His mind day and night. Not like a sponge, or a funnel, or a strainer was He, but like the winnow that separates the chaff of sin from the wheat of the Word, by which our souls are nourished for time and for eternity.

"Have this mind among yourselves."

Prayer Suggestions

Pray that through the Holy Spirit's power you may love God with all your heart, soul, and mind.

Appreciating What We Have

The woman was bitter—resentful against God because her son had died. Efforts at consoling and counseling her seemed ineffective. Then one day a friend said to her, and the words bore weight; "I never had a son."

Sometimes we become aware of blessings we've had when we note that others have far less, as someone has said, "I felt sorry for myself for not having shoes, Then I saw someone who didn't have feet."

When we have losses, it is good to take inventory of what we still possess—personal assets that many fellow human beings may be lacking: daily bread, a place to live, a family, friends, a purpose in life to be fulfilled, good health, a sound mind, bodily members and organs that function. Must we wait until we see a blind person before we appreciate our eyesight? Or an amputee before we thank God for our arms and legs? Or the homeless, ragged, emaciated refugee of East Asia before we are grateful for our ample food?

We have riches exceeding the value of our physical assets, one of which is membership in the household of God. By faith in Jesus Christ we become a part of God's family. As God's children we are heirs and have the promise that under divine direction, all things, suffering included, work together for our good. We are so richly blessed because God spared not His own Son but delivered Him up to the cross for our salvation, full and free.

So, although we may have lost a dear one or are like the woman who never had a son, we are under the umbrella of God's grace; we have God's own Son as Redeemer and Friend.

Prayer Suggestion

Pray that God may remove all bitterness from your heart and fill you with thankfulness for all His gifts.

Delayed Gratitude

One July day in 1980 Matt Urban of Holland, Michigan, was invited to Washington, D.C., to receive at the President's hands the Medal of Honor for heroism in World War II—36 years after the event. Somehow the letter recommending the recognition was misplaced. Among human beings gratitude is frequently delayed.

"I remember my faults today!" exclaimed the butler when Pharaoh had a dream and wanted to know its meaning. Two years had gone by since Joseph had given a favorable interpretation to the butler's dream when he was a fellow prisoner with Joseph. Freed and restored to his position, the butler had forgotten to express his gratitude.

Let's look into our lives and try to remember our benefactors. Have years gone by and we never said thank-you to mother, father, brother, sister, neighbor, or friend for favors performed? It is time to express thanks now, before it is too late.

Now is the time to say thanks to God for His goodness—time to exclaim with the psalmist David: "Bless the Lord, O my soul, and all that is within me, bless His holy name! Bless the Lord, O my soul, and forget not all His benefits, who forgives all your iniquity, who heals all your diseases!"

In His Son, Jesus Christ, God has blessed us beyond measure. He has forgiven us our trespasses, for Christ atoned for them when He was made to be sin for us. He has healed our souls and in so many instances also our bodies. Although two years may have passed since He helped us, as in the case of the butler, or 36 years, as in the case of our nation before recognizing a heroic man, gratitude to God is always in place, even when delayed.

Prayer Suggestion

Pray that the Holy Spirit may bring God's many kindnesses to your remembrance and make you thankful for them.

Dollars in the Exercise of Discipleship

Should a follower of Jesus have and use money? Some have said no, giving away everything and taking the vow of poverty. Some have misunderstood the Bible, as though money itself is an evil, when the fault is greed in the human heart. Still others have thought it improper to associate money with God. For that reason President Theodore Roosevelt in 1907 ordered the "In God We Trust" motto taken off the ten- and twenty-dollar gold coins. He said that the reference to God would be cheapened by putting it on coins.

On the other hand, Martin Luther included "money" and "goods" as blessings of God we pray for when we say: "Give us this day our daily bread." John Wesley preached a sermon on the theme "The Christian's Use of Money," stressing these three points: (1) Earn all you can, (2) Save all you can, and (3) Give all you can.

Jesus Himself owned no money; what people gave was put into the treasury of the Twelve. When He sent out the apostles for the first time, He told them not to take money along. But when commissioning them as apostles after His resurrection, He did not forbid them, nor the people who heard them, to have and use money. He expected the people to have money, so that they could render to Caesar and to God the appropriate sums.

Money is entrusted to us as wise and faithful stewards. With it we serve God and help needful people. "God loves a cheerful giver," writes St. Paul. Christians give cheerfully and, as John Wesley said, all they can, because they are thankful to Jesus Christ, who redeemed them and all people, not with gold or silver, but with His blood as the Lamb of God.

Prayer Suggestion

Ask for God's help in becoming a better steward or administrator of your earthly goods.

Refreshed at God's Fountain

"You are dust," God said to Adam after He had made his body out of the dust of the earth. God could just as well have said, "You are water!" for that is what our bodies mostly are. Our blood is 83 percent water; our muscles, 75 percent water; our bones, 25 percent water.

Not only *are* we water, but we also *need* water. People cannot survive long in the heat of a desert unless they have water to drink.

As our bodies need natural water, so our souls need spiritual water—water that comes from God, water that *is* God. The psalmist exclaims: "As a hart longs for flowing streams, so longs my soul for Thee, O God. My soul thirsts for God, for the living God." As natural water comes into our homes through pipes, so God comes to us in and through His Word, He comes to us as refreshing, living water.

At Jacob's well near Sychar in Samaria Jesus had an instructive conversation with a woman, telling her that He was the Messiah who had come to bring salvation, peace with God, forgiveness, eternal life. He told her that all who receive His living water will never thirst again—that it will become in them "a spring of water welling up to eternal life."

Jesus is but repeating the invitation of Isaiah: "Ho, everyone who thirsts, come to the waters." The fourth to the last verse of the Bible says the same: "Let him who is thirsty come, let him who desires take the water of life without price."

The Bible you have in your home—perhaps right there by your bed—is like a pitcher of fresh, cool water. The Bible bears witness that Jesus Christ lived, died, and rose again to provide for you the water of eternal life. Have some!

Prayer Suggestion

Pray that God may refresh you with the water of His Word and help you share it with others.

Growth in Christ

The yellow school bus has replaced the little red schoolhouse as a symbol of education. In rural and small-town areas buses bring children to the schools of consolidated districts. In many cities, bus transportation is considered a means of effecting integrated, or racially balanced, education.

There is another kind of integrated education, and this kind is up to homes and churches to provide: Christian education. It is growth in learning going hand in hand with growth in Christ. This makes for a balanced, complete education, for coordinated mental, physical, spiritual, and social growth. This is how the boy Jesus was educated, for He "increased in wisdom and in stature, and in favor with God and man."

This symmetrical growth of the total person is in a sense integrated education. Secular knowledge and spiritual knowledge are not kept in separate drawers, but they are together in one package. Faith in the Savior Jesus Christ and love for Him motivate learning and everyday living.

Both the home and the church have a stake in integrating the Christian faith with the learning process. St. Paul tells parents to bring up their children "in the discipline and instruction of the Lord." Such instruction centers in the Gospel, with all the good news it tells us about salvation in Christ. The church too has to be involved in the responsibility and privilege of bringing children to the Lord Jesus and keeping them with Him through Christian education. The public schools cannot provide religious education.

When Jesus said, "Teach them to observe all that I have commanded you," He was pleading for this kind of integrated education.

Prayer Suggestion

Pray that the Holy Spirit may enrich all your learning by leading you to a stronger faith and deeper Christian life in Jesus Christ.

Teaching and Learning with Love

Susan Elizabeth Blow, 1843—1916, is gratefully remembered as the teacher and educator who opened the first kindergarten. She did this in St. Louis. In the kindergarten young children learn basic skills and social behavior as a happy, joyful introduction to school as a teaching-learning community.

Teaching children is a noble calling. It is so especially when it is done in the context of the Christian faith. It was also kindergarten teaching—and home teaching preceding and following it—that Jesus had in mind when He said shortly before ascending into heaven; "Teach them to observe all that I have commanded you."

What Jesus commanded covers a wide range of truths, truths that must be taught, for human beings do not know them by nature. Put in briefest form, what Jesus commanded is that we love one another as He loved us.

It is showing love when parents and teachers make children aware of their selfishness and other sins. To ignore or gloss over sin is not doing anyone a favor. Christian love prompts us to call attention to and help pupils cope with their behavioral drives that often go in the wrong direction.

More than that, it is showing Christian love when parents and teachers lead the young to the Savior Jesus Christ, who, as the simple hymn line has it, "died to make us good," died and rose again for the forgiveness of our sins so that we can be reckoned as good, just, and holy in God's sight. Through His Word and Holy Spirit Jesus enables children to grow in the goodness of Christian character.

Children of kindergarten age are not too young to be taught this. Someone asked a rabbi when to begin the religious instruction of a child. He replied: "Nine months before it is born."

Prayer Suggestion

Ask God for a greater measure of grace to bring up our little ones in the love of Jesus.

Blue Collar Turns White

During a 30-year span, from 1947 to 1977, the number of blue-collar workers dropped from 41 percent to 33 percent of our U.S. labor force, while white-collar workers increased from 33 percent to 50 percent.

The type of one's work, whether symbolized by the blue or the white collar, is pleasing to God—and should be pleasing in our own eyes—if it is honest, useful to people and to oneself, and in keeping with one's training and God-given talents.

Manual work is no disgrace. Long before the idea of being a worker-priest was born, St. Paul testified that with his own hands he ministered to his needs and the needs of others. A learned scholar and great missionary apostle, St. Paul was not ashamed of his trade as a tentmaker.

As the work of hands is not to be despised, so should mental work not be dismissed because it is nonphysical and sometimes invisible. Such is the work of teachers, architects, bank tellers, computer programmers, and others who work with their brain.

Through the fulfillment of our vocation and the performance of honest work we earn our daily bread and, in St. Paul's words, are "able to give to those in need." Such purposeful activity glorifies Jesus Christ, who endured the labors of the cross to redeem us, and who declared: "We must work the works of Him who sent Me, while it is day; night comes, when no one can work."

The writer of Ecclesiastes has well said, "Whatever your hand finds to do do it with your might." Now is the time to do it; when night comes, it will be time to rest.

Prayer Suggestion

Ask God to bless your work and the time you set aside for rest and recreation, that His name be glorified and your fellow human beings benefited.

Mind Openers

Few persons have been as close to one another as Helen
Keller and Anne Sullivan Macy, her teacher. Born deaf and blind,
Helen Keller became educated and led a useful life, due largely
to her teacher, who opened her mind. Mark Twain said of the
two: "It took the pair of you to make a complete and perfect
whole."

Many things remain closed and sealed to us unless someone
opens them to our understanding. Think how on the first Easter
day two men, totally confused and saddened, made their way to
Emmaus! But a Stranger joined them and in the ensuing conversation opened to them the Scripture so that they now understood that Jesus had to be crucified and to rise again for the
salvation of the world. This Stranger was the Lord Himself, the
same Lord who on many other occasions opened not only the
eyes of the sightless but also the minds of the spiritually blind.

Opening minds is a role everyone can play. Parents are in a
unique position to explain and interpret life's meaning to the developing minds of their children. Young people can render an
equally important service when by example and kind word they
keep minds of older people open—to the message of God and
of those He sends to teach us.

An open mind, of course, is not like a funnel or a sieve
through which everything runs. Some things it can forget; others
it must retain if there is to be mental and spiritual growth. The
open mind lets hateful remembrances flow through and vanish.
Its value lies not only in this, but also in its likeness to unlocked
doors and windows that let the fresh air of truth come in. This
hymn stanza sums it up: "Lord, open now my heart to hear, And
through Your Word to me draw near; Preserve that Word in purity
That I your child and heir may be."

Prayer Suggestion

Pray that the Holy Spirit may open your heart to the wonders of
God's love in Christ.

Some Things Are Not for Sale

A reporter of a metropolitan newspaper asked people what one thing they would try to save in case of a fire. Most of them said it would be something that money can't replace: a keepsake, a family heirloom, the Bible with the family record, the picture of their parents.

Yes, there are many things in life that money cannot buy. This may come as a surprise to the individual who tries to buy his way into all the things or achievements he desires: a political office, a home he considers comfortable, the respect of the community. And when a traffic officer stops him for speeding, he offers money to avoid a ticket.

It bears repeating: some precious things in life are beyond buying and selling. One cannot buy peace and harmony in marriage; one cannot purchase the love of children with expensive toys offered as replacements for parental concern. All the virtues we value highly and need to make life livable are not purchasable merchandise. The writer of Proverbs in chapter 31 extols the virtues of a good wife and mother. He declares, "A good wife who can find? She is far more precious than jewels."

"Money talks," people say. But it does not talk with God, for all the wealth of the world and all private fortunes are His already. With money one cannot buy God's favor. No one can negotiate his or her way into heaven with the checkbook or with generous donations. Forgiveness of sins and peace with God are not for sale.

Thank God that this is so! Thank God that they are free! Jesus paid the price of everyone's salvation with the blood He shed on Calvary's cross. Salvation is free—free for the asking.

Prayer Suggestion

Pray that God may help you discover what is truly valuable in your life.

Mercy—Like a "Gentle Rain"

Mercy is a human quality often lost in the give and take of daily living. In an age of "me first"—of emphasis on self-fulfillment and personal rights at all costs—being merciful sems out of date.

Showing mercy is something spontaneous. In *The Merchant of Venice* Shakespeare has Portia say to the man demanding a pound of human flesh as his due: "The quality of mercy is not strained [is not forced]. It droppeth as the gentle rain from heaven upon the place beneath; it is twice blest; it blesseth him that gives and him that takes. . . . It is an attribute to God Himself. And earthly power doth then show itself most like God's when mercy seasons justice."

Mercy cannot be commanded. It is not a sign of personal weakness but of strength rooted in a combination of strong conviction and tender compassion. It comes in response to the appeal of God's mercy to all people. It lets the family resemblance show, that is, our likeness to God, as Jesus said: "Be merciful, even as your Father [in heaven] is merciful."

Mercy, as Shakespeare said, blesses both the giver and the receiver. Also this truth comes from the mouth of Jesus, who said: "Blessed are the merciful, for they shall obtain mercy." With Christians, this is the sequence of events: God had mercy on them when He ordained His Son, Jesus Christ, to be the Redeemer of the human race by His life, death, and resurrection. Knowing and believing this, Christians are moved to be merciful to others. They are merciful because they have obtained mercy, and as a reward of divine grace they will obtain mercy. Christian mercifulness is an effect and a cause. Who can go wrong being merciful?

Prayer Suggestion

Pray that God, beginning with you, may melt hearts of stone so that mercy may prevail.

Christ Makes Us God's Friends

In many situations of life we need a go-between. A federal mediator helps management and striking workers come to an agreement. A real estate agent brings seller and buyer together. A matchmaker introduces future marriage partners. In the musical *Fiddler on the Roof* such a go-between is called Yente, and she tries to negotiate marriages for Tevye's five daughters.

The role of a go-between is especially important when people are on the outs. Such was the case when the first human beings, Adam and Eve, fell into sin by disobeying God. They knew they had done wrong; their conscience accused them. Instead of welcoming the presence and friendship of God, they hid from Him.

So it is still with the descendants of Adam and Eve today. Like their first parents, they are sinners, estranged from God. By nature they have neither the willingness nor power to be friends with God. So God has to take the initiative in effecting a reconciliation. To Adam and Eve God promised a Savior—the woman's Seed, who would crush the serpent's head—to break the power of Satan and sin.

Jesus Christ, the Son of God born of the Virgin Mary, is the woman's Seed. He came to be, as St. Paul declares, the Mediator between God and man. He became the Go-Between, the Reconciler, when He rendered full satisfaction for the sins of the whole human race. Through faith in Him we are again the forgiven sons and daughters of God and the heirs of salvation.

Today's English Version of the Bible states this reconciliation in a way we can all understand: "All this is done by God, who through Christ changed us from enemies into His friends, and He gave us the task of making others His friends also." How wonderful to be a friend of God, and a friend-maker in His behalf!

Prayer Suggestion

Pray that you may have greater zeal and joy in sharing with others the friendship you have with God through Christ.

A Journey of Joy

In a Missouri State Park along the Mississippi River is the grave of Princess Otahki, the daughter of a chief. Along with hundreds of others, she died when the Cherokees were taken in winter from their native southern states to Oklahoma, then called Indian Territory.

That forced march, known as the "Trail of Tears," is reminiscent of the journey of life, often marked by sadness. Said St. Paul: "We must through much tribulation enter into the kingdom of God."

On the other hand, thanks to God's gracious intervention, life is also a joyful journey. There was joy when the children of Israel, after their 40-year pilgrimage, entered the Promised Land. There was joy when the believers journeyed to Jerusalem for the high festivals. The psalmist declares: "I was glad when they said to me, 'Let us go to the house of the Lord!' Our feet shall stand within your gates, O Jerusalem!"

Also our journey to God's house is one of joy, for there we pray, praise God in our hymns, and hear the good news of salvation in Jesus Christ. Also the return journey to our homes is joyful, for in church we have visited with Christ, our dearest Friend. The homeward way of the Wise Men of the East was much easier, for they had worshiped Christ. Of the traveling Ethiopian official it is said, after the evangelist Philip had baptized him: "He went on his way rejoicing."

As you count your blessings, taking note of what you have going for you—family support, friendships, health, opportunity to work and to serve, peace with God—you too will find that life, its tears notwithstanding, is a journey of joy.

Prayer Suggestion

Pray that God may wipe away your tears and give you the joy of salvation in Jesus Christ.

The Four Horses

Visitors in Venice usually go to see St. Mark's Basilica, where four bronze horses are on display. They are very old, brought from Constantinople as loot around A.D. 1200. How old they were then, nobody knows.

The Book of Revelation in the Bible also speaks of four horses. In chapter 6 the writer, St. John reports that in his vision he saw, in turn, four horses: a white horse, a red, a black, and a pale one. The colors are symbolic: red stands for war and bloodshed; black, for hunger and starvation; pale, for death.

The white horse, as we are led to believe, stands for Christ's victory. In chapter 19 the rider of the white horse is called "Faithful and True." Though clad in "a robe dipped in blood," He is crowned with many diadems, signifying His conquest of sin, Satan, and death. He is also called "the Word of God," in keeping with the opening verses of John's gospel: "In the beginning was the Word . . . The Word became flesh and dwelt among us." This is Jesus Christ, the Son of God born of the Virgin Mary that He might bring us peace with God.

Jesus told us about the evils that three of the four horses represent, but He has conquered them all. As long as this world of sinners continues to exist, there will be wars and rumors of war, hunger not only in third-world countries but even in our own land of plenty, and the pallor of death resulting from natural causes and deeds of violence. It is a comfort for us to know that Jesus has redeemed us from all evil and has promised us eternal life. He is the Rider on the white horse.

Prayer Suggestion

Pray that we may be delivered from all evil and preserved for our Lord's heavenly kingdom.

The Human Race, One Family

When you look at a world map, you get the idea that certain parts of the world belong together—that South America, for example, was once part of western Africa but seemingly broke off. In 1912 the geographer Alfred Wegener went a step further and said all continents were once one continent. He called it Pangea: "All Land."

Whether or not that may be, one thing is true: we are one human race, one family created by God. Preaching on Mars Hill in Athens, St. Paul declared that God made of one blood—from one human ancestor, Adam—all the nations of the earth. That one family of God has grown into millions of people, living under different circumstances, speaking many languages, developing various cultures. Also physical changes have come about in stature, skin color, and the like. But underneath we are all one human race, one family.

Regarding God's new, spiritual creation, Malachi asks: "Have we not all one father? Has not one God created us?" The answer, of course, is yes. This one God and Father sent His Son, Jesus Christ, to redeem all people, for all have sinned. God is not a racist; He shows no favoritism. He equally loves the whole world—all humanity as made up of individual persons like you and me. He loved to the extent that He gave His Son into death so that all might have eternal life.

God the Father created all, the Son redeemed all, and the Holy Spirit seeks through the Gospel to bring all to saving faith in Jesus Christ. This means missions. This is what our Lord wants. He commands His disciples in all ages to make disciples of all nations by baptizing them into the name of the Triune God and teaching them.

The world may show that our earth is divided into many parts, but the people inhabiting it are one human race, one family. Let us act like it!

Prayer Suggestion

Pray that wars may cease and that true peace may weld together the nations of the world.

What God Wants Us to Do

Converted to Christianity, Saul the Pharisee asked: "What shall I do, Lord?" He realized he must quit persecuting Christians. He knew also that he must do something beyond plying his trade as a tentmaker. He was soon to learn of his new role: to be an apostle of Jesus Christ and to bear witness to Him.

God may not communicate with us as directly as He did with St. Paul, but He does communicate. When we ask: "What shall I do, Lord?" He tells us: "As far as your salvation is concerned, you need do nothing to earn it; I have suffered, died, and risen again to obtain it for you." If we then ask: "Shall we then just sit, Lord, and do nothing?" "Oh, no," He replies, "I want you to be My disciples and do works of love in My name, not in order to be saved but *because* you are saved."

We may ask further: "Do You, Lord, want me to become a traveling missionary or evangelist like St. Paul?" For some Christians it is Christ's will that they be just that. For most of us, however, it is His declared will that we bear witness to Him in and through our vocation, our daily work. What that vocation is to be depends on a number of things: our talents and interests, opportunities, results of aptitude tests, the advice of people who know us, and the like.

In our changing times it is often necessary to change vocations. But doing so is not always easy. At a social gathering the wife of a general told author George Bernard Shaw that her husband would retire from the army and become a writer. "Strange," Shaw replied, "I was thinking about doing the opposite: Retire from writing and become a general." The point is: Each vocation requires preparation—you don't just walk into it.

What does God want you to do? This is what He wants: do a good job in whatever you are now doing. He will let you know if you are to enter a new field. So considered what He says in His Word and pray for guidance.

Prayer Suggestion

Pray that God may direct you in the way He wants you to go.

265

God's Unchanging Truths

The concept people have of moral values varies, and the more people follow their own opinions, the more their values vary.

Our present morality is somewhat like a coin whose value changes. At a rare-coin auction in Lexington, Kentucky, someone paid an enormous sum of money for a silver dollar dated 1794. When coined, it was worth a dollar, but when sold as a rare coin, it brought $34,500.

Monetary values go up and down everyday—in an age of inflation, mostly down. Is this what is happening to our moral values? Has inflation set in with the increase of pornography, gambling, contempt for marriage, violence, a me-first philosophy of life?

It is inevitable: when people cut themselves off from their religious roots, they have nothing else to fall back on than human opinions, and human opinions on what is right and wrong vary widely. Quite often those who yell the loudest or can muster a majority get their way, regardless of what God has revealed about it in His Word.

Sometimes even misguided religious people turn God's law upside down. God's commandment says: "Thou shalt not kill." But some religious fanatics want to kill others, as Jesus foretold to His disciples: "The hour is coming when whoever kills you will think he is offering service to God."

As we see moral truths established by God being exchanged for immoral human opinion, we recognize more and more the need—and the blessedness—of adhering to the Word of God. Where God has spoken, the thing is settled, and human opinion must yield.

Truly God has spoken in His Word, not only in His law but also the Gospel. He has spoken to us in and through His Son, Jesus Christ, who loved us and gave His life to gather us together as the people of God. This truth abides unchanged.

Prayer Suggestion

Ask God that His Word may increasingly overrule false human opinions in our world.

Laying the Foundation for Peace

Sometimes buildings, erected in a previous age, can be converted to modern use, especially a use that serves peace and peaceful pursuits. In Paris, France, for example, visitors can see a 16th-century arsenal now serving as a library. Also, what used to be a military fortress is now a world-famous museum—the Louvre.

It would be wonderful if all institutions and instruments of war could be turned into aids for loving, learning, and the upbuilding of the human race. Some people hope that the words of the prophets Isaiah and Micah in the Bible can be literally fulfilled: "They shall beat their swords into plowshares and their spears into pruning hooks; nation shall not lift up sword against nation, neither shall they learn war anymore." We have a good example of this, they say, in the vehicle called the Jeep. It was developed for war use but has found many peacetime functions.

How shall we work toward peace? There are many ways. The United Nations is one. We need to take all these efforts seriously. But topping them all is the restructuring of the individual— from one who follows his passions and inclines toward violence into one who is at peace with God and consequently at peace with himself and with his fellow human beings. Such a change of heart comes only through the Gospel, which is and has the power of God to turn people from hatred to love, from enemies of God to friends, from rebels to His children. Jesus Christ is the Mediator, Reconciler, Peacemaker. He atoned for sin, broke down the partition between God and sinners, and made us one family in Christ.

Peace with God, which is what Christianity is all about, expresses itself in outward peace in the community, state, nation, world. It turns, so to speak, arsenals of war into Christian schools and hospitals.

Prayer Suggestion

Pray that God will give you peace through faith in Christ and enable you to share it with others.

Not Insults, but Commendation

In an Idaho city a child was born with only 85 percent of its brain. The brain stem was there, but the main organ was missing—a great deprivation!

The brain is a gift of God. People who have a healthy brain and sound mind, to go with it sometimes fail to use it rightly. Or they may misuse it. A state penitentiary guard in Huntsville, Texas, told a touring group that some of the shrewdest, brainiest people, including business persons and bankers, were within these walls. The criminal wears not only a blue but also a white collar. What God wants is that we develop and use our brains for greater usefulness in this world and to the glory of God.

It is a sin, a cheap shot, and an insult to call a normal person "brainless," perhaps after a mistake was made or something was overlooked. The Bible makes this clear. In the Sermon on the Mount Jesus condemns sinful namecalling, usually done in anger, such as saying "You fool!" or "Raca!" The latter word, from the Aramaic, was a term of contempt and reproach. It meant worthless, empty, as if to say: "You empty head!" or "You brainless fool!"

Those born with an incomplete brain, like that Idaho baby, or whose mind is deficient, are deserving of our Christian love and concern. Those whose brain functions all right, but not always to our liking, are not to be made the targets of demeaning insults. If their thinking is out of line, the epithet "brainlessness" will not help. But words of correction spoken in Christian love, will help, especially if they are accompained by commendations for what is done right. Our good example also helps. Our Lord wants us to approach the problem in this way. St. Paul reminds us that Christ died for weak and erring persons. They are precious in His sight.

Prayer Suggestion

Pray that the mind [mind-set] that was in Christ—a mind functioning in truth and love—may dwell also in you.

Above and Beyond the Call of Duty

The following help-wanted ad for a garage foreman once appeared in an issue of a St. Louis, Mo., newspaper: "Qualifications: Patience of Job, leader of men, a lover of people, nerves of steel, six hands, twelve ears, ability to be in four places at once. Experience. See John H . . ."

It is evident that the garage owner resorted to an over-statement, even to a touch of humor, in listing the qualifications. But he also made it plain that an employee would at times be called upon to render services above and beyond the call of duty.

The Lord is that kind of an employer. When Jesus called twelve men to be His disciples and later His apostles, He didn't promise an easy life or work that would always be pleasant. Instead He said this: "I send you out as sheep in the midst of wolves; so be wise as serpents and innocent as doves."

Christ's full-time workers today—the called and ordained servants of the Word, the church's pastors—know that their work doesn't always fall into a neat, nine-to-five daily schedule. They are prepared to agree to the aforementioned qualifications of the garage foreman: "Patience of Job, leader of men, lover of people . . ."

But what about lay people? All Christians, as servants of Jesus Christ, are expected to go above and beyond the call of duty, to extend themselves, to endure hardships, to be hassled and harassed in Christ's behalf and for the good of His brothers and sisters. Why are they willing to go the second, even the third and the fourth mile? Because they believe that this is what Jesus did in their behalf. He endured suffering, even death on the cross, for their eternal good.

Christ died also for you. You too can be that kind of a disciple.

Prayer Suggestion

Pray for strength to render that extra Christian service in critical situations.

Facing Life's Changes

Perhaps no previous age has seen so many changes as ours in one lifetime. Some changes are for the better. Everyday living is in many respects made easier by the inventions of science.

Other changes in our culture are for the worse. Many who were brought up in a right-and-wrong value system are bewildered by what is happening. One is reminded of lines in Marc Connelly's play *The Green Pastures*, where the Lord is quoted as telling Noah what will happen when the Great Flood comes: "The levees are going to burst, and everything that's not fastened down is coming loose."

The new life-styles, the abandonment of moral standards, people doing their own thing, widespread pornography—all make it seem that a rampaging flood has been released. Some try to escape the changes by fleeing to remote places in the world, or by isolating themselves and retreating into their own private world.

There has to be a better way of coping with changes. Christians keep their balance by realizing that God is still in charge of His universe, and His Word abides. The psalmist declares: "The counsel of the Lord stands forever." Changes come about in our world, but God doesn't change; He is the same. And Jesus Christ is the same yesterday and today and forever. The Gospel is still the power of God for salvation to all who believe in Christ as Savior. Sin is the same, as is God's cure for it.

Assured of this, we can begin to evaluate our times, accepting the changes that are good and resisting those that cause sin and evil to increase. Knowing *who* we are, and *whose* we are, why we are here and where we are going, namely, to our heavenly home, we will not be washed away by the flood of changes. We will have learned to roll with the punches and survive, continuing to be God's people: the salt of the earth and the light of the world.

Prayer Suggestion

Ask for God's help in keeping up with the changes in your life and in using them to good advantage.

There is a Better Way

In many instances old ways have yielded to better ways. The inland barge canals, so needed for transportation, became obsolete when the railroads come. In 1860 the first of the 400 Pony express riders reached San Francisco. In less than two years this mode of communication gave way to the telegraph.

Usually changes are not made for the sake of change but because they represent a better way. When there are problems in our personal lives, we tend to worry and fret. But there is a better way. The Bible says: cast all your cares and anxieties on God, for He cares for you.

Some people are jealous of others, as was the case in the church at Corinth, because not all had the same spiritual gifts: prophesying, healing, speaking in tongues. So St. Paul told them he would show them a "more excellent way." And what was that way? It was the way open to all, the way of love, which the apostle then explains in one of the great chapters of the Bible: 1 Corinthians 13.

From ancient times the rule was: an eye for an eye, a tooth for a tooth. It was the way of revenge, of hating one's enemies and trying to get even. But here comes Jesus who tells of a better way: love your enemies. That is better for them and better for you. But most of all, it is the right way.

In this respect Jesus is not only our Teacher or our Example, that we should love as He has loved, He is also our Enabler. He Himself is the way to peace with God, to peace with one another, to peace within oneself. He died for our sins and rose again, and through His Holy Spirit He brings us to faith in Him so that we can follow the better way: the way of love and peace.

Prayer Suggestions

Pray that in every situation God may show you the better way and help you walk in it.

Christians, a Pilgrim People

Christians are people on a journey. From the time they are born they are on the trip of life. Every passing day finds them closer to their destination: their ultimate home in heaven.

Christians are described in the Bible as "strangers and exiles on the earth." Some people are persecuted and cast out of society or country because of their faith in Jesus Christ. Such were the people in Asia Minor to whom St. Peter wrote his First Epistle, calling them "strangers and pilgrims." Aside from external opposition, people like this have to cope with many temptations that come from within.

Christians as pilgrims are a cross section of society—people in all walks of life. In his *Canterbury Tales*, written some 600 years ago, Geoffrey Chaucer delineates the character of people making a pilgrimage to a shrine in Canterbury. The group includes a knight, miller, clerk, cook, sailor, cook, monk, merchant, housewife, steward, parson, and others. In their pilgrimage today Christians are of a great variety: young and old, rich and poor, learned and unlearned, and of many ranks and races.

But they are all one in their faith in Christ Jesus. All were redeemed from sin by His precious blood. All constitute the members of His body, the church, having been called by the one Holy Spirit to one hope, one Lord, one faith, one baptism, one God and Father of all.

Christian pilgrims have much in common; they invite others to join them on their journey. They want to help one another, as the hymn writer has stated: "Before our Father's throne We pour our ardent prayers; Our fears, our hopes, our aims are one, Our comforts and our cares."

Prayer Suggestion

Ask God to give you strength to follow in Jesus' footsteps on life's pilgrimage.

If at First You Don't Succeed . . .

The expression to "be with it" needs to be followed by one just as important: "Stay with it." Discouraged because of initial failure, many people are inclined to give up, to throw in the towel, to try something else entirely. Perhaps all they need is a different approach.

As a young baseball player in the major leagues, Walter Alston was a failure. In his only time at bat he struck out. But instead of quitting the sport, he became a very successful manager.

The Bible is full of encouragements to us, not only to persist but to be flexible. If one door is locked, try another. After his conversion, St. Paul had no success as a missionary. He had to flee Damascus by night. In Jerusalem he ran into all kinds of difficulties. But he did not quit missions because certain places seemed to be closed to him. He went elsewhere to preach the Gospel. In Ephesus, he writes, "a wide door for effective work has opened to me."

During His earthly ministry even Jesus ran into an occasional brick wall—like in His own home community, where He could do no mighty works. But He continued His work so that, in fulfillment of God's plan for the salvation of us all, He performed the mightiest work of all: He sacrificed Himself on the cross in our behalf and then rose from the grave.

Also in our lives some rain will fall: all kinds of discouragements, rebuffs, setbacks, closed doors. But with faith in the promises of God, we not only try again but stay out of a rut by viewing our work from a different vantage point and trying a new approach. Such wise persistence God will bless.

Prayer Suggestion

Pray that God may lead you to the right door for the opportunity to serve Him joyfully and effectively.

The Right Self-fulfillment

"Self-fulfillment" is a word often heard in today's conversation. It can stand for something good and right. God has given each person natural talents, and He wants them developed and put to good use. The mind should not be wasted. We all would be less well off if Thomas Edison, or Alexander Graham Bell, or Madame Curie had not applied their talents.

"Self-fulfillment" can also be a cover-up word for plain, old selfishness and pride. Members of the "me generation" care only about their own interest. If they say, "Me first, then you," not only is their grammar suspect but also their moral character.

A boy came home from school and proudly announced to his mother that he was the best-looking in his class. His mother asked, "How do you know this? Did someone tell you?" The son replied, "There was no need for that; I saw the others myself." It is the nature of conceit to base its judgment of self on its own opinion or on wishful thinking.

The Christian religion teaches humility—not an abject self-contempt or self-depreciation, but a healthy, wholesome humility linked with Christian love. St. Paul dwells on this subject often in his letters. He tells the Philippians to avoid selfishness and conceit, to seek also the interest of others, to follow a "You First" way of life, to "count others better than yourselves."

In this connection he speaks of letting the mind [mind-set] of Christ be in us. What was the mind of Christ? In great humility He became a servant and was obedient unto death, even death on a cross. Thus he redeemed us from all sin, also the sin of pride and selfishness. What is more, He set us free to become servants to Him and others.

Prayer Suggestion

Pray that because of love for Christ you may gladly serve Him and others in Christian humility.

Warm Love or Frosty Fear?

Sometimes children write books about their famous parents, including movie stars. While much of what is written is a critical recital of half-truths, one does occasionally come upon a grain of truth, as when a son wrote this about his stern father: "You can't love anyone you fear."

How is it with our heavenly Father? Can we both love and fear Him? The expression "fearing God," as used in the Bible, generally means to have reverence for His holiness. Respect for God goes well with love. In fact, we show love for God when we respect His holy will and keep from displeasing Him by sinning.

But the word "fear" can also stand for terror, for fright that causes one to shake and tremble. That kind of fear is incompatible with love, for you can't really love someone whom you fear. The apostle John writes in his First Epistle: "There is no fear in love, but perfect love casts out fear."

St. John is an excellent expounder of love. He was the disciple whom Jesus loved and who in turn loved Jesus. He put on record many of our Lord's discourses on God's love, including these beautiful words: "God so loved the world that He gave His only Son, that whoever believes in Him should not perish but have eternal life." And in his First Epistle: "God is love, and he who abides in love abides in God, and God abides in him."

How is it with us? Are we afraid of God? Do we shake in our boots at the mention of His name as though He were a condemning judge, a taskmaster, a drill sergeant? If so, we don't really know God. In Christ God has become the Father who loves us. When we love Him in return after the Holy Spirit has kindled faith in our hearts, our hearts will grow warm, and this warmth will drive out the frost of fear.

Prayer Suggestion

Pray now that you may so grow in your love for God that you regard Him as the heavenly Father who loves you.

Eating and Drinking to God's Glory

It is well known that many people have a drinking problem, but what is perhaps not so obvious is that others have eating disorders. To the latter, medical science gives names. Anorexia is a starving disease. The other extreme is bulimia, which in its literal meaning is "the hunger of an ox." This disease is marked by a constant, insatiable hunger. The one afflicted goes on an eating binge, then purges.

The Bible, while it is not a medical textbook, has something to say about eating and drinking. On the one hand, it recognizes that some people overindulge in food and drink, to the detriment not only of their physical health but also of their spiritual well-being. St. Paul speaks of these sins as excessive feasting, debauchery, carousing, revelry. This is not the normal eating and drinking of people. This is, as Martin Luther translated in the German Bible, the *Fressen* and *Saufen* associated with animals.

The Bible has good things to say about the right use of food and drink. It tells us that Jesus, the Son of Man, "came eating and drinking." Jesus was not a fanatic about fasting; He did not practice total abstinence. Instead He set us a good example in the right use of God's gifts: food and drink. But Jesus is more than our Exemplar. He is our Redeemer, who by His death in our behalf earned forgiveness and gives us strength to lead God-pleasing lives. Now we can follow this guideline of the apostle: "Whether you eat or drink, or whatever you do, do all to the glory of God." Eating and drinking, when it stills normal hunger and thirst, is to our welfare and to the glory of God. God helps us to use His gifts rightly, including our daily bread. God gives us His Holy Spirit, who works His fruit in us: love, joy, peace, and self-control.

Prayer Suggestion

Ask God for strength to use His gifts of food and drink with moderation.

Confidence in Our Children

When Randolph Churchill was no longer Chancellor of the Exchequer, an official from the British parliament came to the house to collect his official robes. But Mrs. Churchill refused to give them up, saying, "I am saving them for my son." Her son was Winston, who did indeed rise to high government office during England's critical years.

It is good when a son can continue his father's work. In the Bible we read that King Solomon succeeded David to the throne. But not only in government but also in other areas of life it makes for continuity when children walk in their parents' footsteps.

Sometimes fathers and mothers throw up their hands in despair when their teenage sons and daughters seemingly want to strike our on their own instead of continuing their parents' work—perhaps on the farm or in business. One has to bear in mind that their talents and interests may lead them in another direction. In all cases, it helps to give our young people a vote of confidence.

Risks are involved in the upbringing of children in our day and age, but if we teach them the Word of God and lead them to their Savior Jesus Christ, we can expect that they will do honor to their parents. St. John has a word for fathers and sons: "I am writing to you, fathers, because you know Him who is from the beginning. I am writing to you, young men, because you have overcome the evil one." It is evident that St. John had confidence in Christian youth.

Had someone asked the heavenly Father to take away what lay in store for Jesus: the purple robe, the crown of thorns, the cross, He could well have replied: "No. I am saving them for My Son, so that He can be the Savior of the world."

Prayer Suggestion

Pray that as a Christian parent you will never lose faith in your growing children.

Facing the Facts

Some facts are hard to face, and death is one of them. Long after Prince Albert, the husband and consort of England's Queen Victoria, had died, his devoted wife continued to have his clothes and a basin of fresh water brought in for him every day. She wore mourning clothes for nine years.

Other realities of life are easily ignored, and sin is certainly one of them. States the holy writer: "If we say we have no sin, we deceive ourselves, and the truth is not in us." St. John goes on to say: "If we confess our sins, God is faithful and just, and will forgive our sins and cleanse us from all unrighteousness." We can confidently trust in God's forgiveness, for in the preceding verse the apostle declares: "The blood of Jesus His Son cleanses us from all sin."

The reality of God's grace to all who confess their sins and in faith turn to Jesus Christ for salvation enables us to be honest with ourselves and with others. We can face the facts and adjust our life accordingly. Someone who has a drinking problem can quit pretending and can seek help. People with other personal problems, perhaps in their sex life, can come out of the closet and go to counselors for aid. All this is made much easier if we face the fact that by faith in Jesus Christ we are right with God.

So let us be honest and truthful with ourselves and the people around us. We will not lose face by doing this. It is no disgrace to be poor; why pretend we can freely spend money to keep up with the Joneses? In whatever we say or do, whether in drawing up a job résumé, planning for the future, making purchases with credit cards, or building a home, it never pays to ignore the facts of our economic status and get in over our heads.

At peace with God and rich Him, we can afford to be truthful and face life's facts.

Prayer Suggestion

Pray for the courage to face up to life's challenging problems, asking Jesus' guidance.

Worship Before the Family Altar

In his lengthy poem *The Cotter's [or Cottager's] Saturday Night* Robert Burns narrates how a Scottish father conducts a family devotion. The Bible lies open, and "the priest-like father reads the sacred page." He reads in the Old Testament about Abraham, Moses, Job, Isaiah. Turning to the New Testament, the father reads about Christ's sacrifice: "How guiltless blood for guilty man was shed; how He who bore in heaven the second name, Had not on earth whereon to lay His head." Burns goes on to say, "Then kneeling down to heaven's eternal King; The saint, the father, and the husband prays."

How strong our families, our communities, and our nation would be if scenes like this were enacted in today's homes! The Christian family is Christ's little church, forming the foundation of Christendom at large.

In the first century, Christ's followers could not worship in beautiful church edifices, for there weren't any. Yet Christianity was then a movement that moved and shook the world—this because people fostered it in their homes. There is where Christian cell groups were. St. Paul repeatedly refers to house churches. Philemon, to whom he writes a letter in behalf of Onesimus, a runaway slave, had a church in his house, and so had Mary, the mother of John Mark, in Jerusalem. The centurion Cornelius regularly gathered his family and household for worship in his home.

Christianity fares best when it flourishes at the grass roots, that is, in the home. The family group is the best nursery for Christian faith and life. God's blessings fall abundantly on a house where the Bible is read and prayers are spoken. This is the family altar, where worship is translated into a life of love, as the apostle bids us: "Be kind to one another, tenderhearted, forgiving one another, as God in Christ forgave you."

Prayer Suggestion

Pray for God's guidance in making your home a bastion of Christian faith and life.

The Book We Need

It is interesting to know that one of the all-time best sellers, *Gone with the Wind*, is the only book Margaret Mitchell of Atlanta ever wrote.

It has been said: "The Bible is the one and only Book God wrote." This is true. Of course, God did not write it with His own hand, for He is a Spirit. To get His book written, God employed a great many writers, from Moses, who wrote the first five books of the Old Testament, to St. John the Divine, author of Revelation, the last New Testament Book. He did not use the dictation method; if He had, all the writers would have written in the same style. God inspired the writers—the prophets in the Old Testament, and the apostles in the New. St. Peter declares: "Men moved by the Holy Spirit spoke from God"—and wrote from God. St. Paul adds: "All Scripture is inspired by God."

We cannot know or explain the process of the Bible's divine inspiration, but we do know what the Bible is: the Word of God. We also know why it was written: "to instruct us for salvation through faith in Christ Jesus." Our Lord Himself said: "The Scriptures bear witness of Me." They testify that Jesus Christ is God's Son, who came into the world to die for our sins and to rise again.

Because the keynote of salvation is so clear in the Bible, it was not necessary for God to write other books on this theme. The one Holy Scripture is all we need. Whatever is clearly and concisely stated in creeds, confessions, and catechisms is drawn from the Bible; they are not bibles to be added to *the* Bible.

Do we need the Bible—the one book God wrote? We certainly do. It shows us the road to heaven through faith in Christ, and shows us how we may lead God-pleasing lives in this present world. No other book from the pens or typewriters of human authors can ever replace the Bible. It is important to study it, individually and in groups.

Prayer Suggestion

Pray that the Holy Spirit may enlighten you as you read God's Word and draw you closer to Jesus.

Taking the Right Road to Heaven

The last line in Anton Chekhov's play *The Three Sisters* reads, "If only we knew, if only we knew." So said the three sisters who had long planned to go to Moscow but who never made the trip.

All kinds of things can keep us from doing what we had intended: procrastination, preoccupation with other interests, the intervention of people. Some persons miss out on education because they keep on delaying their entry into college. Some never harvest a crop; they failed to sow the seed. Others never get around to visiting the members of their family, near or far.

Every minister has heard people say after he has called on them, "Pastor, you'll see us in church one of these Sundays," but they never come. Jesus and His apostles heard people promise to hear and learn more of the Gospel, but those promises fell through. To a discerning scribe Jesus said, "You are not far from the kingdom of God," but this man's attitude still left him outside the kingdom. St. Paul heard King Agrippa say after the apostle had pleaded Christ's cause: "Almost you persuade me to become a Christian."

"Sure, I want to go to heaven," someone may tell you. "I want someday to enter that beautiful heavenly city." But that is where it stops. Others say with Chekhov's three sisters: "If only we knew"-"If only we knew for sure that there is a hereafter; if only we knew what it is like to be in heaven; if only we knew the way to heaven!"

Well, we do know! Jesus tells us: "I am the Way." He is the only way to the Father's house. Believe in Him as your Savior, and you are on the right road.

Prayer Suggestion

Pray that God's Spirit may lead you on the road to eternal life and enable you to invite others to come with you.

God Blesses the Peacemakers

Some people seemingly can't help being troublemakers. They stir up ill will wherever they are: in the home, in school, in the community, in the church. Some thrive on controversy.

It is all too evident that trouble breeds more trouble, misdeeds invite to misdeeds, violence begets more violence. In 1790, on the ship *Bounty*, Fletcher Christian led a mutiny against Captain Bligh. With his rebellious group he settled on Pitcairn Island, but not to a peaceful existence. Three years later a squabble arose among the mutineers, and they turned on their leader and killed him.

In the Bible we read this about Ishmael: "His hand [is] against every man, and every man's hand against him." In Job's words, he was "born to trouble." "Are you the one who troubles Israel?" King Ahab asked the prophet Elijah. The question was misdirected; it was Ahab who troubled Israel with his idolatry. St. Paul complains several times about people dogging his footsteps in the mission fields in order to undermine his preaching of the Gospel.

But here are also peacemakers, of whom Jesus declares: "Blessed are the peacemakers, for they shall be called sons [and daughters] of God." They are like their heavenly Father, the "God of peace." They are the brothers and sisters of Jesus Christ, of whom we read in Ephesians: "He is our peace, who has made us both one . . . so to make peace and . . . reconcile us both to God in one body through the cross." The immediate reference is to the first-century dispute over circumcision, but in every conflict, chiefly in the sinners' conflict with their righteous God, Christ is the Mediator, the Peacemaker, the Prince of Peace.

Be a peacemaker in the circles within which you move! God will bless you for it!

Prayer Suggestion

Pray that Christ may fill your heart with peace and make you a peacemaker.

Faith Persistent in Prayer

In a gun factory there was an 8-foot steel bar weighing 500 pounds and hanging by a chain. Next to it was a cork suspended from a silk thread. The cork was made to strike the steel bar in a regular rhythm. After half an hour of this persistent motion the cork caused the bar to move.

Persistence counts also in our spiritual lives. So Jesus taught us. He told in a parable how a legally wronged widow got a reluctant judge to act in her behalf—by calling on him persistently. Our Savior spoke of a faith that could move mountains, again by persistence. St. Paul experienced how amid physical weakness faith prevailed because it relied on the power of God. He had an ailment—a thorn in the flesh—about which he prayed. God answered his prayer, not in the precise form he desired, but in a much better way. God exercised His strength through St. Paul's weakness, saying: "My grace is sufficient for you, for My power is made perfect in weakness."

Weak as we are, we too can do great things by a faith that draws its power from God. God has sent Christ, His Son, into our world to take all our sins, griefs, and weaknesses upon Him, carrying the burden to Calvary's cross. Our faith in Christ Jesus and in His Gospel, which is the power of God unto salvation to all who believe it, gives us the confidence we need as we pray and as we turn our problems over to God. It may seem at times that our problem is like that 8-foot, 500-pound steel bar and, measured against it, our own ability seems like a cork on a silk thread. But by persistence in faith and prayer we can move it, not by our own strength but by the power of God.

Prayer Suggestion

Ask God for enduring strength to cope with your problems, and the confidence that He will hear your prayer.

Christians:
Christ's Representatives in the World

In a church edifice stood a beautiful statue of Christ. Through the years the worshipers admired it. When the time came to remodel the church, the statue was taken outside and temporarily placed along the curb. There, according to someone's estimate, more people saw the Christ figure than had ever seen it inside the church.

Many individuals don't attend church regularly to hear about Christ. So it is up to Christ's people to bring Christ, so to speak, from their church seats to the streets, so that through their example people may see Christ.

Our Lord said to His disciples, "He who hears you hears Me." He could also have said, "He who sees you sees Me." When non-Christians see God's children leading Christian lives, they should get some idea of what the loving Father in heaven, is like. This is letting the family resemblance show. Said St. Peter: "Maintain good conduct among the Gentiles so that . . . they may see your good deeds and glorify God."

It has been said, "The world doesn't read the four gospels—the gospels according to Matthew, Mark, Luke, and John—but it does read the fifth gospel: the gospel according to you." St. Paul told the Christians in Corinth that they were a letter from Christ, known and read by all people.

Those who never see the inside of a church, where Christ may be pictured in colored windows or other art forms, nevertheless see Him when Christians become "little Christs" in the world. Martin Luther said, "I will give myself as a sort of Christ to my neighbor as Christ gave Himself for me." That is the right motivation, as St. Paul also said: "I live by faith in the Son of God, who loved me and gave Himself for me."

Prayer Suggestion

Pray that through God's Word and Spirit you may become more Christlike from day to day.

Losses and Gains in One's Christianity

David Livingstone, England's great benefactor and missionary to people in Africa, was back home to be decorated by Queen Victoria. Malaria, dysentery, and other diseases had made him old and weak before his time. A lion had clawed one of his arms. His wife lay buried in an African jungle. Yet, he said, he had not made sacrifices for Christ. He considered it a privilege to serve Him.

Livingstone stands in the line of great heroes of faith, such as St. Paul, who wrote: "Whatever gain I had, I counted as loss for the sake of Christ. Indeed, I count everything as loss because of the surpassing worth of knowing Christ Jesus, my Lord. For His sake I have suffered the loss of all things, and count them as refuse, in order that I may gain Christ." Again, he writes: "I live by faith in the Son of God, who loved me and gave Himself for me."

In our own lives we may have sustained what seem to be losses, disadvantages, and defeats because we are Christians. This happens not only in Communist countries, where Christianity is suppressed; it can happen right here. Such so-called sacrifices may involve bearing ridicule: or, what is just as demeaning, a condescending attitude. Our commitment to the Christian faith may create tension in the family, in school, at work, in community living. It can cost us a boyfriend or a girlfriend. It may mean being passed over when a job promotion is made. It may spell social ostracism.

When this happens, we think of St. Paul and David Livingstone. In comparison with their sacrifices, ours may be very small indeed. But whatever our losses, they cannot compare with the great gain we have in Christ: forgiveness, peace with God, a purposeful life.

Prayer Suggestion

Ask God to show you the great spiritual riches you have in Jesus, the best friend your soul ever had.

Good Medicine for the Soul

Dr. Kilmer's Swamp Root, Dr. King's New Discovery, Peruna, Water of Life—these are some of the patent medicines of the past. Similar concoctions are still being sold to the public today. These remedies, sometimes laced with a little alcohol, may give temporary relief. All the while they are only "quack medicines."

Useless, as well as harmful, remedies are offered for the *soul* as well. Satan was the first to peddle them when he came to Adam and Eve in the Garden of Eden and gave his prescription for happiness and human fulfillment—a prescription of disobedience—in direct contradiction to what God had said. That is always the nature of false religion. It proclaims sweet-tasting, easy-to-take, quick-curing remedies for the spiritual ailment: sin. It offers the miracle drugs of man-made religion: salvation by good works, a formula offering you God's love without you loving Him, meditation, mysticism, magic, occult arts, even Satan worship. This is all bad medicine for the soul.

But available to us is the good medicine for what ails us spiritually, the remedy that truly helps and heals. It is the medicine Jesus, the Physician of the soul, dispensed when He said to the paralytic man: "Take heart . . . your sins are forgiven." This is the prescription for inner peace, for when our sins are confessed and forgiven for Jesus' sake, we are right with God—we are at peace with Him, and from it follows peace with others and peace with ourselves.

Jesus has the right to pronounce forgiveness, for He is the one who went to Calvary's cross to obtain it for us. Our faith in Him reaches out and receives this gift. What healing words are those written by St. Paul: "Since we are justified by faith, we have peace with God through our Lord Jesus Christ." What good medicine!

Prayer Suggestion

Pray that God may heal you daily by reassuring you of His love in Christ.

All Is Forgiven

At the end of the baseball season, statisticians can add up not only the player's hits and runs batted in, but also his errors.

Can a person—or someone for him or her—keep track of the number of his or her moral errors—errors we call sin, trespasses, trangressions, debts? Apparently Augustus M. Toplady, better known to us as the author of the hymn "Rock of Ages," tried to do this. He at one time estimated that someone 20 years old had sinned 630 million times in thoughts, words, and acts. He computed further that at age 50 the number of sins committed had climbed to a billion and a half. That is an astronomical figure, like that of our national debt, if you add to that the sins of others.

Of course, no one can really keep score of human sins. One problem is that we are not always clear on what is a sin. St. Paul confesses that he had not known that lust was a sin until he heard God's law tell him: "You shall not covet." Likewise today many think that only crimes like murder or robbery are sins. Further, mind and memory often fail us, so that we must exclaim with the psalmist: "Who can discern his errors?"

What to do? Instead of trying to count, and instead of trying to make up for our errors by good deeds and exemplary behavior, we simply confess that we have indeed sinned much and then, as the hymn writer suggests, lay our sins on Jesus, the Lamb of God who bore them for us. "Not the labors of my hands can fulfill thy law's demands," writes Toplady in "Rock of Ages." He adds that the blood of Jesus is the "double cure" for sin. So it is. So God has spoken. We can trust that for Jesus' sake God will forgive all our sins.

Prayer Suggestion

Tell God you are sorry that you have sinned, and ask Him to forgive you for Jesus' sake.

287

Joining Others in Their Grief and Gladness

One day little Mary, who had been sent on an errand, came home late for supper. She explained, "I met Sue along the way and saw that she had a broken doll." The mother asked, "Did you help her fix the doll?" "No," said Mary, "I helped her cry."

Mary was a partner in her friend's grief. This was very human of her. This was what the apostle Paul encouraged when he said: "Weep with those who weep:" and "If one member suffers, all suffer together." "Jesus wept," says the shortest verse of the Bible. But it is long in content. It shows us that the Son of God was moved by the feeling of our infirmities—in this case, moved to tears over the death of His friend, Lazarus, and grief of his sisters, Mary and Martha.

Much of what takes place in our world today—death, disappointment, loss—creates sorrow. We can help others bear their burdens as we participate in their grief, speaking words of comfort, praying with and for them, and rendering help to ease the burden.

But joy also comes into the lives of people with whom we live—joy over the birth of a child, joy at the celebration of a wedding anniversary, joy over a good fortune, such as a valuable scholarship attained, a good crop harvested, a successful business deal completed, a good job obtained. Some cannot suppress jealousy when this happens, and they express it in belittling remarks. But that is not the Christian way. This is: "Rejoice with those who rejoice." "If one member is honored, all rejoice together." Jesus rejoiced, for example, with the young married couple of Cana. He is Himself the heavenly Bridegroom who woos and weds His bride, the church, for as St. Paul writes, "Christ loved the church and gave Himself up for her." He bids us all to be with Him in faith, and to rejoice with Him.

Prayer Suggestion

Pray for a love that makes you a partner in the sorrows and joys of God's people.

Repeat Performance

Sigmund Freud spoke of "repetition of culture," by which he meant that in many instances children do what their parents did before them.

This can have a bad side and a good side. First the bad news. It is known that many people who abuse their children were in childhood themselves abused by their parents. The Bible speaks of people walking in the wrong footsteps of their fathers and mothers. Stephen the Martyr said to his accusers: "You always resist the Holy Spirit. As your fathers did, so do you."

On the other hand, much good can be said about children, adolescents, young adults, and persons in every stage of maturity who follow the *right* instruction and example of their parents, dead or alive.

It is a much better home in which to live where children learn from their parents to work together, to assume personal responsibility, and to love and forgive one another. It is a much better school in which to learn when children follow through on the three R's because of the head start their parents gave them at home. It is a much better shop to work in when both employers and employees are honest, diligent, and considerate as their parents were before them. It is a much better country in which to live when each rising generation imitates previous ones in obeying the laws.

Christian parents realize the privilege and responsibility resting on them to bring up their children in the faith that calls for mutual love, concern, forgiveness, as St. Paul teaches: "Be kind to one another, tenderhearted, forgiving one another, as God in Christ forgave you." When people give this way of life a "repeat performance," we all face a bright future and a more pleasant world in which to live.

Prayer Suggestion

Ask God to help you to "hold fast what is good" in your Christian heritage.

Performing Helpful Services

Some people do not use good judgment in the choice of services they want to perform. In the 1890s a wealthy New York drug manufacturer thought it would be a good idea if all the birds mentioned in Shakespeare's plays were represented in the U. S. So he introduced also the starlings, which have since become a pest in some parts of the country.

The wrong kind of service sometimes goes beyond a nuisance and becomes a crime, as Jesus told His disciples: "The hour is coming when whoever kills you will think he is offering service to God." Saul the Pharisee considered it a God-pleasing deed to persecute Christians. His outlook changed when Christ appeared to him on the road to Damascus and made him St. Paul the Apostle, a proclaimer of salvation in Christ.

This apostle writes: "I beseech you therefore, brethren, by the mercies of God, that ye present your bodies a living sacrifice, holy, acceptable to God, which is your reasonable service." Christian service follows from one's commitment to Christ, who in love served us and gave His life a ransom for all. Christian service is, in a sense, worship by which God is glorified. It is a continuous chain of loving words and works that benefit fellow human beings. Here we have a definition of a good work in God's sight: whatever God's children do, speak, or think, in faith, according to the Ten Commandments, for the glory of God and the benefit of their fellow human beings.

A helpful service is a far cry from mistaken or foolish ideas gone astray. It is right action flowing from right thinking and right believing. In Christian service the saving faith works in love.

Prayer Suggestion

Ask God, by His holy Word and Holy Spirit, to prompt and empower you to render Christian service.

God's Boundary Line of Right and Wrong

In the early days, prior to the Revolutionary War, the colonies of Maryland and Pennsylvania had a dispute over their boundary line. So two surveyors from England, Charles Mason and Jeremiah Dixon, worked for five years to establish the 312- mile-long line, marking every mile with a limestone. It came to be known as the Mason-Dixon Line, which played so prominent a part in United States history.

Lines of demarcation are necessary in all areas of life, especially in the area of right and wrong in morals. You hear people ask: "Where does one draw the line?" In fact, God has drawn a line in the Ten Commandments. The Commandments clearly declare where God Himself draws the line, not only to check sin, or to identify what sin is, but also to serve as a guide for righteous living in thoughts, desires, words, and deeds.

Because God has established the line, we have a sure standard or norm by which to determine what sin is. Sin is stepping across the line. God has put up a sign, so to speak, in regard to our attitudes and actions toward Him and other human beings. The sign says: No Trespassing! But people do it nevertheless. That is sin. Sin is transgression of God's moral law. Sin is every departure from the rule of the divine law. It entails a penalty, for "the wages of sin is death."

Is there an escape? Yes, for Jesus Christ came to undo what human beings have done wrong. He was obedient to God's law for us—He walked a straight line. What is more, He paid the penalty for our sins by the shedding of His blood.

God's moral Mason-Dixon line is still there, but it cannot condemn us, for Jesus fulfilled its demands. It is now helpful to us as a reference line for righteous living. Thank God for His law, but above all, thank God for His Gospel—the good news that Christ has redeemed us from the curse of the Law and has put all of life into a new perspective—the perspective of faith, love, and joyful obedience.

Prayer Suggestion

In your spontaneous prayer ask for light and strength to live according to God's holy will.

291

Reverence for Age

Early in 1975, when author P. H. Wodehouse died in a Long Island, N.Y., hospital at age 93, he was working on his 97th book.

We need to have high regard for elderly people. That regard is more apt to be forthcoming when aging persons themselves have self-esteem and high regard for their maturing talents and powers of body, mind, and spirit.

People who live in retirement can continue to be active in church and community. They can, in the words of the psalm, "still bring forth fruit in old age." The man Moses was Israel's leader for many years beyond threescore and even fourscore years. Anna the prophetess, age 84, was an active worshiper in the temple, and having found the Christ Child there, she witnessed to all who were awaiting the redemption of the Messiah. The same can be said of aged Simeon. The prophet Joel had foretold that not only the young but also "old men" shall receive and declare God's revelation.

Reverence for oneself and for the life God has given is catching. Those who in their golden years grow in self-esteem, knowing that God has for so many years preserved them, that Jesus Christ has redeemed them at great cost, and that the Holy Spirit makes their bodies His holy temple, will find that younger people will honor them all the more for their spirit. They will, without direct command, "rise up before the hoary head," as the Bible bids them.

God has promised, and His Word stands: "Even to your old age I am He [your gracious Lord] and to gray hairs I will carry you."

Prayer Suggestion

Pray that God may continue to give you the strength to remain active in His service.

The Assertion of Life

A common saying has it that death and taxes are certain. Before the Civil War battle of Cold Harbor, Va., where General Grant was about to attack the entrenched position of General Lee, it seemed obvious that there would be many casualties. In a diary entry dated June 3, the day of the battle, a Union soldier wrote, "I was killed today." His prediction was right. In fact, during the first eight minutes Grant lost 7,000 men.

While death is a dread reality for every Christian, its opposite—life—is also a certainty. Jesus, the Son of God, came into the world not only to declare the reality of life but also to effect it. He said, as the Good Shepherd concerning His sheep: "I came that they may have life, and have it abundantly." He goes on to say how He was to effect life for all by His self-sacrifice on the cross: "I am the Good Shepherd. The Good Shepherd lays down His life for the sheep." Jesus is truly the Way, the Truth, and the Life.

The life He wants to share with us supersedes physical death, which we must all experience. All the while, as the Conqueror of death, He holds out to us the gift of life. Even now we have the fullness of life that transcends the cares and worries of this world that has meaning and purpose and that puts us in fellowship with our Savior and with one another as brothers and sisters in the faith. The life we have in Him extends from the present time into eternity and is therefore rightly called eternal life.

The soldier at Cold Harbor recorded his death in advance: "I was killed today." In behalf of all who are joined to Him by faith, our Lord makes also this diary entry: "They live today, for I, their Redeemer, live."

Prayer Suggestion

Pray that the Holy Spirit may draw you closer to Christ, the Source of all life.

Letting God's Will Be Done

In his youth John Steinbeck, the Nobel Prize winning author of more than 25 books, including the novel *The Grapes of Wrath*, enrolled at Stanford University to study marine science. In his freshman English course he received a "C." This student didn't seem to be an author in the making.

In the lives of many people a change of direction takes place. The Bible tells us of many instances when God turned things around. Quite often He overrides the plans of people, guiding them to fulfill His will for them. Joseph tells his brothers in Egypt: "You meant evil against me; but God meant it for good, to bring it about that many people should be kept alive."

Few people have experienced a turnaround like that of Saul of Tarsus. He studied to become a Pharisee. In misguided zeal he persecuted the Christians, sending them to prison and to death. Then Jesus confronted him on the road to Damascus. Suddenly all his life's plans were changed. He was converted to Christianity and became its chief spokesman. It was true what Christians said: "He who once persecuted us is now preaching the faith he once tried to destroy."

Perhaps God has plans to change your life for the better. Don't fight it! Let His good and gracious will be done. Go along with what God tells you in His Word. Believe in Jesus Christ as your Savior and follow His guidance. Listen to the good advice of fellow Christians. Learn the dimensions of Jesus' love. Do some thinking and a lot of praying. Remember that God "is able to do far more abundantly than all that we ask or think."

Prayer Suggestion

Ask God to make His will known to you and to give you the strength to do it.

Jesus Benefactor and Friend

Many Christians, including prominent persons, have expressed their fondness for the hymn of simple faith: "What a Friend We Have in Jesus." President Eisenhower called it his favorite. And abroad, when Chiang Kai-shek of Taiwan passed away in 1975, a brass band played the hymn in the funeral procession. A white lily wreath in the form of a cross gave further evidence of his Christian faith.

We could not claim Jesus as a friend if He had not first befriended us. He said: "Greater love has no man than this, that a man lay down his life for his friends." One's life is the greatest gift anyone can give for his or her friends. But Jesus did more: He laid down His life on the cross not only for His friends but also for His enemies. That is the greatest love, as St. Paul testifies: "God shows His love for us in that while we were yet sinners, Christ died for us." "While we were enemies, we were reconciled to God by the death of His Son."

In love and friendship, which spring from His heart without any inducements on our part, Christ goes on to tell us, His disciples: "You are My friends . . . No longer do I call you servants." What is more, He calls us His brothers and sisters, for that is what we are when we are the sons and daughters of God.

The love and honor Jesus bestows on us prompts us to exclaim: "What a Friend we have in Jesus!" Because He not only calls us His friends but made us this by laying down His life for us, we are privileged to call Him our Friend, love Him, serve Him and confidently take everything to Him in prayer. We can say to others: "Come with us, and we'll introduce you to the One who is also your dearest Friend, Jesus Christ!"

Prayer Suggestion

Pray that the Holy Spirit may lead you into a closer friendship with Jesus.

Dealing with Good and Evil

A good or evil act usually prompts a reaction, which may take one of these four forms:

(1) The first way is to repay *good with evil*, and this kind of an exchange is devilish. God had done good to all the angels He had created, but a group of them, led by Satan, disobeyed. The devil prompts people to do the same today.

(2) The second way of responding is to reward *evil with evil*. This is brutelike, as when a tiger bites the trainer who abused him. The tit-for-tat instinct is also in people. Hence the resolve to demand an eye for an eye, a tooth for a tooth. This is jungle warfare.

(3) The third way of reacting is to reward *good with good*. This, by human standards, is considered noble. But it isn't too difficult. People give us gifts, and we give them gifts. Friends invite us to dinner, and we return the favor. Many friendships are based on the expectation of mutual rewards. While we are not critical of this, it is also true that no great virtue is involved.

(4) There is a fourth way, that is to reward *evil with good*. That is Christlike, that is divine. We do this when we pray for our enemies and bless those who curse us. For this we have not only the example of Jesus but also His imparted power. St. Peter writes: "Christ also suffered for you, leaving you an example." What is more, from Christ comes the new heart, the new mind, the new power to do what He has done, for St. Peter continues: "By His wounds you have been healed." We are healed from sin and the desire for revenge, healed by the best medicine that has ever been administered for our good spiritual health: the love of Christ.

To repay good with evil, or evil with evil—this is out. To repay good with good is natural. But as Christians we can do even better: to repay evil with good.

Prayer Suggestion

Pray that you have a share in the love of Jesus, which conquers evil.

Seeking the Good of Your Community

The poet, playwright, and literary critic T. S. Eliot, born 1888 in St. Louis, Mo., became a British citizen and member of the Church of England in 1927. In whatever country he lived, he was an influence for good. One of his memorable sayings is: "No community can become Christian unless it is a community of Christians."

This is worth keeping in mind. It is important to improve our communities in whatever ways we can. But it is not better *things* but better, spiritually reconstructed *persons* that raise the moral standards of our towns and cities.

Being a good influence in one's surroundings isn't always easy. It wasn't easy for God's people when held in the Babylonian Captivity. But through the prophet Jeremiah God said: "Build houses and live in them; plant gardens and eat their produce. Take wives and have sons and daughters . . . Seek the welfare of the city where I have sent you into exile, and pray to the Lord on its behalf, for in its welfare you will find your welfare." God's people were to lead normal lives, in the mainstream of state and society, to uphold them with their piety and prayers.

Some people, even when they are not in need, seek welfare *from* the city. But God means something else: seek the welfare—the good—of the city. Jesus put it like this: "You are the salt of the earth . . . You are the light of the world." Instead of withdrawing into their own enclaves, Christians desire to be active in public life to the good of all. They want to show love, which is the fruit of their faith in God, who in love gave His only Son, Jesus Christ, for the salvation of all.

Have you been a light lately in your community?

Prayer Suggestion

Pray that God may bless your efforts toward improving life in your community.

Letting God Do Something with Your Life

George Washington Carver, born near Diamond Grove, Mo., in the same year that the Civil War began, did not have a good start in life. His parents were slaves; his father died early; he was a sickly boy. Having escaped with his mother, his master bought him back for $300, the price of a good horse. Carver became a famous agricultural chemist, teaching and doing research in seed and soils at Tuskegee Institute in Alabama. He was a pious, Christian man, asking God to help him to develop the lowly peanut. Hundreds of uses were found for the peanut, and even a former president of the United States, Jimmy Carter, calls himself a peanut farmer.

The Christian faith helps us to evaluate, develop, and apply our varying talents. It motivates us to use our powers of body, mind, and spirit to glorify God and open doors for fellow human beings. As Christians we are given goals and are promised the help of God to achieve them. Through the Word of God and prayer we remain in close fellowship with our Maker and Redeemer, who helps us make our lives count.

Jesus Christ redeemed us—bought us back—from sin, not with $300 or the price of a good horse, but with His own precious blood, so that we might belong to Him and serve Him.

George Washington Carver could have thought of scores of reasons why he could not do much with his life. But he put himself into God's hands and became a credit to his Maker and to humanity. Shouldn't you try to do the same?

Prayer Suggestion

Ask God to make His grace and power perfect amid your weakness.

Music: God's Gift to Us

In Sedalia, Mo., around the turn of the century, Scott Joplin developed a new syncopated style of music. For lack of a better term, it is called "ragtime," although Scott himself considered it a serious branch of classical music. There is new interest in it today.

Music and musical instruments are mentioned in the Bible. Young David played his harp as therapy for King Saul's depression. David wrote many psalms to be sung to the accompaniment of instruments. When the prodigal son returned in repentance, the grateful father threw a party with the playing of music.

Music is God's gift. As the author of it, He seemingly built music into His universe when He created sound and rhythm. Pythagorean philosophers originated the doctrine of the music of the spheres. Through Job God declares that at the creation "the morning stars sang together and all the sons of God [angels] shouted for joy." In our world birds sing, and what is far more, people sing and play music. It is God's gift to them, given in lesser or greater degrees. Martin Luther ranked music next to theology—next to God's gift of the Word.

Not only in His revelation in nature but also in that of His Word, God commends music, especially music that can be rendered by that other divine gift, the human voice. Through St. Paul He declares: "Let the Word of Christ dwell in you richly, teach and admonish one another in all wisdom, and sing psalms and hymns and spiritual songs with thankfulness in your heart to God."

In the glimpses into heaven given us in the Book of Revelation, it is Jesus Christ, the Lamb that was slain for the sins of the world, who is the content of the songs of saints and angels. Jesus is still the heart and soul of the music by which we praise God today.

Prayer Suggestion

Pray that God may open your heart and mouth to sing to His glory.

Christians Are Realists

William Inge went from the teaching of drama at Stephens College, Columbia, Mo., to the writing of successful plays. In *Come Back, Little Sheba* he portays a woman who wants to cling to her romantic dreams, complaining that the "years have vanished—vanished into thin air." Then she likens them to Little Sheba, her dog that has disappeared, never to return.

It's no use living in a make-believe world, or daydreaming about the good times beyond recall. Christians are a "now" people, as the apostle declares: "*Now* is the acceptable time . . . *now* is the day of salvation."

As people living in the *present*, we are concerned for—but do not worry about—the *future*, as Jesus said: "Take no thought for the morrow." By the same token, there is no call for worrying about the *past*, or wishing it to return. What is past is past; all we can do is to ask God for Jesus' sake to forgive our failings and remember them no more.

As people aware of life in the present, we are realists, calling a spade a spade. We have to be honest with ourselves, avoiding cover-ups or self-delusions. There is the reality of sin, as St. John declares: "If we say we have no sin, we deceive ourselves and the truth is not in us. If we confess our sins, God is faithful and just, and will forgive our sins and cleanse us from all unrighteousness." How clean? The preceding verse says: "The blood of Jesus His Son cleanses us from all sin."

As realists, we believe this, and consequently can be honest with ourselves; we have nothing to hide. We need not yearn for past years to return, good as they may have been. Let the figurative Little Sheba stay away; we have something better. Said the poet Browning: "The best is yet to be."

Prayer Suggestion

Ask God to help you be completely honest with yourself in the conviction that He forgives.

Overcoming That Sinking Feeling

Margaret Tobin had a humble beginning at Hannibal, Mo., but she was plucky and colorful, married James J. Brown, lived in wealth in Denver, and died in New York. In her life she survived many things, including the sinking of the Titanic. She was popularly known as the "unsinkable Molly Brown."

Few of us, if any, will ever have that sinking feeling as we struggle to survive in an ocean. Peter the disciple had that feeling when, walking on the water of the Sea of Galilee—as Jesus asked him to do—he saw the high waves and became afraid. Beginning to sink, he cried out: "Lord, save me!"

The sinking feelings we may have will, very likely, occur on land, perhaps in a place we consider safe. It may come as a result of bad news. It may occur in a doctor's office when we get the results of a physical examination. It may occur when we open our pay envelopes and find a proverbial "pink slip" in them.

What to do? Of course, it won't help to resort to drugs and drinking; these only make things worse. We have to avoid panic, keeping our heads clear and our hearts courageous. It helps to seek counsel and aid from family members and friends.

The best Friend of all is the one Peter called out to on the water. In his hymn "Jesus, Lover of My Soul" Charles Wesley exclaims in prayer: "Lo, I sink, I faint, I fall; Lo, on Thee I cast my care."

Jesus cares; therefore we can cast all our cares on Him. Jesus cared for our present and eternal well-being, for which reason He went to a cross, drawing us up to Him and raising us up from our sinking feeling. Now you and I, as Christians, are unsinkable.

Prayer Suggestion

When feeling low, ask the Holy Spirit to whisper words of hope in your heart.

Caring About People

Resting in Bellefontaine Cemetery, St. Louis, is General William Clark, who with Meriwether Lewis led a two-and-a-half-year expedition to the Pacific Ocean. One remarkable thing about the Lewis and Clark expedition through wild country was this: of the nearly 50 people in the party, only one man died. He had a ruptured appendix and might have died even if he had stayed behind in St. Louis.

Those are good leaders who look after the welfare of people committed to their care. In His high-priestly prayer, spoken the night before He died, Jesus gave this accounting to the heavenly Father: "I have guarded those whom Thou hast given Me, and none of them is lost but the son of perdition"—that was Judas Iscariot, who destroyed himself.

Those are good parents who look after their children with love and concern. They will be able to say in heaven, "Here we are, Lord, and the children whom You have given us." Of course, like Judas, sometimes a son or a daughter goes astray, in spite of the parents' efforts, and that is not the parents' fault.

Those are good teachers who love the children in their classes and who try not to lose a single one to indifference or to a dropout status.

Are you in charge of workers in your shop, factory, or place of business? If you are faithful, you will look after them and seek their well-being as best you can.

"Faithful?" you say? Who can teach us this? The answer is: Jesus Christ, who gave His life that He might gather all of God's people together "as a hen gathers her brood under her wings." He was lifted up on a cross that He might draw all people to Himself. From Him we learn true soul accounting.

Prayer Suggestion

Pray that you may always have the proper concern for the people in your life.

Our Heavenly Father Knows

"Only God knows why he should die so young," wrote General William T. Sherman when his 9-year-old son, Willie, died of typhoid fever in 1863. The next year an infant son died—one he had never seen. Both rest with their parents in Calvary Cemetery, St. Louis, Mo.

Only God knows! How true that is of the many events in today's world—and in our own lives! Our vision is limited. We can't understand why there are so many victims of wars, disease, fires, floods, tornadoes. We are at a loss to explain why misfortunes come our way.

But our heavenly Father knows. What is more, He knows how to make all things work together for good to those who love Him. Sometimes already in this life God gives us a glimpse, so that we can begin to find meaning in what was formerly a total mystery, as Jesus said to Peter: "What I am doing you do not know now, but afterward you will understand." That "afterward" will come, if not in this life then in the life to come.

God knows the design of your life, like a rug weaver knows the eventual pattern of his product, although for awhile there is a tangle of threads. Let God proceed with His plan. Follow where He leads you. Accept His Word as a lamp to your feet and a light on your path. Pray for guidance. Always trust that God will supply you with all you need for life's journey. Always bear in mind: "He who did not spare His own Son but gave Him up for us all, will He not also give you all things with Him?"

General Sherman was grieved to give up two young sons. It helps, in situations like that, to know that God, too, gave up His Son for the good of us all.

Prayer Suggestion

Pray for God's assurance that He is leading you the right way.

Our Changing Faith

Customs change! During the 1904 world's fair in St, Louis, Mo., a woman doctor from New York City was refused admittance to the ladies' lounge because she was wearing a pants suit.

For both men and women, changes occur—in dress, in life's daily routine, in the roles they play. Outward customs may vary from one group to another. In one religious community the men show respect to God by keeping their hats on in the house of God, in another, they take their hats off. The showing of respect for God is basic, how that is done can change from place to place, or from time to time.

The Christian hymn writer declares: "Change and decay in all around I see; O Thou, who changest not, abide with me." God does not change. "Thou art the same," says the psalmist, "and Thy years have no end." With the Father of lights, writes St. James, "there is no variation or shadow due to change." And Jesus Christ is the same yesterday, today, and forever.

As God doesn't change, neither does His Word. God has not retreated from a single revelation of His will. Sin is still sin, and all that God has said about it—and about death as its consequence—still stands. However, His promise of salvation from sin is likewise in effect, and all His promises find their completion, their fulfillment in Jesus Christ.

Because God's Word is unchanging, our faith in its promises of peace and forgiveness in Christ is likewise unchanged. Of course, from the beginning misguided individuals have tried to change it, and such attempts can result in the loss of faith entirely. St. Jude tells us in his New Testament epistle to contend earnestly for the faith once for all delivered to the saints.

Changes occur in our life-style, and sometimes these are for the better, but faith anchored in Christ remains.

Prayer Suggestion

Pray that God may help you remain true to the changeless Christ your Savior.

God Knows Who You Are

The historic city of Hermann, Mo., along the Missouri River was in 1842 the scene of a tragedy when the river boat *Big Hatchie* exploded and many passengers lost their lives. Some bodies were never recovered, and 35 lie buried in unmarked graves in the burial plot overlooking the city. One can say of the victims what we say of unknown soldiers: they are known only to God.

Yes, God knows—knows not only the dead but also the living—the many millions of people now living on earth. What the psalmist wrote centuries ago is still true: "The Lord looks down from heaven, He sees all the sons of men; from where He sits enthroned He looks forth on all the inhabitants of the earth . . . He observes all their deeds."

God is all-knowing, with a mind far exceeding ours, and with a memory-bank that excels all the world's computers combined. God's knowledge is infinite. As Creator and Preserver He is aware of all people, sending rain and sunshine also on the ungodly. His special love goes out, however, to those who by faith in His Son, the Redeemer Jesus Christ, have become His sons and daughters. He has a record of them; their names are written in the Book of Life. Full forgiveness and eternal life are theirs.

The day will come when all nations will be gathered before the Lord's judgment throne—those still living and those raised from the dead. On the day of Christ's return all graves will be opened, all those bearing the dust and ashes of people known and unknown, including the 35 unidentified ones buried on a hill overlooking Hermann, Mo. The Book of Revelation adds that also the sea will give up its dead.

God knows all the people. He knows who we are, and His heart and heavenly home are always open to us.

Prayer Suggestion

Pray in behalf of those who do not know God as their heavenly Father.

Learning to Live Together

Damon and Pythias, David and Jonathan, were close friends. In American history, William Clark and Meriwether Lewis were together 1804—06 when they made their historic expedition to the Northwest—up the Missouri River. They got along well together. When Clark had a son born to him in 1809, he named him Meriwether Lewis Clark. Father and son, both generals, lie buried in Bellefontaine Cemetery, St. Louis.

Some people are not compatible. They get on each other's nerves. They cannot reconcile their differences of opinion. Such was the case with St. Paul and Barnabas, who had been together on the first missionary journey. When preparing for the second journey, says the Book of Acts, "there arose a sharp contention, so that they separated from each other" because Barnabas wanted to take Mark along but Paul was against it, since Mark had left them during the first journey. In later writings Paul indicated that he was again on good terms with Barnabas and his cousin, Mark.

"Be reconciled to your brother," Jesus tells us, and St. Paul states: "Do not let the sun go down on your anger." Christians know the basis that exists for friendship and for reconciliation. St. Paul teaches, as translated in the Today's English Version (2 Corinthians 5:18-19): God "through Christ changed us from enemies into his friends and gave us the task of making others His friends also. Our message is that God was making all mankind his friends through Christ." A few verses later: "Christ was without sin, but for our sake God made Him share our sin in order that in union with him, we might share the righteousness of God."

When we are at odds with others in the home, in school, at work, or even in the church, let us make every effort to be reconciled, on the basis of Christ's reconciliation of us with God.

Prayer Suggestion

Pray that you may live in peace with other people and seek reconciliation when differences arise.

Delivering God's Message

At St. Joseph, Mo., stands a monument honoring the 400 men and boys who were Pony Express riders. The colorful William Cody, known as Buffalo Bill, was one of them. The route established in 1860, began at St. Joseph, its eastern terminal and extended to San Francisco, the gold country. However, this system soon gave way to the telegraph.

The spread of Christianity is another, far more significant chapter in communication. Jesus initiated it when He told His disciples to go and make disciples of all nations, to proclaim the Gospel to the whole creation, to be His witnesses in ever-widening circles. The emphasis was on "express," on haste. At the empty tomb the angel said to the women: "Go quickly and tell His disciples that He has risen from the dead." The disciples in turn, after Pentecost, went quickly into all the world as messengers of the risen Christ. They traveled on foot and on ships, always under this urgency: "We cannot but speak of what we have seen and heard." "The love of Christ constrains us."

The Pony Express riders carried dispatches concerning important events: new discoveries of gold, the state of the Union, the approach of the Civil War, Abraham Lincoln's election to the presidency. What news did the apostles have to tell? Bad news and good news. The bad news pertains to sin and death as its wages, for the union between God and the human race was broken; there was war. The good news is that "God so loved the world that He gave His only Son, that whoever believes in Him should not perish but have eternal life."

There never will be a time when this is no longer good news. The message of salvation is still God's power to establish peace. Each one of us can be a messenger to tell this Good News.

Prayer Suggestion

Ask God to show you how you can be a teller of the Good News of Jesus' love.

Safety in Our Cities

Cities large and small are often hit by calamities—fires, floods, tornadoes. In 1849, for example, St. Louis experienced double trouble: a devastating fire and a cholera epidemic claiming some 4,000 people.

When St. Paul wrote that he endured perils in the city, he very likely did not have in mind the rampages of nature. He referred to perils people create: "danger from robbers, danger from my own people, danger from Gentiles . . . danger from false brethren." These dangers are experienced today in the cities, where many people congregate.

Many explanations are offered for crimes of the city, both the street crime and the white-collar crime. Poverty is not always the reason. Many people shoplift for the thrill it gives them. The California millionaire who had an illegal device installed in his home to avoid paying for long-distance telephone calls could not plead poverty. Regrettably many violent crimes are committed by drug addicts.

Obedience to the law and better law enforcement are necessary, but the ultimate cure lies in better relationships among people, based on the right relationship with God. Such a change is not effected by laws—as necessary as laws are—but by conversion, that is, by the rebirth of the individual through the Gospel. Such an individual is willing and able to say: Jesus Christ is my Lord; He died for me, and now I live for Him.

The more this change in persons comes about, the greater will be the safety in our cities.

Prayer Suggestion

Pray that God may keep you safe in your city or community.

Prospecting for Christ

A group of Indians from Missouri, en route to Washington, D. C., to see the President, camped on a farm at Chillicothe, Ohio. The farm's owner, Thomas James, saw that they had a red substance, hematite, smeared on them. He knew that this mineral contained iron, traced the hematite to its source, and in 1826 opened productive iron works.

Similarly, a man read in the Bible that the little basket in which the baby Moses lay had been waterproofed with pitch. He said: "Where there's pitch, there's oil." His company explored the area in Egypt and soon had three oil wells in production.

Seemingly insignificant events or observations can lead to important discoveries. Such was the case with St. Paul. On the basis of even scant information he went prospecting for Christ. In a vision a man of Macedonia said to him: "Come over and help us!" The apostle went, his missionary journey taking him into the continent of Europe, to Philippi and other cities where he planted the banner of the cross.

There is a message here for us: follow the clues, and they can lead us to sharing the Gospel with someone. A question someone asks can open the door to do some prospecting for Christ. St. Peter tells us to give an answer to those who ask about the reason for our hope. We can reply: "Christ died for us all and rose again that we may have the sure hope of salvation." Again, someone's great sorrow or great joy, misfortune or good fortune, work we do with others, traveling together, conversations over the back fence—all these are points of contact and opportunities to prospect for Christ.

What a great blessing it is—far beyond the discovery of gold, silver, iron, or oil, when by the power of the Holy Spirit a person is brought to Christ through us.

Prayer Suggestion

Pray that God may open your eyes to opportunities to witness about Jesus' love. Ask Him for the power and courage to take advantage of those opportunities.

Many Cultures, One Christ

It doesn't take a child long to realize that there are people of other cultures, races, and religions, perhaps right in his or her own neighborhood. Customs of people vary; they have different priorities; they eat different foods; they speak other languages. The illustration of a melting pot has been used, to describe this country, as if to suggest that it is necessary for ethnic groups to merge into one. Perhaps a better illustration is that of a mosaic, with the individual units keeping their color, their identity, but together forming a beautiful, larger design.

A drama reflecting the collision of two cultures is *The King and I*, the story of an English woman, Anna Leonowens, going to Bangkok, Siam, in the 1860s to teach the children of King Mongkut. The conflicts were pronounced, mostly because there was no common basis on which the two would come together. Anna and the king both were set like cement in their own cultures.

It is hard to think of a better common ground for all cultures than the Christian faith. The Gospel of salvation in Jesus Christ both transforms and transcends culture. It spans race differences. When people of whatever background bow before a common Savior, who by His redeeming merit has made God their Father, cultural differences no longer cause static. This does not mean that ethnic qualities cease to exist; it means that a higher order supersedes them.

Whatever the factions, St. Paul declares that in Christ all are made one. Problems are not papered over; no rose garden of perfect harmony and beauty is promised. But this is guaranteed: as many diverse members—eyes, ears, hands, feet—form one body, so in Christ we all form one body, whatever our cultural origin.

Prayer Suggestion

Pray for a stronger bond to tie you to Christ and to your brothers and sisters in the faith.

Keeping One's Balance

We have trouble keeping our balance when our footing is unstable. Someone leaning out of a window or over a ledge too far is in danger of falling. The situation is even more risky when our moral and spiritual balance is lost. This happens when greed, for example, overwhelms the individual, as St. Paul writes: "The love of money is the root of all evil; it is through this craving that some have wandered away from the faith and pierced their hearts with many pangs."

Money itself is not evil; we need it to buy life's necessities. The evil is the *love* of money. It causes people to lose their equilibrium. So it is with other things people crave. One too many drinks can be the cause of a person losing control of himself or herself and having a tragic accident.

Visitors to Italy like to view the leaning Tower of Pisa. Every year it comes a little closer to losing its balance. Every year it tilts about another five-hundredths of an inch. Unless measures are taken, it is only a matter of time before the tower will fall.

There is a lesson here for persons who have dangerous leanings: greed, violent tempers, uncontrolled cravings. For a while, perhaps for a long while, they are seemingly coping with their problem. But they may eventually lose their balance and come down with a crash.

This need not happen, for God gives us the means for keeping our spiritual balance. In Jude we read: "To Him who is able to keep you from falling . . . to the only God, our Savior through Jesus Christ our Lord be glory . . . ." Faith in Jesus Christ keeps us from falling. That's why Jude tells us earlier in his letter that we should earnestly contend for the faith once and for all delivered to the saints.

Keep close to Jesus, and you will keep your balance!

Prayer Suggestion

Pray that God may sustain you in times of temptation.

God, Our Refuge

Tennessee Williams' first successful play was *The Glass Menagerie*. In it a very shy young woman, Laura Wingfield, finds refuge in glass figurines and in playing old phonograph records.

For many people, preoccupation with some things or activities is more than a hobby—it is retreat from the world around them; it is withdrawal into their inner selves. Another kind of escapism with more dire consequences is taking refuge in alcohol and other drugs. Sometimes things become substitutes for God, as is certainly the case with those who idolize gold and silver or whose highest goal in life is the attainment of honor or pleasure.

But nothing can really take the place of God, our highest good. Said Charles Wesley in his hymn "Jesus, Lover of My Soul": "Other refuge have I none; Hangs my helpless soul on Thee." The thought is taken from the Bible. The Book of Proverbs declares: "The name of the Lord is a strong tower; the righteous man runs into it and is safe." Psalm 46, on which Martin Luther based his hymn "A Mighty Fortress Is Our God," says, "God is our Refuge and Strength, a very present Help in trouble."

We take refuge in God when we trust His name, entrust our lives into His hands, and pray to Him. God is great and mighty, not a created idol of wood or stone, of gold or silver. God is loving and kind; He is "merciful and gracious, slow to anger, and abounding in steadfast love and faithfulness."

God's steadfast love came to full expression in Jesus Christ, whom the Father sent to redeem a fallen world, and through whom we have access to the throne of mercy. We join the disciples in saying, "Lord, to whom shall we go? You have the words of eternal life."

Prayer Suggestion

Pray that the Holy Spirit may draw you closer to Jesus, in whom we are safe.

Take Time to Talk

Dr. John Staupitz, vicar of the Augustinian Order at Witten-
berg University, exercised a deep influence on Martin Luther. In
Here I Stand Roland H. Bainton writes, "One day under a pear
tree in the garden of the Augustinian cloister—Luther always treas-
ured that pear tree—the vicar informed Brother Martin that he
should study for the doctor's degree . . . and assume the chair of
Bible at the university."

Where do we give advice to one another? It may not be
under a tree. It may be over the back fence, in the family room
at home, or at the supper table. It may be at the shop where two
are working or eating their lunch. It may be while walking home
from school. The important thing is that people who seek another's help have the opportunity for uninterrupted conversation. The
welfare of a person for the rest of life may be at stake.

One of the unpleasant features of our urban culture is isolation, aloneness, loneliness because of distant and impersonal
relationships. There are too many invisible walls. We do need to
talk to one another when important decisions have to be made,
or to get someone else's opinion on important subjects.

So we ought to cultivate the neighborly pear tree, so to speak.
There we can not only speak to one another but also address our
Lord in prayer. Wherever we may be—in our private rooms, while
working in the garden, or when sitting and resting under a shade
tree, we can speak to Jesus, and He hears us. Our needs and
wants meant so much to Him that He suffered and died to redeem
us. Although He ascended into heaven, His promise still stands:
"I am with you always." Do take the time to speak to Him!

Prayer Suggestion

Pray that God may speak to you through the truths told you by
the people around you.

Just Passing Through

Quite a few years ago an American tourist visited a world-renowned religious leader in Poland. The American was surprised to see that the man's living quarters consisted only of a simple room containing a table and chair and many books. "Where is your furniture?" the visitor asked. It drew the counterquestion: "Where is yours?" "Mine?" the American asked. "I'm only a visitor here; I'm just passing through." The man replied, "So am I."

"Here we have no lasting city, but we seek the city which is to come," declares the writer of the Letter to the Hebrews. We are all pilgrims, visitors, tourists passing through. Therefore we travel light, wanting to take along for life's journey only the essentials.

Sometimes God gives us more than what we actually need, sometimes even riches. Such wealth may have been given us as a test. What will we do with it? When we love money and all that money can buy—love it more than God and the neighbor—wealth is a spiritual liability, a burden. Then it keeps us from making spiritual progress. It is like a tourist wanting to take along too many things for a journey: his or her total wardrobe, the grand piano, the TV console, even the kitchen sink.

As we pass through life we let ourselves be guided by God's Word, nourished by Jesus Christ as the Bread of Life, refreshed by Him as the living Water, and clothed by the robe of His righteousness. As tourists we need the Savior, for He is the Way, the Truth, and the Life.

Prayer Suggestion

Ask God to keep you mindful of your tourist status and to provide you with what you need as you are passing through.

Endowed to Serve

Samuel Morse was a gifted man. A college professor, writer, literary critic, and portrait painter, he is best known for his invention of the telegraph. On May 24, 1844, this richly endowed man sent his first message over the new medium of communication. It read, "What hath God wrought!" a quotation from Numbers 23:23. Professor Morse, a Christian man, served God with his gifts, contributing to church schools and mission societies.

God has endowed us all with gifts—perhaps for music, for mathematics, for writing, for repairing a motor. What is more, to natural talents the Holy Spirit adds a variety of spiritual gifts. Whatever the endowment, it comes from God, and we must exclaim when we see the good people have done with their divinely bestowed gifts: "What hath God wrought!"

As people who are alive in Christ we are urged, challenged and invited to use our gifts to serve, as did Samuel Morse and many others. We have the best reasons for wanting to serve God and humanity with our endowments, for we were, as St. Paul puts it, "bought with a price." We were "redeemed with the precious blood of Christ as of a Lamb without blemish and without spot." What else can grateful people do but serve God and humanity with their talents?

Whatever our gifts and our accomplishments, we remain humble, realizing that God blesses us as we put our powers and energies to work. We are endowed to serve, God working in us both to will and to do His good pleasure.

Prayer Suggestion

Thank God for His gifts to you, asking Him also to guide you in their right use.

Mental Inflation

The cost of goods and services keeps rising. The value of the dollar keeps shrinking. For many, life's savings are dwindling away. This is due to economic inflation.

"Knowledge puffs up, but love builds up," writes St. Paul. This reference is to another kind of inflation—the inflation of the mind. The Greek verb used for "puffs up" means to inflate, to blow up (as we do a balloon), to make proud and arrogant, to become conceited.

False knowledge, or knowledge held for its own sake, contributes to the inflation of a person's ego. It results from an unrealistic, proud concept of what one knows or thinks one knows. It does nothing for the individual except to inflate the mind and spirit.

By way of contrast, how wonderful is true love! In all our relationships with others it "builds up." In 1 Corinthians 13, that wonderful chapter on love, St. Paul writes, "Love is not jealous or boastful; it is not arrogant or rude. . . . Love bears all things, believes all things, hopes all things, endures all things." Love lets the air of pride out of a person's heart and fills it with the solid substance of trust in God and concern for the neighbor.

"We love, because God first loved us," writes St. John. God showed His love in that He sent His Son as the Savior of the world. This love has reached us personally. Far from being inflated with pride, we now model ourselves after our God, and likewise show love. "Love builds up, " says the apostle. In love we lay aside pretenses and walk before God in truth.

Prayer Suggestion

Pray that false pride may yield to reliance on Jesus Christ for becoming right with God.

Your Right Image

A word in our everyday vocabulary that has taken on distinctive meaning is "image." Psychology stresses the importance of a right self-image. Public relations people talk a great deal about projecting a good image. Sometimes this refers more to a good front rather than a genuinely good character.

It is one thing to impress people around us, and another to pass inspection with God. God is concerned with what we truly are, not with what we seem to be.

To have the right image with God means to be like Him. In the beginning people were made like God. They were created in the image of their Maker, that is, in blissful knowledge of God and in righteousness and holiness.

But this image was lost when our first parents fell into sin. In its place came another kind of image, that of sin and death, the image of the Evil One. Jesus did not hesitate to say to those who rejected Him and His Father: "You are of your father the devil."

When sinners are converted to faith in Jesus Christ they are then renewed in the image of God. They become new creations in Christ, discarding the old evil nature and putting on the new nature. Then they know God to be their Father, just as Adam and Eve in the state of perfection had intimate knowledge of God. In this new nature the Christian strives to grow in holiness, always after the example, model, and image of the holy and righteous God. As St. Paul told the Colossians: "You . . . have put on the new nature, which is being renewed in knowledge after the image of its Creator."

Prayer Suggestion

Ask for the Holy Spirit's power to renew your life every day so that it may conform more and more to the image of Jesus Christ.

Spiritual Littering

Many people litter. Wherever they go they leave waste paper, empty cans and cartons, and food morsels that attract roaches and rodents. The result is that God's world is marred.

There is also spiritual littering: people cluttering up the scene with indiscreet, sinful lives. Is it not a form of littering to scatter abroad one's unbelief and doubts? Does it not spoil things for others to use obscene and profane language, to disseminate gossip, to spread gloom?

Considerable spiritual littering went on among the Corinthians in St. Paul's day. People made a mess of things with their contentions and party spirit. Think of the rubbish one man left behind for others to clean up when he slept with his father's wife!

Because there was so much disorder—so much littering due to religious and moral messiness—St. Paul wrote: "All things should be done decently and in order." He also wrote that God is not the author of confusion and disorder but of peace.

Is there litter in our lives too? Yes, indeed, for we are all sinners who fall short of the holiness and wholesomeness God desires. But, thank God, Jesus Christ came among us to take away all the rubbish and refuse of our sinfulness. He is the Lamb of God whose blood cleanses us from all sin. He tells us today that our lives are "made clean by the Word" which He speaks to us. God saved us "by the washing of regeneration and renewal in the Holy Spirit, which He poured out upon us richly through Jesus Christ our Savior" (Titus 3:5). Our lives are clean; let's keep them that way.

Prayer Suggestion

Ask God for the desire and the ability to keep His world and your life clean.

Obsession with Obscenity

In our day the preoccupation with sex—mostly abnormal sex—is both amazing and disgusting. Many bookstores for adults feature pornographic material. A movie that does not border on wanton is a rarity. Obscenity is an obsession for many. It is also big business.

Obscenity is not for Christians. St. Paul writes, "Put them all away: anger, wrath, malice, slander, and foul talk from your mouth." Note how obscene language, oral or in print, is put into the same category with other improper emotions.

For language to improve, it is necessary for the *heart* to be cleaned up first, for it is out of the abundance of the *heart* that the mouth speaks or the hand writes. The human heart is changed when through the Gospel the Holy Spirit brings a person to faith in Jesus Christ as Savior, so that this person loves Him as his or her best Friend and desires to serve Him out of a pure heart. Then all things become new with that individual.

Can laws help? A community may find it necessary to protect itself against moral pollution by passing antiobscenity ordinances, just as it may find it necessary to protect itself against the pollution of air, earth, and water. But it bears repeating that moral renewal cannot be legislated. Reform must begin with the complete change of the heart. "If anyone is in Christ he is a new creation; the old has passed, behold, the new has come." So writes St. Paul.

The more true Christians make their influence felt in a community, the better will be its moral tone. Moral improvement begins with us, here and now.

Prayer Suggestion

Pray that through the Gospel of Jesus Christ God may create in you a clean heart and renew a right spirit within you.

What Shopping Centers Say

Very much a part of the present-day suburban sprawl are the shopping centers with their street-level shops, landscaped malls, and acres of parking space. Shopping centers are the modern counterpart of bazaars and market places of the past. While shopping, people conferred socially. There children played as their parents shopped. Jesus compared His generation to "children sitting in the market places and calling to their playmates."

Shopping centers, over and above all the spoken words and the reams and reams of advertising, have a distinctive message for today's consumers. The message says: sin reigns here too! Purchasers have to be on the lookout for shoddy goods and for services that are promised but not performed. Credit cards make it easy to buy, and that is one of the reasons why many go head over heels into debt to everyone's unhappiness. The psalmist says, "Oppression and fraud do not depart from the market place." This is true today.

All the wonderful goods on display in shopping centers—foods, drinks, garments, shoes, tools, appliances—what would they tell us if they had the power of speech? Surely this: "Man shall not live by bread alone." And the same principle applies to all merchandise: Man does not live by TV sets alone, by sports gear alone, by power mowers alone, by home furnishings alone.

To be truly alive, people need Jesus Christ. He is the living Bread, the Food and Drink for our souls. As bread is broken and drink is poured out, so was His body broken on the cross and His blood was shed for the forgiveness of our sins and for new life in Him. Are you alive in Christ?

Prayer Suggestion

Pray that in everything you do, also in buying and selling, you may reflect faith in Jesus Christ, who with the price of His own blood bought you to be His own.

Old Before Your Time?

News stories tell about children who suffer from progeria, a sickness that ages their bodies, so that a 10-year-old boy, for example, is physically an old man.

Is it also possible for people to age prematurely mentally and spiritually? If so, what means are available for staying young in spirit?

The psalmist declares that God, through His Word, does wonderful things for people: He forgives all their iniquity, heals their diseases, redeems their life from an early grave, crowns them with steadfast love and mercy, satisfies them with good as long as they live "so that their youth is renewed like the eagle's."

Undoubtedly sin and the evils connected with it are aging factors, for they cause worry, which can lead to illness of body and mind. For this, the Gospel of Jesus Christ is a spiritual remedy. The Gospel declares that through faith in Christ, who died to atone for the sins of the whole human race, your sins are forgiven, and you have peace with God.

It belongs to our daily renewal that we grow in this saving faith. There is a difference between a *childish* and a *childlike* faith. A childish faith is stunted. A childlike faith is reliance on God's promises. It grows as one learns more and more of what God has revealed in His Word.

Of Jesus it is said that He grew in four ways: physically, mentally, socially, and spiritually. As we mature in these areas we become, in Tennyson's words, a tower that stands "four-square to all the winds that [blow]."

Prayer Suggestion

Ask the Holy Spirit to keep you young and vigorous in your faith.

Confession—The Better Option

In Tennesee Williams' play *The Glass Menagerie*, Laura Wingfield is the shy, physically handicapped young woman who escapes from real life into a make-believe world of glass figurines and old phonograph records. She engages in a form of self-deception, a failure to reckon with reality and truth.

There is much self-deception in people's spiritual lives. Much of it stems from the knowing or unknowing denial of facts. St. John, in his First Epistle, cites a case in point: "If we say we have no sin, we deceive ourselves, and the truth is not in us." The denial of sin is one of the greatest of all self-deceptions.

Sin is a dreadful reality. It is disobedience. It is every transgression of the holy will of God as expressed in His holy Word. No one can keep God's law, the Ten Commandments, perfectly and thus cannot earn divine favor and be rewarded with eternal life. The fact is : "Surely there is not a righteous man on earth who does good and never sins." To deny this truth is to engage in self-deception.

The only way out of the deceptive trap of self-proclaimed sinlessness is to confess one's sins honestly. Denial of sin leads to self-deception and gets us nowhere. But confession does, as St. John goes on to say, "If we confess our sins, He is faithful and just, and will forgive our sins and cleanse us from all unrighteousness." God forgives, not because He overlooks or ignores sin, for He is just. He forgives, because Jesus Christ has atoned for all our sins and made us clean before God. By what means are we cleansed? St. John writes in the preceding verse, "The blood of Jesus His Son cleanses us from all sin."

So what is the better option: denial of sin and self-deception, or confession?

Prayer Suggestion

Pray that God may remove all self-deception from your heart and lead you to confess your sins, knowing that Jesus has died for them.

Liberated Women

Much has been written, said, and done in recent years by members of the women's liberation movement. These crusaders have called for equal employment opportunities and compensation for women. They have rightfully protested every demeaning custom and practice, such as the portrayal—sometimes the *pornographic* portrayal— of women as sex symbols.

Long before there were feminist movements, God led a women's liberation movement of His own. Such liberation became necessary because Adam, the first man, and Eve, the first woman, had enslaved themselves by falling into sin of their own free will.

Our first parents and all who came after them were incapable of liberating themselves from the slavery of sin. As the writer to the Hebrews states, all "were subject to lifelong bondage."

It was up to God to free man and woman from sin, and this is what He did. At the fullness of the time He sent His Son Jesus Christ to be "born of a woman, born under the Law, to redeem those who were under the Law." This liberation applies to women as well as to men. It applies to them equally, for the apostle Paul states, "There is neither male nor female; for you are all one in Christ Jesus." Women participate equally in God's forgiveness and saving grace. In this respect Christianity differs radically from some other religions in which women are held to be inferior to men and sometimes are excluded from the so-called "salvation" they offer.

In Christ, people are liberated from sin and from self-serving commitments. They are completely free to serve in love. God Himself is the Leader of this liberation movement.

Prayer Suggestion

Express your thanks to God that in Jesus Christ He has redeemed women as well as men—and children too—so that all serve one another to His glory.

Easing the Identity Crisis

Many people in our loosely knit, massive urban society have an identity crisis. Lacking distinctive self-images, they see each other as lonely faces in the crowd, and these faces are mostly masks. They live in quiet desperation, asking, "Who am I?" Over the grave of many a person one could speak the line from Arthur Miller's play *The Death of a Salesman*: "He never knew who he was."

We *can* know who we are, for God made us; we are His people, His children. He acted to give us identity when He sent His Son Jesus Christ among us to be our Redeemer from sin, which had estranged us from God. God has made us His children; we can now live a life of service in His kingdom. By faith in Jesus Christ we are workers together with God, we share in Christ's ministry, for we are crucified with Him. By Baptism we are buried with Christ and our sins are taken into His grave. And with Him we are raised from the deadness of sin to glorify and serve the living God.

This newness of life casts us into a new role as the children of God and as brothers and sisters to one another. St. John writes, "To all who received Jesus Christ, who believed in His name, He gave power to become the children of God." We who were once spiritual orphans were adopted into the family of God. This relationship gives us identity and a proper self-image.

We are no longer like shipwrecked people tossed to and fro on a stormy sea; we are no longer strangers and foreigners, but equal citizens in God's kingdom, members of God's family, people who belong. Since we are God's children, we are also heirs of eternal life. This is who we are.

Prayer Suggestion

Pray that the Holy Spirit may strengthen your self-image as a child of God by drawing you closer to Jesus Christ, your dearest Friend and Savior.

Jesus Christ Is for Real

Many people, even in this enlightened age, are being deceived by the proponents of quack medicines. In the past, people were offered "Hadacol," "Swamp Root," "Water of Life," and "Alpine Herbs" as cures for whatever ailed them. Sufferers from rheumatism were sold "magnetic belts" to ease the pains. Medical charlatans are especially cruel when they deceive the aged and the incurably ill.

Deception takes place also in the name of religion. St. John writes in his short Second Epistle: "Many deceivers have gone out into the world, men who will not acknowledge the coming of Jesus Christ in the flesh." Here the apostle takes note of such who claim that the Son of God did not become a true human when He came to this earth. They say He was a make-believe man. He may have seemed like a true human being, and looked and sounded like one, but in reality was a totally spiritual being, a kind of sublime apparition.

In calling these false teachers not only deniers but *deceivers*, St. John is saying that they under a guise of true Christian teaching were misleading the people. Deception is involved, for the followers of such a religion are not getting what is true and what is truly needful for their salvation. They are being deceived into regarding Jesus as a great humanitarian and philanthropist, a Jesus so full of cheap grace and forgiveness that He requires no repentance and self-denial, a Jesus who saves by His moral example rather than by His shed blood on Calvary's cross. Only as the One *come in the flesh* could Jesus shed His blood for us.

Jesus Christ is for real, not only because He is true God but also because He is true God *come in the flesh*.

Prayer Suggestion

Ask the Holy Spirit to keep you from being deceived, to lead you into all truth, and to strengthen your faith in Jesus Christ, God's Son come in the flesh.

Closing the Gap

We are living in an age of almost instant communication, thanks to our highly efficient news media. Messages via satellite make the world a small community, an intimate whispering gallery. The information gap is nearly closed.

Nearly 2,000 years ago, Jesus instructed His disciples to go into all the world and proclaim the Gospel to everyone. Lacking newspapers, radio, and TV, you would think they couldn't get the job done. But they did. The opponents said, soon after Pentecost: "You have filled Jerusalem with your teaching."

Beyond Jerusalem lay Judea, Samaria, Galilee, the Mediterranean Sea area, and the world beyond that. How did the first disciples fare in communicating the Gospel of the crucified and risen Jesus Christ? Time and again the Book of Acts reports at key points in its mission narrative: "The Word of God grew and multiplied." Christianity received a big boost when St. Paul, the missionary especially to the Gentiles, came upon the scene. He did more than anyone else to close the communication gap in behalf of the Gospel.

We close the gap today when we send missionaries into all the world, when these messengers faithfully preach the Gospel, when we ask the Holy Spirit to lead people to believe the Word of salvation and serve Jesus Christ.

Locally there may still be a communication gap, and that is because we do not witness to our Lord at home, in school, at work, in our communities. We close that gap when we, in St. Peter's words, are "ready always to give an answer to every man that asketh you a reason of the hope that is in you." Perhaps this very day you too have witnessed to Jesus Christ and thus built a bridge to others.

Prayer Suggestion

Pray that God may help you to sense the impact of His Word and then to share the Good News with neighbors.

Closer than Cousins

Jesus and John the Baptist were relatives. Their respective mothers, Mary and Elizabeth, were kinswomen or, as the King James Version translates, "cousins." That would make Jesus and John second cousins.

But their closeness to one another exceeded a blood relationship. John was the herald and forerunner of Christ. To this day he prepares our heart to receive the Savior by preaching repentance and faith. He preaches to us still, and not only the Law but also the Gospel, saying: "All flesh shall see the salvation of God." In pointing to Jesus he said: "Behold, the Lamb of God who takes away the sin of the world." How close was this witness bearer to Jesus!

And Jesus was close to John, by whom He was baptized. In John 5:35 He calls John "a burning and shining lamp." He also said: "Among those born of women, there has risen no one greater than John the Baptist." For a while Jesus lingered in the background. But after His baptism in the Jordan He came to the fore to begin His public ministry. Then He increased, and John decreased. But they were always close to one another.

Jesus Christ shed His blood on the cross to redeem all people, including you and me. He wants to be close to us, closer than a cousin. He wants us all to be His brothers and sisters, with Himself as our older Brother under our common Father. "There is a Friend who sticks closer than a brother," states the book of Proverbs. Jesus is that Friend, and He is very close to us. But how close are we to Him? Is He someone far away, someone unreal like a figure in a colored church window, or does He live in our heart?

Prayer Suggestion

Turn a well-known hymn stanza into a prayer by asking the Friend you have in Jesus to bear all your sins and griefs.

Another Kind of Capital Punishment

Following a Supreme Court ruling in 1972, some states discontinued capital punishment. The rising crime rate has given some state legislatures second thoughts, however.

Whatever the pro's and con's of this important issue, there is another, altogether different kind of capital punishment of which the Bible speaks. It is the punishment for all people's sins meted out to Jesus. And since this penalty brought Him death, we might call it capital punishment.

At the very beginning God told Adam and Eve that they would surely die if they disobeyed His specific command not to eat of the tree of knowledge of good and evil. Sin calls for the death penalty, as also St. Paul has written: "Sin came into the world through one man and death through sin," and "The wages of sin is death."

Our first parents and all their offspring to this day should have died, for all have sinned. But God's love found a way out, not by ignoring the demand of the Law that all sinners die but by sending a Substitute to be punished with death in the sinners' stead. That, in brief, is what the Christian Gospel is all about, as St. Peter writes, "Christ died for sins once for all, the Righteous for the unrighteous, that He might bring us to God."

The first Adam sinned. But he and all his descendants need not die because Jesus Christ, God's Son, the Second Adam, was penalized in their stead with the death sentence. This means life for you. Surely this is the best news you have heard all day!

Prayer Suggestion

Build a prayer of resolve on these hymn lines: "I lay my sins on Jesus, The spotless Lamb of God; He bears them all and frees us From the accursed load."

Two Visitors at Your Door

Some people who have suffered a lot or have reached old age with its weaknesses wish to die but must live on. In the Bible, Job, the man of many afflictions, asks: "Why is life given to the bitter in soul, who long for death but it comes not?" In *The Living Relic* Ivan Turgenev, the Russian author of a century ago, has death come to a sick peasant, to say: "I am sorry I can't take you now."

But others the grim reaper seems only too anxious to take, whether they want to go or not. An unwelcome visitor at life's door, it knocks insistently and will not leave until its intended victim accompanies it. Death is no respecter of persons. It practices no discrimination with regard to age, sex, race, social standing, ethnic heritage, and the like. The grave claims them all, in the words of William Cullen Bryant: "the youth in life's green spring, and he who goes in the full strength of years, the matron and the maid, the speechless babe, and the gray-headed man."

But there is another visitor at the door, Jesus Christ. He is always a welcome Guest, for He is our Savior, the Conqueror of death, the Giver of life. He died on the cross and rose again so that death itself might die. He is the Resurrection and the Life. This Friend tells you today: "Behold, I stand at the door and knock; if anyone hears My voice and opens the door, I will come in to him and eat with him, and he with Me."

Prayer Suggestion

Pray that the Lord Jesus may abide with you with the gifts He brings: forgiveness, peace, eternal life.

A Sound Marriage Formula

On the 88th anniversary of the late President Eisenhower's birthday, his wife, Mamie, laid a wreath at the base of his statue at Gettysburg College. She let the simple act speak for itself. She made no speech. All she said was, "He was my life." And that spoke volumes!

For husband and wife to share each other's life, to love not only *with* but also *for* one another, to bring personal love and devotion to that basic one-to-one relationship—marriage—this is a sound formula.

Here are no gimmicks, no long lists of do's and don'ts, no quick suggestions for surface solutions. Here is what is fundamental to every marriage: husbands and wife living for one another.

This they will do and can do if in their hearts they have the right kind of love, a love that survives and grows when the excitement of romance has faded. That kind of an enduring love exceeds human accomplishments. It is a gift of God. Jesus Christ had it first when out of love for His bride, the church, He gave Himself for her. That kind of divine love is not only a *model* for marital love, it is also the *medium* for achieving it. We love Him and one another because He first loved us. Faith in Jesus brings this love with it.

Now can follow what the apostle Paul urges: "Husbands, love your wives [and by the same token, "Wives, love your husbands"] as Christ loved the church."

Not a footnote to Mrs. Eisenhower's life, not only a part of it or an appendage to it, but, as she said of her husband: "He was my life."

Prayer Suggestion

Ask God's help so that as husband and wife you may share each other's life.

Bringing in the Sheaves

By this time of the year we have harvested our crops. It is a time of rejoicing; it calls for thanksgiving. The ancient Israelites observed festivals of rejoicing after they had completed their harvest and had gathered in the produce. God's people have always been glad and grateful to the heavenly Provider for giving them daily bread and all associated blessings through the course of nature. As for the future, the promise still holds: "While the earth remains, seedtime and harvest, cold and heat, summer and winter, day and night shall not cease."

We ourselves are, in Isaiah's words, "the plantings of the Lord." The new spiritual life in us sprang from the seed of God's Word, which St. Peter calls "imperishable" and "living and abiding." Through the same Word the Holy Spirit nourishes our faith so that we can grow in grace and the knowledge of our Lord Jesus Christ. God tends and cultivates His planting so that we can bear fruit. In Christ Jesus our Savior, who died and rose again for our salvation, God has created us for good works, which He prepared beforehand, that we should walk in them. Note the loving forethought of God—how He planned ahead for us—as expectant parents do before their baby is ever born.

It would be a disappointment to God to come to us looking for fruit but not finding any. But how pleased He is to find us fruitful in every good work! And someday He will bring in the sheaves. He will bring us, His harvest, into His heavenly home. "Even so, Lord, quickly come To Your final harvest home, Gather all Your people in, Free from sorrow, free from sin, There, forever purified, In Your garner to abide. Come with all Your angels, come, Raise the glorious harvest home!"

Prayer Suggestion

Ask the Holy Spirit to work in you love, joy, peace, patience, kindness, and all His other fruits.

Thinking and Thanking

Two closely related words that come from the same Anglo-Saxon root are "think" and "thank." In sequence, the one follows the other. The more we *think* about God's good gifts, the more we will want to *thank* Him.

The psalmist declares, "Know that the Lord is God! It is He that made us, and we are His; we are His people." This is an invitation to do some thinking—to fix certain facts in our minds and go over them thoughtfully from time to time. Who is God, and who are we? To these questions much thought should be given. The God whom we worship is the Lord, who is not only the Creator of heaven and earth but also *our* Maker. "It is He that made us." Consequently, we are His people; we belong to Him. God provides His people with so many blessings: first of all, life itself and then so many things in support of life. Three basic physical needs are food, clothing, and shelter. But we have received so many more divine gifts: health and medical services, education and schools to provide it, peace in the land and a stable government to maintain it, friendship and many good people to foster it.

St. Paul exhorts us to think about whatever is true, honorable, just, pure, lovely, gracious. Think especially about God's greatest gift: His Son Jesus Christ, our Redeemer and Reconciler.

What happens when we count our blessings one by one—when we *think*? We are moved to *thank*. The psalmist bids us, "Enter into His gates with thanksgiving, and into His courts with praise! Give thanks to Him, bless His name." That is what the Thankgiving season is for: to gather in our homes and churches, that we might praise Him from whom all blessings flow.

Prayer Suggestion

Think of people who have meant so much in your life, and then thank God for them.

Giving God What We Owe: Thanks

When young Abraham Lincoln was clerking in a New Salem, Illinois, store, he once inadvertently overcharged a customer by a few cents. That evening he walked miles to return the money—another reason why he was called "Honest Abe."

The Bible tells us about another man who walked a considerable distance to return something. He was the Samaritan, one out of the ten men whom Jesus had healed of leprosy. He felt that he owed something to Jesus for restoring his health—not money, but something more precious to Jesus: thanks. We are told that he "turned back, praising God with a loud voice; and he fell on his face at Jesus' feet, giving Him thanks."

Returning to God what we owe—our thanks for His many kindnesses—is not always easy. It may require effort, as it did for the Samaritan who walked back. It may mean that we have to leave undone or postpone something else we would rather do than to give thanks. The other nine men were probably so anxious to return to their families and to resume normal life that they neglected their thanksgiving.

Giving thanks is hard for some because pride keeps them from acknowledging their indebtedness to benefactors. Someone has said, in cynicism, to be sure: "If you want to make an enemy of someone, do him a favor." Because of the high threshold of egotism, many stumble over their pride and fail to give thanks to God and to other people.

What people are thankful for the salvation God has given them in Jesus Christ, the Healer of the leprosy of sin? Surely those who lay aside pride and pretense and who acknowledge both their sinfulness and their total dependence on God for forgiveness and new spiritual life.

Prayer Suggestion

Ask God to give you a thankful heart for all His benefits to you, especially for the gift of His Son, Jesus Christ the Savior.

Our Letter of Thanks

A man working in the dead-letter section of the Post Office Department said that every year thousands of undeliverable letters addressed to Santa Claus are received there—letters in which children say what they want for Christmas. He recalled but one thank-you letter.

Human beings are by nature much more acquisitive than thankful. They can be eloquent in saying what they want, but they become almost mute when it's time for thanksgiving.

God changes all that when by His Holy Spirit He makes people a new creation in Jesus Christ. Very likely the people in the ancient city of Philippi were like other people—self-centered, grasping, materialistic, pleasure-minded. But when St. Paul came there and through the Gospel made of them converts to Christianity, the Philippians became different.

The Philippian Christians, thankful to God for their salvation in Christ, were thankful also to St. Paul. When he was in prison elsewhere, they sent him a gift, perhaps an offering of money. The apostle, in turn, was grateful and sent them a letter of thanks, his well-known Epistle to the Philippians. He writes, "I thank my God in all my remembrance of you, always in every prayer of mine for you all making prayer with joy, thankful for your partnership in the Gospel."

Before the day ends, let us send a letter of thanks to someone who has befriended us. And by all means let us thank God in a special communication to Him. No postage is required. Just tell your thanks in prayer. Then back up your thanksgiving with thanks-living.

Prayer Suggestion

Thank God for His goodness, asking Him also to help you express your gratitude in thanksliving.

Thankfulness to Match Our Enrichment

Once, at a recent public occasion President Carter enumerated what he said were the seven deadly sins as stated by Mahatma Gandhi: wealth without work, pleasure without conscience, knowledge without character, commerce without morality, science without humanity, worship without sacrifice, and politics without principle.

The list could, of course, be extended. One could add also this sin couplet: reception without thankfulness, or enrichment without gratitude.

The Bible tells us of people who in various ways showed their thankfulness for what God had entrusted to them. Abraham, in the Old Testament, was a wealthy man. He was also a thankful man. Returning victoriously from a rescue mission, he gave Melchizedek, the priest of God Most High, a "tenth of everything."

In the New Testament, Joseph of Arimathea and Nicodemus were men of substance, and they showed their thankfulness for what Jesus meant to them by decently and tenderly burying His body in Joseph's tomb. Not nearly that well-to-do, in fact, very poor was the widow who put two copper coins into the temple treasury because she was thankful for what God had given her. And the woman who anointed Jesus' feet was thankful; as Jesus pointed out, she had sinned much and was forgiven much.

It is the same for all of us: we have sinned much, but for the sake of the restitution made by Jesus Christ, God has forgiven us much. In fact, He offers total forgiveness, full and free. And He has given us so much of everything else.

Prayer Suggestion

Tell God that you appreciate His many blessings of the day and that you intend to use them to His glory.

God Opens His Home

Rostropovich, the Russian-born conductor of the National Symphony Orchestra, Washington, D. C., has a story of thankfulness to tell.

In 1934 his parents moved to Moscow so that their talented children could get a musical education. But there was no place to live. Finally an Armenian woman took them into her small apartment. Rostropovich recalls, "There was only space to be in the beds at night. If you have a palace of ten rooms, and you give one room to somebody else, it is not such a great thing. But if you have two small rooms for three people and take in four other people, that is incredible. The woman kept us for nearly three years—and without asking for money."

That landlady gives us a glimpse of the love of God. He took us into His household, as St. Paul writes, "You are no longer strangers and sojourners, but you are citizens with the saints and members of the household of God."

Yes, God took us in, right off the street, as it were. He saw our desperate circumstances; He knew we had no money to pay. But He made us members of His family anyway—made us equal partners with those already there. That is what salvation by grace means. "God showed the immeasurable riches of His grace in kindness toward us in Christ Jesus. For by grace you have been saved through faith; and this is not your own doing, it is the gift of God—not because of works, lest any man should boast."

Rostropovich is thankful for the hospitality his family received. We too are thankful and bow our knees before the Father, from whom the whole family in heaven and on earth is named.

Prayer Suggestion

Express your gratitude to God for receiving you into His family, asking Him to keep you always in His grace.

Consumers of God's Goods

Private and public agencies are giving much help these days to consumers of all kinds of goods. In the light of so much information and guidance available, consumers can be more discriminating purchasers and get their money's worth.

In relation to God, who supplies us with all we need, we are not *customers*, for we are not paying for the gifts we receive from Him; we are *consumers*—users—of His blessings. This is what God wants. St. Paul tells Timothy that God "richly furnishes us with everything to enjoy." Again, the same apostle declares, "The living God who made the heaven and the earth and the sea and all that is in them . . . did good and gave you from heaven rain and fruitful seasons, satisfying your hearts with food and gladness."

In Deuteronomy 28, Moses identifies God's gifts to us as one's earning in the city as well as the fruits of the ground, the increase of cattle, and the full basket. We are not really the creators of these goods; we are consumers. Even in our day of urban life God's gifts to us are everything we might include under "daily bread," that is, "food, drink, clothing, shoes, house, home, field, cattle, money, goods." These are entrusted to us as consumers who are wise and faithful stewards.

We receive also many spiritual blessings. St. Paul speaks of them so eloquently in the opening verses of his letter to the Ephesians: "Blessed be the God and Father of our Lord Jesus Christ, who has blessed us in Christ with every spiritual blessing in heavenly places." We can't pay for these blessings, but we can be thankful for them and show this by sharing the Gospel with others.

Prayer Suggestion

Pray that God, the Giver of all good gifts, may give you wisdom, so that you may not waste these gifts but use them wisely.

Christ Fills All Our Needs

Our times have witnessed an upswing of interest in the occult: Satanism, magical rites, sorcery, witchcraft, astrology, and the like. The occult arts were practiced long ago in pagan society. The Scriptures of the Old and New Testaments mention many forms of occultism, showing that the Word of God is not compatible with magic.

In Ephesus, the Book of Acts tells us, the converts to the Christian faith made a big bonfire of books dealing with the black arts, consuming a collection having a commercial value of 50 pieces of silver. Also then occultism was big business.

Why is there a rebirth of occult practices in our time? It is safe to say that when interest in the Christian religion declines, cults have a tendency to flourish. Nature abhors a vacuum, say the physicists. It seems that also *human* nature abhors a vacuum. When people turn from the worship of the true God, it is not uncommon for them to try to satisfy their spiritual hunger with substitutes for true and valid religion.

When the people in Ephesus consigned expensive books to the flames, they indicated their conviction that they had now found something much more precious: the Gospel of Jesus Christ. All who have been led to discover Jesus Christ as the Savior who died for their sins and rose again—as the Friend who fulfills all their needs, as the One who is for them "the power of God and the wisdom of God"—need no would-be religious substitutes or supplements. In Jesus Christ we have all we need for the life now and for the life to come.

Prayer Suggestion

Thank God for having called you out of darkness into the marvelous light of Christ's Gospel, asking Him to give you guidance for sharing the light with others.

"If I But Knew"

Amy E. Leigh, a poet, felt a kinship to nature, particularly the forest. So she exclaimed in a poem: "If I but knew what the treetops say Whispering secrets night and day If I but knew . . ."

"Had I but known!" What a world of regrets these words enclose! During a tragic fire in a Kentucky supper club some 160 persons lost their lives. In the rush to get out, a husband and wife were separated, but both made it to safety. But neither one knew that the other was safe. So each in turn went back into the burning building to look for the other. In so doing, both were burned to death.

"If I but knew." Spiritually speaking, many are eternally lost because they didn't know Jesus Christ as the Way, the Truth, and the Life. Much agony and despair resulting from sins committed could be avoided if people only knew and sincerely believed that there is forgiveness with God. Many misdeeds would never be committed if people knew what is involved. In writing to the Corinthians, St. Paul speaks of the glorious salvation that God from all eternity ordained for His people, and he then adds: "which none of the princes of this world knew; for had they known it, they would not have crucified the Lord of glory."

"If I but knew!" or "Had I but known!" are expressions of regret you and I need never voice concerning our rightness and peace with God, for we *know*—we know the grace of our Savior Jesus Christ; we know that our Redeemer lives. Now it is a matter of letting others know.

Prayer Suggestion

Thank God for having made known to you the way of salvation in Jesus Christ, and ask Him to make you His instrument for telling others.

Speaking and Listening

Speaking and listening go together; they make verbal communication among people possible. What wonderful gifts of God are tongues that can speak and ears that can hear! How hard it would be to convey thoughts and feelings to one another if we couldn't speak! And what sounds we would miss if we couldn't hear—couldn't hear a mother's voice, the songs of birds at dawning, a Beethoven sonata!

Speaking and hearing have their function also in the exercise of our faith. First, there is speaking.

God speaks to us in His Word, telling us of His love for us in Christ Jesus, whom He sent from heaven to redeem us. In whatever form this Word comes to us: in Scripture readings, sermons, hymns in church or as we read and speak it to one another at home, it is God who speaks. And also we speak to God and to one another in His name, as St. Paul has written: "Let the Word of Christ dwell in you richly, as you teach and admonish one another in all wisdom, and as you sing psalms and hymns and spiritual songs with thankfulness in your hearts."

The correlative or corresponding part of speaking is hearing, and it too plays a part in our Christianity. Jesus said, "Blessed are they that hear the Word of God and keep it." As we enter church or are about to begin family devotions we say with young Samuel: "Speak, Lord, for Thy servant hears." Or we can pray the words of the hymn: "Lord, open now my heart to hear, And through Your Word to me draw near."

Prayer Suggestion

Pray that God may open your heart and mind so that you may hear Him speaking to you from His written Word.

Taking the Galilean's Hand

An interesting book is Joseph Heller's *Catch-22*. It tells of a man's attempt to avoid military combat by pleading insanity. But the plan defeats its own purpose, for it is argued: if one is able to figure out such a strategem, he is sane enough for combat duty.

So frequently in life do people fall into their own trap, also in their plotting against God. St. Paul writes, quoting words from the Book of Job: "The wisdom of this world is folly with God. For it is written, 'He catches the wise in their craftiness.' "

The supreme example of man's wisdom having the opposite effect from what was intended was the act of crucifying Jesus Christ. Thereby His enemies did not at all succeed in getting rid of Him. Instead, they were the unwilling, unwitting instruments in carrying out God's plan for the salvation of the world. Again, it didn't work when wise men in St. Paul's day called the Gospel foolishness. They were caught in their own trap, for the more they agitated against the Gospel, the more it was revealed as the wisdom of God and the power of God to save many.

So many times schemes against Jesus of Galilee backfire! In the fourth century an unbelieving emperor, Julian the Apostate, did everything he could to reverse the progress Christianity had made under Constantine the Great. But it was all in vain. Mortally wounded in a battle with the Persians, he menacingly lifted up his arm to heaven and exclaimed, "You have finally won, Galilean!"

Why raise a hand, a balled fist, against the Galilean? He wants to be our Friend. So put your hand in His hand.

Prayer Suggestion

Pray that the Holy Spirit may through the Gospel of Christ's forgiving love warm cold hearts, so that their enmity or indifference may be turned into friendship.

Too Much Sitting in the Kingdom?

A churchman has said, "Most of us are singing about standing on the promises, and we are just sitting on the premises."

Perhaps that is what the mother of James and John wanted for her sons when she came to Jesus and asked, "Command that these two sons of mine may sit, one at Your right hand, and one at Your left, in Your kingdom." Note her words: "may sit." She wanted them to help Jesus rule, give Him advice from both sides, share the honor, but not really exert themselves. The request was altogether contrary to the very nature, aim, and purpose of Christ's kingdom.

Yes, there were times when Jesus Himself sat—sat in Peter's boat when He taught the people by the seashore, sat on a beast of burden as He rode into Jerusalem, sat with His disciples at the Passover table. But He certainly did more than sit. He was busy from morning to night helping and healing the people. He walked many weary miles to proclaim the Gospel in towns and villages. At the end He walked to Calvary to suffer and die on the cross for all people's sins. This was hard work, as the prophet Isaiah indicates when he speaks of the Messiah's "travail of soul."

In the lives of Christ's disciples there are times to sit—sit when they rest, eat, converse with one another, and listen to God's Word in church or at home. But then they also arise to do their God-given work, to do the works of Jesus, saying with Him: "We must work the works of Him who sent Me, while it is day; night comes, when no one can work."

"Then all that you would have me do Shall such glad services be for you That angels wish to do it too. Christ Crucified, I come."

Prayer Suggestion

Ask the Lord Jesus to increase your love for Him so that you may gladly witness for Him and do His work.

Singing to the Son

Legend has it that the sun in the sky was one of the fallen angels and was cast out of heaven. The sun was so distressed and downcast over this that it would not rise in the morning to shine unless someone would first sing to it. Giving material form to this legend is a statue sculpted by Carl Milles, called "The Sun Singer."

We sing to the Son (S-o-n). Why? A long time ago the devil and his angels were cast out of heaven because of disobedience. St. Jude speaks of them as kept by God in eternal chains as they await the judgment on the Great Day. Although restricted, they have enough freedom of movement as to tempt people into sin.

We can be sure there was someone greatly distressed and concerned about the fall of people. That would be the Son of God, who is the Light of the world, the Daystar, the Sun of righteousness with healing in His wings. In fact, He cared so much that at the fullness of the time He became man that He might live obediently in our stead, suffer and die for our salvation, and rise again as the certified Victor.

It is true: we ourselves could not have induced Him to rise from His heavenly throne and come into this world by singing to Him; His own love for us was the one sufficient motive. But now that He has come and redeemed us, we can be Son singers. We can show our appreciation for what He did by serving Him, living for Him, and singing to Him in joyful thanksgiving. Praise Him by singing songs you have learned like this one: "We praise you, O God, our Redeemer Creator; In grateful devotion our tribute we bring. We lay it before You, we kneel and adore You; We bless Your holy name, glad praises we sing."

Prayer Suggestion

Pray that the Holy Spirit may help you recall the blessings that are yours in Christ, and then give thanks.

Different, Yet Alike

People differ, not only in looks and size but also in moods, thoughts, and conditions under which they do their best work. We see this, for example, in the way the song "Lead, Kindly Light" came about. John Henry Newman, on a voyage to improve his health, wrote the words while on a ship that was becalmed in the Mediterranean Sea. The music was composed by John B. Dykes while he was bumping into people on one of London's busiest streets, the Strand.

God kept this from being a dull world by making all persons creative in their own way. He wanted no exact duplicates, no clones.

Yet people have so much in common! All were created by the same God. All became sinners when Adam and Eve disobeyed God in the Garden of Eden. The Bible teaches, "There is no distinction, since all have sinned and fall short of the glory of God" (Romans 3:21-22).

People are equals also in the plan God has prepared for their salvation from sin. St. Paul carries through the "no distinction" theme as he goes on to say, "They are justified by God's grace as a gift, through the redemption which is in Christ Jesus." That's the road to heaven for rich and poor, wise and unwise, young and old, and for all people in-between.

Alike in our creation and redemption, we have in common also our sanctification, that is, the new life the Holy Spirit has given us and the goal He has set. The apostle writes, "He died for all, that those who live might live no longer for themselves but for Him who for their sakes died and was raised."

We are individuals, each one different, but we are all surrounded by the same love of God in Jesus Christ. How wonderful it is!

Prayer Suggestion

Pray that the one Holy Spirit may through the one Word and Baptism bring you to a stronger faith in the one Lord and Savior Jesus Christ.

To Know and to Do

An interesting encounter of two fowls is described in the school song "The Robin and Chicken." The two looked at each other, and each wondered what a strange creature the other was, not only because their looks were different but also because the robin couldn't crow and the chicken couldn't sing. The bottom line reads: "And each thought the other knew nothing at all."

This is a parable about people, who often misjudge one another because they don't look alike and don't know how to do the same things. Someone has said, "We are all ignorant, but not in the same things." That can also be turned around: we are all knowledgeable, but not in the same things. A mechanic with tools, the musician with an instrument, and a cook in a kitchen know what they want to do and how to do it. Now if a mechanic can't play a violin, or a musician can't repair a motor, this does not prove that they know nothing at all.

God distributes His gifts and the capacities for knowledge and skills variously. He does not require equal accomplishments, or equal proficiency in the same fields. What He does desire is that all be faithful in the use and further development of their entrusted talents.

Of the lad Jesus it is said that He "increased in wisdom." It is well for us that He did, for when it was time for Him to enter upon His redeeming ministry, He knew what He was doing—knew what the heavenly Father wanted Him to do. This is what God said through Isaiah the prophet: "By His knowledge shall the Righteous One, My Servant [that is Jesus the Messiah], make many to the accounted righteous, for He shall bear their iniquities."

Let God help you to know what you should do and then to do it!

Prayer Suggestion

Thank the Holy Spirit for the knowledge you have and ask Him to prompt you to be faithful in putting it to use.

Uncounted Forgiveness

Jerald Jellison, a social psychologist, has estimated that on an average every American lies 200 times a day. How many times a day would a person sin if one were to add anger, profanity, disobedience, covetousness, lovelessness, disregard for others? Of course, no one can tell.

While sinning is certainly a matter of concern to us, it isn't important that we keep count. Neither is it possible, for we have to say with the psalmist: "Who can discern his errors? Clear Thou me from hidden faults." What is important is that we daily repent, ask God for forgiveness, and resolve with God's help to improve the moral quality of our lives.

"Where sin increased, grace abounded all the more," writes St. Paul. How thankful we are that God doesn't keep count of the sins He forgives! He has laid them all on Jesus, who as the Lamb of God bore the sin of the whole world. In Christ God casts our sins behind Him. He buries them in the depth of the sea so that they are out of sight and out of mind.

Perhaps you are hearing this devotion toward the close of day. If so, you will all the more appreciate the words of George W. Doane in his evening song "Softly Now the Light of Day." "Thou whose all pervading eye Naught escapes, without, within, Pardon each infirmity, Open fault and secret sin." Then specifically addressing himself to the Savior, the writer goes on: "Thou who, sinless, yet hast known All of man's infirmity; Then from Thine eternal throne, Jesus, look with pitying eye."

Such a prayer God hears. With that we can confidently rest our case.

Prayer Suggestion

Ask God to help you fight against sin and to rely completely on Jesus Christ for forgiveness.

One Step at a Time

John Henry Newman, an English churchman, had gone through a personal crisis. In his hymn "Lead, Kindly Light" he speaks of "th' encircling gloom," asking God to guide him. He doesn't demand instant enlightenment, nor the immediate ability to see the whole picture in clear perspective. "I do not ask to see," he declares, "the distant scene; one step enough for me."

One step at a time—a step in the right direction: sometimes this is the most we can ask of God. We build ourselves up to disappointment when we request the whole package at once. Quite often God distributes His blessings one at a time—in sickness, a little improvement every day; in mental depression, today a little brighter and more hopeful than yesterday; amid life's problems, a little more understanding now and day-by-day growth in faith.

Saul of Tarsus, an enemy of Christianity, was converted before the gates of Damascus, and from that day forth his life was changed. He no longer lived for himself, but for Jesus Christ, who for his salvation died and rose again. Yet it took quite a bit of time for the newborn man, St. Paul, to reverse a misguided life. He spent years of meditation and prayer in Arabia to put the pieces together. Then he emerged a complete apostle, a missionary who preached the Gospel to many people, especially the Gentiles.

Are you encircled by gloom? Are you in a tight situation? Don't despair; remain hopeful. Pray as Newman did, "Lead, kindly Light." Pray that God may help you to take one step forward. Let that be enough for now.

Prayer Suggestion

Pray that God for Jesus' sake may give you the light of His Word to guide you as you face life's problems.

The Plumb Line in God's Hand

Many years ago it was found that the 404-foot spire of the magnificent Salisbury Cathedral in England was beginning to lean, and measures were taken accordingly. In order to detect leaning in the future, a plumbline was suspended from the top of the spire, extending all the way to the floor of the nave. In drawing a moral lesson, a message nearby says that by a plumb line "God judges the hearts of men—whether they are upright or crooked, true or false."

In a vision the prophet Amos saw that "the Lord was standing beside a wall built with a plumb line, with a plumb line in His hand." As God measured His people then to see whether they were in line with His law, so He today lowers His plumb line among us. This line is true and reliable. It does not curve, bend, or budge. "It tells it like it is."

Some people think that things in the moral sphere are at best only relatively true, or were true years ago but not now, or are true only when it suits their fancy. To them two and two is sometimes five. But that is not God's way. His plumb line stands for moral absolutes. It shows human deviation, human crookedness. It warns a person ahead of time that the tower he or she is building is beginning to lean and may soon fall.

But God does not leave us in despair. He holds another plumb line in His hand, that of the Gospel. The second plumb line takes into account the perfect obedience of Jesus Christ in our behalf. He straightened out the crooked walls of our life by fulfilling all the demands of God's law and undoing the damage. Now the plumb line of the Law can no longer judge or condemn, for, as St. Paul declares, "it is Christ Jesus who died, yes, who was raised from the dead."

Through His Word and Spirit Christ helps us restructure our lives in keeping with the principles of truth and love.

Prayer Suggestion

Ask God to help you correct what is wrong in your life and then to assure you that for Jesus' sake all is right in your life.

Why Were You Born?

Visitors to the grave of Sir Winston Churchill at Blenheim Palace in England can purchase a booklet in which these tongue-in-cheek words of the prime minister are written: "At Blenheim I took two very important decisions: to be born and to marry. I am happily content with the decisions I took on both those occasions."

The man of the Bible who was greatly afflicted, Job, was not that happy about his birth. These were the first words he spoke when friends came to comfort him: "Let the day perish wherein I was born . . . Let that day be darkness! May God above not seek it, nor light shine upon it!"

The question occurs to everyone: "Why was I born?" Looking beyond our troubles we can see so much in our life that is purposeful, uplifting, and full of opportunities to serve. We cannot but bless the day in which we were born, and bless even more our spiritual birthday, that is, the day when we were born again to faith in Jesus Christ.

As for His life and mission, Jesus knew the reason for it. He said to Pontius Pilate: "For this I was born, and for this I came into the world, to bear witness to the truth."

In the light of these words we see the reason for our own life, for we are participants in everything that is Christ's. That is more than going to work every day, earning a few dollars, eating and drinking, marrying and giving into marriage. It is reaching for the higher truth, the truth that Jesus Christ personified and proclaimed, namely, that in Him we have the forgiveness of our sins and peace with God.

When we believe the words of Jesus and bear witness to His truth, we are fulfilling the prime purpose for which we were born.

Prayer Suggestion

Pray that the Holy Spirit may bring you closer to Jesus Christ, whose Word and work give meaning to your life.

Home Is Where the Heart Is

In Stratford-on-Avon, England, William Shakespeare was born and died. He was baptized and buried in the local Holy Trinity Church. Although the playwright won great fame in London, he in his later years returned to Stratford. That was his home. There his father had owned a glove-making shop. There also was the home of his wife, the former Anne Hathaway.

Other people, no matter how far they have roamed in the world in pursuit of a career, eventually return to their original home. Some who don't return nevertheless retain fond memories of their home, as did John Howard Payne, who wrote, " 'Mid pleasures and palaces though we may roam, Be it ever so humble, there's no place like home."

Home is where we are with our loved ones, and that can be most anywhere: in the city, in the country, in a small town. Home is where the heart is, and that makes it a beautiful place.

Christians have also a spiritual home, for they are "members of the household of God," members of the Holy Christian church, the communion of saints. There they have God as their Father, thanks to the reconciling role of Jesus Christ, through whose atonement they are made the children of God and heirs of eternal life. There they are not alone but have the support of many brothers and sisters in the faith.

The members of God's family love to come together to hear God speak to them in His Word and to speak to Him in prayer. They want to worship with fellow Christians, see them face to face, speak to them, touch them.

Shakespeare in his later years did more than to return to his Stratford home. The time came when he, a confessing Christian, had his heavenly homecoming. The heavenly Father's house of many mansions awaits also you and me.

Prayer Suggestion

Thank God for the many blessings He channeled to you through your parental home, and ask His help in making your present home a source of good.

The Right Cure

In a hospital in Pennsylvania the wrist bands of two women patients were erroneously switched, with the result that the one who had trouble with her parathyroid gland was given back surgery, while the one with a back problem had her gland removed. The patients were treated for illnesses they didn't have. All the while their real problems remained uncorrected.

Can this happen in God's dealing with His people? Does He treat individuals for sickness they don't have, giving one person a cure really meant for another? Does He make this mistake of assigning a heavy burden to one too weak to bear it, and of laying a featherweight load on one who can carry half a ton?

We can be sure that God makes no such switches. The affliction called a "thorn in the flesh" that the apostle Paul had was not meant for John or Peter—it was for Paul. The latter could cope with it, for he had experienced that God's grace is always sufficient; God's strength was made perfect in his weakness.

As the Good Physician, Jesus always administered the right spiritual treatment. He treated Thomas for an ailment he had: doubt and unbelief. After Peter had denied Him and felt sick about it, Jesus forgave him and reinstated him in his apostleship. He didn't have to deal this way with John, for example, for John did not have this problem.

There is a cure that Jesus has for all of us, because all of us have sinned and come short of the glory of God. This is the gift of forgiveness for all who are sorry for their sins and come to Him, the Redeemer, for healing. We can be sure it is the right remedy for us.

Prayer Suggestion

Ask God, for Jesus' sake, to grant you the healing you need by forgiving your sins.

Planting Oaks in Flowerpots

In her novel *Wuthering Heights* Emily Brontë compares the lack of foresight to "planting an oak in a flowerpot and expecting it to grow."

Undoubtedly we sometimes think too small in making plans for the future. The acorns we plant in the flowerpot of our hopes become seedlings that have no chance to succeed because there is not enough earth.

We plant oak trees in flowerpots when we underestimate our ability. The image we have of ourselves may be too restricted. So we locate ourselves in narrow corners and soon find that we can't grow and develop as God wants us to.

Perhaps our problem is, as someone has said, that our God is too small. God, of course, is great and mighty, and all the earth and the heaven of heavens cannot contain Him. But our conception of Him is at times too limited. We say, "God can't do this or that; why pray to Him about it?" We forget that with God nothing is impossible. He can heal sicknesses that medical authorities may call very serious, even terminal.

John Newton declares in a hymn stanza: "You are coming to Your King, Large petitions with you bring; For His grace and power are such None can ever ask too much." St. Paul confronts us with a very important question: "God, who did not spare His own Son but gave Him up for us all, will He not also give us all things with Him?"

When we consider that God created us, redeemed us, and made us temples of the Holy Spirit, we dare not sell ourselves short. God's promises attend His children. Let them not plant oak trees in flowerpots.

Prayer Suggestions

Pray that God may help you plan your life in accordance with His gracious will.

Marble or Mud?

In his novel *The House of the Seven Gables* Nathaniel Hawthorne traces the ups and downs, the strengths and weaknesses, the fortunes and misfortunes of the Pyncheon family of Salem, Mass. He draws the general conclusion: "Life is made up of marble and mud."

The Bible speaks to us about permanent and impermanent things in life. It helps us to distinguish between treasures and trifles, between what is precious and what is purposeless. Much of the earthly wealth people accumulate at great effort is not a durable palace but a mud house that disintegrates in the rain. Jesus bids us build the house of our life on the rock foundation of His Word and work. He invites us to trust in Him who with His own life redeemed our lives and made them both precious and permanent—like marble.

It is said of the saints that their deeds follow them—that their deeds live on and on, long after the doers of them are gone. That is so because these people built with marble rather than mud.

It is building with marble when we let the Word of Christ dwell in us and our children. Two women mentioned in the New Testament did this when they shared the Word with young Timothy, to whom St. Paul writes, "I am reminded of your sincere faith, a faith that dwelt first in your grandmother Lois and your mother Eunice." That same Christian faith is still alive today.

On the tombstone of poet John Keats it is written: "Here lies one whose name was writ in water." That need not be the summary of anyone's life, and it will not be when faith and love live on in our hearts and we share this love with our fellow human beings.

Prayer Suggestion

Take a moment to ask God for guidance to make your life a thing of beauty and a joy forever.

The Grapes of Love

Long before John Steinbeck wrote *The Grapes of Wrath* Jesus told the story of angry grape growers. It is His parable of the tenants of a vineyard who spitefully abused the servants whom the owner had sent to collect the rent. They went so far as to throw the owner's son out of the vineyard and to kill him. Then it was the owner's turn to become angry. Moved to wrath by the defiance of the sharecroppers, he threatened them with the loss of their tenancy.

The meaning of Christ's parable is very clear. God's people in the Old Testament age were defiant and rebellious. They refused to pay God His rightful dues. The various messengers He sent—Moses and the prophets—were turned empty away. Then the Lord of heaven and earth resolved to send His own Son to make the ultimate appeal. What was the outcome of this mission? Jesus knew in advance of the first Good Friday what it would be: the ungrateful tenants of His vineyard of love and grace would kill the Son. And so they did. So did we all.

Despite our ungratefulness, God still offers His grace. How pleased He is when instead of the grapes of wrath His people bring forth the fruits of faith and serve Him with these evidences of thankfulness. The fruits of the Holy Spirit are "love, joy, peace, patience, kindness, goodness, faithfulness, humility, and self-control." This is what we as tenants owe to God, and when we love Him, these dues are a joy to pay. Further, when these Christian virtues take the form of words and works that further the kingdom of God on earth, then the heavenly Father rejoices, too, for it means that His Son did not die in vain.

Prayer Suggestion

Pray that God may increase your love for Him and thus enable you to serve Him with gladness.

Safe in God's Granary

In downtown Boston, near the well-known Boston Common, is a historic cemetery called Old Granary Burying Ground. Here Paul Revere, Samuel Adams, John Hancock, and other patriots lie buried. The cemetery bears this rather odd name because it was once the site of a grain storehouse.

Yet the name is not so odd. The Bible often compares people to fields of grain. God is the Sower, who through the seed of His Word provides of Himself a growing crop of people. He gives the rain and sunshine of His redeeming love in Jesus Christ. The people of faith mature and bear fruit. Then, like wheat, they are ready for the harvest. The reapers are the angels, says Jesus, and they bring in the sheaves one by one. For everyone whose life is in Christ, the Redeemer and Reconciler, there is a place in the granary of heaven. Their souls are safe for time and eternity.

As for their bodies, Christ will raise them up when He returns. In a beautiful passage in First Corinthians St. Paul writes, "Someone will ask, 'How are the dead raised? With what kind of body do they come?' You foolish man! What you sow does not come to life unless it dies. And what you sow is not the body which is to be, but a bare kernel, perhaps of wheat or of some other grain. . . . So it is with the resurrection of the dead. . . . It is sown in dishonor, it is raised in glory."

Jesus Himself was sown into a grave, but He rose again to bring forth much fruit in those who believe in Him.

God's people in the Old Granary Burying Ground and all other resting places of the world are safe. They are God's harvest gathered in His storehouse.

Prayer Suggestion

Make a prayer on these lines of the harvest home hymn: "Lord of harvest, grant that we, Wholesome grain and pure may be."

The Way to Forgiveness

Dr. Samuel A. Mudd, a country doctor in Maryland, was sentenced to a federal prison for setting the broken leg of John Wilkes Booth, the assassin of Abraham Lincoln, and letting him go. Later, when a yellow-fever epidemic broke out in the Fort Jefferson federal prison in the Florida Keys, Dr. Mudd rendered heroic services as a doctor. For that, President Andrew Johnson gave him a pardon. He was considered to have "redeemed" himself.

In a baseball game someone makes a costly error, but later he drives in the winning run with a timely hit. People say he "made up" for his error.

Is it possible for anyone, in the sight of God, to make up for his wrongdoing by doing much good? Can we balance off our sins with good deeds and obtain a pardon? Augustus M. Toplady gives us the answer in stanza two of his hymn "Rock of Ages": "Not the labors of my hands Can fulfill thy law's demands; Could my zeal no respite know; Could my tears forever flow, All for sin could not atone; Thou must save, and thou alone."

This is based on Bible teaching—for example, on Ephesians 2:8-9: "By grace you have been saved through faith; and this is not your own doing, it is the gift of God—not because of works, lest any man should boast."

While self-redemption is out of the question, God's saving grace in Jesus Christ is very much in effect. By grace, for the sake of Christ who died to atone for all our sins, through faith in Him God forgives. Then we do good deeds, not in order to be saved but *because* we are saved—because we are thankful for God's gift.

Prayer Suggestion

Speak to your Savior the words of the hymn writer: "Nothing in my hands I bring, Simply to thy cross I cling."

A Surprise Gift

Sometimes good things come to us in unexpected ways. For instance, a Claremont, Calif., woman bought for a dollar what she considered a "pretty dish" at a garage sale and later discovered it was a genuine Hummel plate worth $1,200.

Quite often God deals out His gifts in surprising ways, and that is always a reminder that we have not earned them but that God is pleased to give them. It is like a person praying a one-dollar prayer and God giving him a $1,200 answer, as indeed the Bible declares: God "is able to do far more abundantly than all that we ask or think."

A woman in a Samaritan town went to the well to fetch a jug of water. She met Jesus there and brought back an unlimited supply of the water of life. According to Jesus' parable, a gem merchant looked for good pearls but came upon the find of a lifetime: the pearl of great price. In Jericho a man with a guilty conscience, Zacchaeus, climbed into a tree to catch a glimpse of Jesus passing by. But the penitent tax collector received a far greater gift: Jesus came into his home, forgave him his sins, and helped him start a new life.

How often hasn't it been true in our lives: we ask God for a modest gift, for a small favor, and He overwhelms us with blessings too great to calculate? And if we say that we can't think of any such experience, we need to consider this: God prepared for us the greatest good, our eternal salvation, and this is indeed an undeserved, unexpected, and most surprising gift of God's love, for "while we were yet sinners, Christ died for us." What a wonderful gift!

Prayer Suggestion

Ask that God may open your eyes to the abundance of good things He has granted you.

Ever Since Eve

In 1910 Mrs. Morris Gershwin bought a piano for her oldest son, Ira. It turned out, however, that another son, George, was much better gifted as a pianist and composer. Ira was good at writing lyrics.

Do mothers make mistakes? They have been doing it ever since Eve, the mother of us all. In her footsteps followed others who erred, like Sarah, who laughed when God promised that she and Abraham were to have a son in their old age. "Why, that would be a miracle!" she might have thought.

It was different with Mary of Nazareth. When Gabriel announced to her that she should become the virgin mother of the promised Christ—and what a miracle that would be!—she believed.

Later in life, problems arose. Her suggestion that Jesus do something about the wine shortage at the wedding of Cana may have been wrongly motivated. The reply of Jesus seems to indicate that. When on a later occasion someone reported to Jesus that His mother and kinsmen were outside, wanting to talk to Him, He replied that His true mother and brothers were the people who accepted His Word. We don't know what the family members had in mind, but it is possible that they wanted Him to quit preaching and come home to Nazareth.

Do mothers, even godly ones who love their children, make mistakes? They do—ever since Eve. And what shall we say of unloving mothers who abandon and abuse their children, who set bad examples, who teach children their own unbelief? May God have mercy!

And that is also the *Gospel* truth! God does have mercy on all who see the light, and in faith look up to Jesus, the Lamb of Calvary.

Prayer Suggestion

Give thanks to God for all the blessings He has brought into your life through a pious mother despite her mistakes.

The Prince Will Return

An interesting legend clusters about Kronborg Castle in Helsingör (Elsinore), Denmark, which is, incidentally, the scene of Shakespeare's *Hamlet.* The story has it that in the time of a great national crisis, Ogier the Dane will come out of the castle to fight the enemy. Similar beliefs have been voiced about other national heroes of the past—how they will some day return to free their countrymen.

In the Apostles' Creed we say of our heavenly Prince of Peace, Jesus Christ, who ascended into heaven: "From thence He will come to judge the living and the dead." This belief differs greatly from the legend of Ogier the Dane. Christ is the Son of God, not a mere man, not a national hero. The Bible teaches that He will indeed return, but not to put down His enemies. This He did once for all when He died on the cross and then emerged alive from the grave. St. Paul describes His complete victory: "He disarmed the principalities and powers and made a public example of them, triumphing over them in Him."

When our Lord returns on the Last Day—and this He has promised to do—it is for a different purpose: to take His people home with Him to heaven. His opponents, already defeated, will be judged and given their due reward. But to His own He will say, "Come, O blessed of My Father, inherit the kingdom prepared for you from the foundation of the world."

Christians look forward to the day of their Lord's return. He tells them as they see the signs of His coming: "Look up and raise your heads, because your redemption is drawing near."

Prayer Suggestion

Ask God the Holy Spirit to prepare your heart to receive Jesus when He comes again.

Telling It like It Is

The United States Department of Defense estimates that it takes *three months* to prepare a recruit for combat. It took Jesus *three years* to prepare His twelve recruits for the rigors of apostleship. He could not turn out 90-day wonders, because too much was involved—not only preaching, baptizing, doing mission work, but also the ability to endure spiritual combat as Christ's enemies reviled, persecuted, and uttered all kinds of evil against them falsely for His sake.

Jesus seeks to prepare all His recruits, also us, for discipleship by plainly telling it like it is. Being a confessing, witnessing, working Christian isn't all roses; the thorns go with it. People enlisted in our Lord's spiritual forces can really get hurt, if not physically, maybe mentally and emotionally. In the combat with evil they can expect to be insulted, maligned, discriminated against, slighted, even "pitied."

But the Savior shows us also the other face of the coin. Those who follow Him through thick and thin are truly blessed. He tells them, "Rejoice and be glad, for your reward is great in heaven."

On balance, joy prevails over sorrow in the Christian's life. During these pre-Christmas or Advent weeks we rejoice and are exceedingly glad. Our delight is centered in the Lord Jesus—in Him who comes in the name of the Lord to be our Redeemer from sin and death. We join the Jerusalem throng in singing, "Blessed is He who comes in the name of the Lord."

Prayer Suggestion

Ask that Christ give you the courage and strength to follow Him even when the going is rough.

Christ's Kind of a Kingdom

In A.D. 301, so tradition says, a pious stonecutter named Marinus founded the Republic of San Marino, a small, 24-square-mile country in the Apennines Mountains of Italy.

The Bible tells us how another craftsman, a carpenter but far more than a pious man—God's Son, in fact—founded a kingdom. It was to spread from "all of Judea and Samaria . . . to the end of the earth." This Founder is Jesus Christ, born in a stable of the Virgin Mary. His kingdom is not of this world; it is not political but spiritual. He established it for our salvation by His obedient life for us, His reconciling death, and His resurrection from the dead.

The kingdom Jesus founded and proclaimed was from all eternity intended to be the inheritance of God's children. Those who are God's sons and daughters are also to be "heirs of God and fellow heirs of Christ." How lovingly and tenderly the King speaks to these children and heirs as they are about to pass from the kingdom of grace to the kingdom of glory: "Come, O blessed of My Father, inherit the kingdom prepared for you from the foundation of the world."

Christ's coming to earth to establish His saving kingdom and make us citizens of it—that is what the pre-Christmas or Advent message is all about. We sing in an Advent hymn, "Let Your kingdom, scepter, crown Bring us blessing and salvation." Isaiah prophesied, "Of the increase of His government and peace there will be no end, upon the throne of David, and over His kingdom, to establish it, and to uphold it with justice and with righteousness from this time forth and forevermore." The King invites us all: "Come, O blessed of My Father." Yes, O come, all you faithful!

Prayer Suggestion

Speak words of thanks to Christ for His invitation that you come to Him and be a member of His kingdom.

The Worth of the Word of God

The Word of God is sometimes precious—in the sense that old copies of the Bible are costly. A New York book dealer paid $230,000 for a 13th-century Psalter alone.

Yes, old Biblical manuscripts may have great value, but the Word of God itself is beyond purchasing price. The psalmist declares about God's words: "More to be desired are they than gold, even much fine gold; sweeter also than the honey and drippings of the honeycomb."

The written Word—the Scripture is God's sure testimony concerning sin and grace, concerning the disobedience of Adam and all his descendants, and the forgiveness of God based on the perfect obedience of God's Son, Jesus Christ, the second Adam. The Scriptures bear witness to Him. They say, "As by one man's disobedience many were made sinners, so by one Man's [Christ's] obedience many will be made righteous." The obedience of Christ in our behalf was total; it extended from the cradle to the cross. Christ, the Babe of Bethlehem, was born to be our Lord and Savior in a complete sense.

Because we rejoice in the good news of our salvation in Christ, we cannot stay away from the Book that tells us all about it in ever so many ways. Like the psalmist of old, we are addicted to it; we meditate on it day and night, also during this busy Advent season. This does not mean that we neglect our life's work and engage in a marathon of Bible reading. What it does mean is that we set aside time for reading God's Word and then reflect on it while we work and while we rest, remember it, evaluate it, and grow in it day by day. People who believe in and live by the Word of God are greatly blessed. Great happiness is theirs. It can be ours, too.

Prayer Suggestion

Pray that God, through His Holy Spirit, may increase your understanding of the Scripture, so that you may find Christ the Savior there.

Reconciliation—A Way of Life

In *The Famished Land*, a novel about the great Irish famine, Elizabeth Byrd writes: "In a certain village in Ireland, long ago, so the story goes, there was no animosity between Protestants and Catholics, not even when they were fighting." Regrettably, peace and good will among people is hard to find, and if there is such a village, in Ireland or elsewhere, it would be a unique place.

That makes it all the more wonderful that we have peace with God. In an Advent text God declares to and through Isaiah: "Comfort, comfort My people . . . Speak tenderly to Jerusalem, and cry to her that her warfare is ended, that her iniquity is pardoned, that she has received from the Lord's hand double for all her sins." Because Christ was born—and in due time atoned for the sins of the whole world—there is, in the hymn writer's words, a "double cure" for sin. There is more than enough forgiveness.

Thanks to Jesus Christ, all our sins are covered—not covered up, hid under a rug, or swept behind the door. They are cleaned away, cleansed in Jesus's blood, removed from the sight of God, gone forever. Believe this, and you have total peace with God.

That makes all who grasp the Good News of God's action in Christ blessed persons. They can look into the face of God and call Him Father, for they are at peace with Him. Now they can begin to look into one another's face, banish animosity, and do away with bickering and fighting, for in Christ they are at peace with one another. Blessed is every land, every city, every village, every person for whom reconciliation is a way of life.

Prayer Suggestion

Say to God that you are sorry for all your wrongdoing and ask Him to forgive you for Jesus' sake. God will forgive, and this will bring you peace.

Clothed in Christ's Overcoat

After World War II a Christian man in the United States, a school teacher, gave an overcoat in a clothing drive for victims in war-torn Germany. He put a letter with a Christian message into one of the pockets. The recipient of this overcoat was most grateful, for both the overcoat and the message. When things got better, he and his family moved to Venezuela and got along well. There they found other recent immigrants. Among them and the native Venezuelans he did mission work, founding more than a dozen mission churches.

If a material overcoat, and a worn one at that, can do such wonders, think of what Christ's spiritual overcoat can do! We refer to the righteousness of Christ, which covers us and in which we can stand before God. This righteousness is not just a shirt or a jacket; it is an overcoat, a garment that fully covers our sins. St. Paul tells the Philippians that he wanted to be found in Christ, "not having a righteousness of my own, based on law, but that which is through faith in Christ, the righteousness from God that depends on faith."

Why was the Son of God born among us? Why did He become a human being and live among us? It was so that by His perfect obedience to God and by His death for us He might make us right with God and procure a righteousness that is ours by faith. There are many ways of putting this. Here is another way St. Paul stated it: "You know the grace of our Lord Jesus Christ, that though He was rich, yet for your sake He became poor, so that by His poverty you might become rich." Might become well dressed and acceptable in the sight of God! You don't have to freeze and shiver and suffer because of your sin. You can be clothed in Christ's overcoat.

Prayer Suggestion

Ask the Holy Spirit to lead many to Jesus Christ, so that the cloak of His righteousness may cover them, too.

Caesar Augustus or God?

Augustus was the Roman emperor when Jesus was born. What sort of a person was he, and who were the people who influenced him? John Archibald, a *St. Louis Post-Dispatch* columnist, gives us a sampling: "Livia was the vicious power behind the throne during the reign of her husband, Augustus Caesar, and that of her son by an earlier marriage, Tiberius. The intrigue and debauchery of those eras, plus that of the infamous Caligula, were recorded by the supposedly imbecilic Claudius, who later became emperor himself." These emperors called themselves divine and sent Christians to the lions for not worshiping them as gods.

The true God tells us of Himself: "I am the Lord your God . . . You shall have no other gods before Me." He is a terror to those who hate Him, but He shows steadfast love to thousands of those who love Him and keep His commandments.

To all who believe in Jesus Christ the Reconciler and Redeemer, God is a loving Father. In steadfast love, which remained unaffected by the disaffection and disobedience of humanity, the heavenly Father blessed the world when He "sent forth His Son, born of woman, born under the Law, to redeem those who were under the Law, so that we might receive adoption of sons." Because in Christ we are God's sons and daughters, "God has sent the Spirit of His Son into our hearts, crying, 'Abba! Father!' " The apostle concludes the passage by saying we are no longer slaves, no longer outcasts, no longer orphans, no longer victims of tyranny under cruel emperors like Augustus or Nero. We are under the Fatherhood of God. We are at liberty to shape our public life, our citizenship, our government in keeping with the love of God for all.

The psalmist declares, "Blessed is the nation whose God is the Lord, the people whom He has chosen as His heritage!"

Prayer Suggestion

Ask that God show you how you can help stem immorality and uphold righteousness where you are.

A Faith to Move Mountains

Moving mountains or parts of them is hard, expensive work. Over 5,000 miners worked for nearly a decade to dig the Eisenhower Memorial Tunnel underneath the Continental Divide on Interstate 70 in Colorado. It cost $112 million, or $1,100 per inch for half the job.

When Jesus wanted to stress the power of faith, even when it was like a small mustard seed, He said it would move mountains—the mountains of fear, doubt, and other obstacles in our lives. Such a faith we find in Mary, the mother of Jesus. She believed there would be a fulfillment of what God had spoken through the angel Gabriel, namely, that she would be the virgin mother of Christ. Christmas marks the fruition of Mary's faith.

There were truly mountains—figurative but real—that Mary's faith had to move or remove. One pertained to her lowly station in life. She was poor. She didn't live in Jerusalem where all the important people lived. A much greater mountain pertained to her virginity. She was to conceive and bear the Child as a virgin. Her mind would say that this couldn't be; it was unnatural. But the angel said with God nothing was impossible, and Mary believed it.

Elizabeth, Mary's relative, said of her: "Blessed is she who believed that there would be a fulfillment of what was spoken to her from the Lord." Blessed are all who confidently hold God to His Word, that is, that the Savior would come to save His people from their sins. Blessed are all who accept this Savior in humble faith as did Mary. Blessed are all who throughout life and in the hour of death look to Him for redemption.

Prayer Suggestion

Pray that the Holy Spirit may strengthen your faith by leading you to believe more firmly in Christ as your Savior.

·

That Wonderful Babe of Bethehem

Babies can arouse interest, awaken love, melt hearts of stone. Perhaps you remember how the author Bret Harte opens his short story *The Luck of Roaring Camp*: "There was commotion in Roaring Camp. It would not have been a fight, for in 1850 that was not novel enough to have called together the entire settlement." Harte continues: "The assemblage numbered about a hundred men. One or two of these were actual fugitives from justice, some were criminal, and all were reckless." What brought them together? It was to witness the christening of a baby.

The Baby Jesus attracts a lot of attention as He lies there in His crude manger. The angels were thrilled to announce His birth. The shepherds were deeply moved by the sight of Him. The Wise Men, out of love for the Infant King, opened their treasures to Him. When Mary and Joseph presented the Baby in the temple, Simeon and Anna, two senior citizens, raved over Him.

What is there about this Baby that touches hearts? It is hardly because He can claim royalty, being born of the house and lineage of King David. It is not only His purity and holiness, although He is "holy, blameless, unstained, separated from sinners." It is not only that He is different in that He was conceived by the Holy Spirit and born of the Virgin Mary. It is because in this His Son, God has revealed His love for us all. It is because so great a Gift was given us undeservedly, as St. Paul writes, "God shows His love for us in that while we were yet sinners Christ died for us."

How wonderful is the Babe of Bethlehem! It is still true what a Christian poet wrote in A. D. 413: "Of the Father's love begotten Ere the world began to be, He is Alpha and Omega, He the source, the ending He, Of the things that are, that have been, And that future years shall see Evermore and evermore."

Prayer Suggestion

Tell God in your own words why you are so joyful and thankful over the birth of His Son, Jesus Christ.

Our Pilgrimage to Bethlehem

Today's headline announces to all the world: "Christ the Savior Is Born!" The Child born of the Virgin Mary is unique. He has a true human nature, being the descendant of Hebrew forebears, notably of the ancestor David. Of them "concerning the flesh Christ came," St. Paul says.

But the Child that is born and the Son that is given is also true God, as the apostle continues to say, "Who is over all, God blessed forever." Because He is God we sing of Him in a Christmas carol as "Maker and Monarch and Savior of all." He is the great God and our Savior Jesus Christ, who gave Himself for us all that He might redeem us from all iniquity and purify unto Himself a peculiar people, zealous of good works" (Titus 2:13-14).

As today we join the shepherds in their pilgrimage to Bethlehem's stable, we too want to worship Him who is true man and true God. But where can we find Him, where shall we look for Him? The stable and the manger are long gone. Where is Christ today? We find Him cradled in the Gospel proclaimed to us in the Holy Scripture. Nowhere else is He found—not in the books of human wisdom and science, although He is a friend of true knowledge; not in the chronicles of human conquest, for He did not come as a world conqueror; not in the mysticism of pagan philosophy and ritual. He comes, as Psalm 40 puts it, "in the volume of the Book." He comes whenever you open that Book and read: "God so loved the world that He gave His only Son."

The same Christ who once came to Bethlehem still comes to us in His Word. We welcome Him today and say, "Blessed is He who comes in the name of the Lord."

Prayer Suggestion

Ask that God may grant you joy over the birth of His Son and help you share that joy with other people.

Beyond Silver and Gold

Norah Lofts, an English author, recalls a former custom about children born to England's kings and queens: "Once the royal children were weighed, and their weight in silver given to the poor."

During the Christmas season we continue to hear the announcement of the prophet Isaiah: "To us a Child is born, to us a Son is given." What Isaiah foretold with such certainty is reported by St. Luke as a fact fulfilled: Christ the Savior is born. He was born of Mary, with Joseph as His foster father, and both were of the house and lineage of King David. Royal blood coursed through their veins, and through those of Jesus. Of what benefit is His birth to the people, especially to the poor? Will they receive His weight in gold, or even silver?

Yes, we all receive riches from Him. "You know the grace of our Lord Jesus Christ," writes St. Paul, "that though He was rich, yet for your sake He became poor, so that by His poverty you might become rich." In writing to the Ephesians the same apostle speaks of "the riches of His grace which He lavished upon us."

This wealth, to be sure, is not money, not precious metals or diamonds, not jewelry or gems. It is something better, something that money cannot buy. It is peace with God, forgiveness, a re-oriented life, hope for the future, the promise of eternal life. Even our Lord Himself could not procure these spiritual treasures for us with silver and gold. Only by the shedding of His precious blood could He—and did He—provide them.

How does the coming of Jesus Christ as Savior enrich you? You are offered salvation without money or price, without any IOU's or strings attached. Take the offer!

Prayer Suggestion

Thank God for the gift of His Son, through whom you are enriched with blessings that money cannot buy.

Strength Amid Weakness

When Napoleon Bonaparte was banished as the ruler of France, he vowed that he would return with "the violets of spring." Thus it came about that the shy, little violet, the most modest of all flowers, was adopted as the symbol of a most violent man and his house.

A much greater contrast is evident in the person of Jesus. Once He was a small baby, entirely dependent on His mother and foster father. In later life He said, "I am gentle and lowly in heart," and He proved it when He fondled the babies that mothers carried in their arms, when He gently laid His hands on the sick and healed them, when He in love forgave the sins of the penitent.

Some people confuse meekness with weakness, peacefulness with cowardice. But this they cannot do in the case of Jesus. He who occasionally seemed to be a violet was in fact a mighty oak tree. He showed great strength when He cast the money changers out of the temple, when He withstood His opponents, when with a cross on His back He climbed "Calvary's mournful mountain" to defeat humanity's mortal enemies: sin, death, the devil, and hell itself!

As far as your life is concerned, don't be afraid or ashamed of any physical frailty you may have. Indeed good health and physical strength are God's gifts, and we thank Him for them. But they are not the measure of courageous manhood and womanhood. To keep your head up and your heart strong in the face of adversity—that is walking in the footsteps of Jesus, the Pioneer and Perfecter of our faith. That is like a violet showing the strength of an oak tree.

Prayer Suggestion

Pray that the grace of Christ may be the power made perfect in you to give you strength amid weakness.

From Poverty to Plenty

William de Kooning, born amid poverty in Rotterdam in 1904, later achieved considerable fame and fortune as an American painter. He once declared, "The trouble with poverty is that it takes up all of your time."

The poverty of Mary and Joseph took up much of their time. Being poor, it was hard for them to find lodging during their journey to Bethlehem. It is much easier and more time-saving to buy food and clothing than to have to go around and beg for them. It takes time to look for bargains, to sew patches on patched clothes, to have to count pennies before making even the smallest purchase.

Poverty is no fun. Its present bitterness is not sweetened by the memory of better days. Poverty brings with it the temptation to steal, to become envious of others, to turn against God.

Amid his total loss, Job declared, "The Lord gave, and the Lord has taken away; blessed be the name of the Lord." If we lose our possessions and are poor, it is good to remember that they were not ours in the first place. They are God's and He lent them to us as His stewards or caretakers.

What is more, we pass from poverty to plenty when in the things of the spirit—the things that matter the most—we turn to Jesus Christ. He was born amid great poverty, lived in poverty, and died in poverty to make us the beloved, forgiven children of God and heirs of the treasures of heaven. How wonderful His grace, for by His poverty we have become spiritually rich! Consider how we have passed from poverty to plenty: "The Word became flesh and dwelt among us, full of grace and truth . . . From His fullness have we all received, grace upon grace." Amazing!

Prayer Suggestion

Thank God for your daily bread; thank Him for the Bread of Life, Jesus Christ, who alone can nourish our souls.

Leaving Something for Others

We were born into an orderly world, enjoying the fruit of other people's labor: government and laws, schools, hospitals, the communications media, means of travel. It reminds us of what Jesus said to His disciples: "I sent you to reap that for which you did not labor; others have labored, and you have entered into their labor." Earlier He had quoted the proverb: "One sows, another reaps."

When a French marshall at age 80 left the military to retire to his farm in Lorraine, he told the gardener to plant an orchard. The gardener said, "But the trees will not bear fruit for 20 years." The marshall replied, "Then we must begin planting at once." He wanted to leave something for the next generation.

Much of the good we do will be enjoyed by others—not by us—but we keep on doing it. It is one of the many forms that loving the neighbor takes—not only the neighbor here and now but also the neighbor then and there: a descendant, an heir, a later beneficiary of our labors. It is always a good question to ask: "What, besides money or property, are we leaving for our children?"

A heritage exceeding in value anything that money can buy is the Christian faith. Parents show wisdom and love in bringing up their children in the teachings of God's book, the Bible. How precious are its truths divine, especially the truth that Christ Jesus came into the world to save sinners and by faith to reconstruct them into children of God!

Inflation can deprive us of much of our earthly wealth, but it cannot rob us of the treasures of mind and spirit that the people preceding us have bequeathed to us!

Prayer Suggestion

Pray that God may enable you to see—and cause others to see—that in Christ we have our greatest riches.

Staying Power

Tiberius, the Roman emperor who succeeded Augustus and ruled during Jesus' ministry, was powerful, but also very superstitious and fearful. It is said that during thunderstorms he would crawl under his bed and cover himself with the leaves of a bay tree.

He himself with his fading power was like the bay tree, as the psalmist declares, "I have seen the wicked in great power, and spreading himself like a green bay tree. Yet he passed away, and, lo, he was not; yea, I sought him, but he could not be found."

Human power is never permanent, even though its possessor may spread himself out like a bay tree. Tiberius and his empire are long gone, but Jesus and His kingdom still flourish. The apostles whom Jesus appointed were weak when compared to worldly rulers. Yet their teaching prevailed, because the Holy Spirit worked through them. Said St. Paul, "God chose what is weak in the world to shame the strong."

At first the strong seemed to shame the weak. All seemed lost when the Lord was crucified and laid into a tomb. But all was gained when He rose again—gained was peace with God and life everlasting, for Christ was put to death for our trespasses and raised again for our justification.

In Christ we can live effectively and be made strong no matter what our situation: young or old, healthy or ill, rich or poor. We are not carried away when others by hook or crook become powerful and spread themselves like green bay trees; perhaps the next time we look for them, they will not be found. Here is a promise we claim, given us through St. John: "He who does the will of God abides forever."

Prayer Suggestion

Pray that through His Word Christ may become alive in you.

We're Not Missing a Thing!

In the song "I Think, When I Read That Sweet Story" Jemima T. Luke expresses the wish that she had been present when Jesus blessed the little children. She wishes she had felt the touch of His hand, seen His kind look, and heard His words. While such a wish cannot be granted, we are not cut off from Him, for the author continues, "Yet still to His footstool in prayer I may go, And ask for a share of His love; And if I thus earnestly seek Him below, I shall see Him and hear Him above."

So, while we were not personally present when Jesus ministered here on earth, we are not missing out on anything. Jesus is with us in His Word. In it we hear His voice and experience His love. We have access to Him in prayer. And as for the future, our Lord has made provision for our reunion with Him.

Some Christians in Thessalonica thought they would miss out on the joy of Jesus' final coming if they lay dead in their graves. So St. Paul tells them: No, you will not miss out on anything, for when Christ comes again "with the archangel's call and with the sound of the trumpet of God," no celebration will begin until He has first raised the dead.

The Lord Jesus, at his first coming, made us God's children by reconciling us to God by His atoning death and His validating resurrection. What He did is valid for people of all times and places. The peace He offered His disciples is the same peace He conveys to you and me.

Here we are, late in time and some 2,000 years after the birth of Christ, and yet we're not missing a thing. We have the same Gospel, the same sacraments, the same faith, the same Lord, the same God and Father of all. We have what it takes.

Prayer Suggestion

Ask the Holy Spirit to make Jesus Christ real to you by deepening your faith in Him.

Ten Devotions for Special Festivals and Occasions

Christmas   2 Corinthians 9:6-15

Sharing Our Gifts

Frank and Ruth Swarthout of Deepwater, Mo., received a special Christmas gift from God when on December 25 a daughter, Gladys Swarthout, was born to them. And she herself received a gift from God in her wonderful singing voice. From singing in a church choir she went on to sing in the Metropolitan Opera Company and to teach music on the West Coast.

Children, also those who can't sing a note but can do many other things, are divine gifts. He who gave His Son for our salvation also gives us sons and daughters to bless our marriages and to round out our families. God sets the solitary in families.

God's gifts to us are many and varied: life, health, eyes to see, ears to hear, a voice to sing and speak, a mind to think, hands to work. He adds gifts to gifts when He blesses our efforts, as St. Paul declared: "God did good and gave you from heaven rains and fruitful seasons, satisfying your hearts with food and gladness."

As we see God's blessings all around us, we have to ask with the apostle: "What have we that we did not receive?"

Besides daily bread, God gives us bread for our souls. He nourishes us with His Word, particularly with the Good News of forgiveness and peace through our Lord Jesus Christ, who is the Bread of Life. We cannot but exclaim: "Thanks be to God for His unspeakable gift!"

The best way for us to keep and increase our gifts—strange as it may sound—is to give them away, to share them with others. The famous soprano we mentioned before, Gladys Swarthout, did this with her voice. Both as a performer and as a teacher she shared her talents. That is what we can do. It is in giving that we receive. Try it!

Prayer Suggestion

Pray for more opportunities to let other people benefit from God's gifts to you.

Walking the Crossroad

Jesus had His cross to bear as our Savior, and we, His disciples, also have our crosses to take up.

The large cross, typifying the pain and penalty for all of the world's sin, rested on the shoulders of Jesus Christ. He carried it to Calvary on our behalf. When nailed to it, He accepted its pain. He was "obedient unto death, even death on a cross." The result for us is reconciliation, God "making peace by the blood of the cross."

Now that Jesus has carried the great cross of our redemption, we are relieved of every attempted task and toil of self-redemption by our own efforts. With St. Paul we cannot but exclaim, "Far be it from me to glory except in the cross of our Lord Jesus Christ."

Now that Jesus has borne "the old rugged cross" for our salvation, we find it much easier to bear after Him our crosses: self-denial, ridicule for His sake, sickness, physical and spiritual affliction. True, we cannot escape walking the "crossroad," for Jesus said, "If any man would come after Me, let him deny himself and take up his cross and follow Me." But this cross is not heavy. It corresponds to our ability to carry it. It is but a crucifix.

So we cheerfully take up the cross of our discipleship and follow Jesus. The trip is not too hard, for we know that Christ is the Pioneer and Trailblazer of our faith. He has gone before, and we can follow in His footsteps, as St. Peter said: "Christ also suffered for you, leaving you an example, that you should follow in His steps."

Prayer Suggestion

Pray that God give you the strength to walk in Jesus' footsteps as you carry your cross after Him.

Staying Close to Christ and to His Own

Through the Sacrament of Holy Communion, which Jesus instituted the evening before His death, we are enabled to stay close to Him and be fruitful in all we do. He is the Vine, and we are the branches; without Him we can do nothing, because we are then disconnected. When we are in fellowship with Him who in love gave His life for us, we experience what we so greatly need in our cold world: the warmth of His continuing love. In Christ we have all we need: the forgiveness of sins according to the riches of God's grace, and peace with Him. From this, other blessings flow.

When we stay close to Christ, we will be in fellowship also with one another as brothers and sisters in the faith. Thus we share the warmth of His love.

During the disastrous retreat of Napoleon's army from Moscow in the dead of winter, the soldiers would at night huddle close to one another around the fire. On the following mornings it was often found that those on the outer fringes had frozen to death.

The Christian church is the communion of saints, the fellowship of believers who stay warm in their faith as they teach, comfort, and encourage one another. It is like a bed of glowing coals. When one coal is removed, it soon loses its heat and grows cold. It is good advice that Hillel, a great religious teacher, gave: "Do not separate thyself from the community."

The first Christians in Jerusalem continued steadfastly in the breaking of bread and thus also in fellowship. St. Augustine said of them: "That they might not be frozen with fear, they burned with the fire of love." The writer of the New Testament Letter to the Hebrews states: "Do not neglect to meet together, as is the habit of some, but encourage one another."

This is our response to the warm embrace of Christ's love, in the words of a hymn: "As Thou hast died for me, Oh, may my love to Thee Pure, warm, and changeless be, A living fire!" (*TLH*).

Prayer Suggestion

Pray that through His Word and sacraments Christ may ever draw you closer to Him and make you fruitful in all good works.

Salvation Is Finished

Some people don't live long enough to finish an important project. They, so to speak, leave unfinished symphonies, books without final chapters, incomplete portraits—like the one of George Washington showing a lot of white. Shown in the Academy Gallery in Florence are rough-hewn figures called "The Prisoners," which Michelangelo began for the tomb of Julius II but never finished.

It would not bode well for our spiritual welfare if Jesus had determinedly begun His work to win salvation for us but had left it half-finished. He said: "My meat is to do the will of Him that sent Me, and to finish His work" (KJV). Again: "The works which the Father hath given Me to finish, the same works that I do, bear witness of Me, that the Father hath sent Me" (KJV).

But what if Jesus, despite a good beginning, had not completed His mission to be the Savior of the world? What if He had refused to drain the cup of suffering down to the bitter dregs of death? Then, of course, we would be unredeemed, for half a redemption is as invalid as none at all. Then some might suppose it were up to them to finish their salvation by doing good works. That is indeed what many are trying to do: Let Jesus begin the work of salvation, and they will try to add the finishing touches and claim some credit.

But our Lord shut the door to all futile efforts of self-salvation by proclaiming on the cross before He died: "It is finished." Indeed He could say in His high-priestly prayer, John 17: "I have glorified Thee on the earth; I have finished the work which Thou gavest Me to do" (KJV).

That means: Our salvation is sure.

Prayer Suggestion

Ask the Holy Spirit to strengthen you in the assurance that Christ has fully and freely completed your salvation.

Everything Was in Order

When the tomb of King Tutankhamen of Egypt was opened in 1923, it was found that thieves had been there before, because much of the contents was in disarray. Grave robbers, like house robbers, are usually in a hurry and don't put things back into place.

From the very beginning it was claimed that thieves had entered the tomb of Jesus to steal His body. On Easter morning, when the tomb was found empty, the soldiers, who had been detailed to guard it, were paid money to circulate the rumor: "His disciples came by night and stole Him away while we were asleep."

But the story wouldn't wash, and that for many reasons, the main one being that our Lord had truly risen. The internal condition of the tomb indicated this to be so; it is unthinkable that robbers had entered the grave. St. John reports what he and St. Peter saw when they looked into the empty tomb—"the linen cloths lying there [robbers would have taken the body without unwrapping it] . . . and the napkins, which had been on His head, not lying with the linen cloths but rolled up in a place by itself."

It is evident: Jesus Himself neatly, deliberately, and unhurriedly had laid away the burial cloths after He became alive in the tomb.

We worship no mummy, no human kings like Tutankhamen of ancient Egypt or Caesar of Rome, who claimed to be divine but who remain in the dust of death. Our faith is in Jesus Christ, the King of kings and Lord of lords. He is "the Son of God with power, according to the Spirit of holiness, by the resurrection from the dead" (KJV). This Lord is alive in the world today and makes His power and presence known in our hearts.

Prayer Suggestion

Ask the Holy Spirit to strengthen His witness in your heart that Jesus Christ is not only alive in the world but wants to live in you.

The Presence

In His farewell talks Jesus comforted His disciples with the assurance of His continuing presence. Even after He had ascended into heaven He would be with them in His invisible but very real presence—"always, to the close of the age."

How is Jesus present? Partly in the presence of others—of the least of His brethren who need our help. Also, He assures us of the presence of the Holy Spirit, who, He said, "dwells with you, and will be in you." The Holy Spirit comes through the Word Jesus has spoken.

And then, there is His sacramental presence.

The people of Israel, in obedience to God's direction, provided their place of worship, the tabernacle, with a "table with all its utensils, and the bread of the Presence; the lampstand of pure gold . . . and all its utensils," according to the Book of Exodus, chapter 39. The "bread of the Presence" is translated in the King James Version of the Bible as "showbread." It consisted of 12 loaves, signifying God's presence and His constant communion with the 12 tribes of His people.

Far simpler was the setting in the Upper Room, where Jesus celebrated the final Passover with His disciples and then instituted a sacrament known by various names: Holy Communion, the Lord's Supper, the Eucharist, etc. Yet the scene in the Upper Room is reminiscent of the tabernacle. There was a table, from which comes "the Lord's Table," another term for Holy Communion. And there were bread and wine, which Jesus consecrated and through which He communicated His body and blood. Thus we speak of His true presence in the Sacrament.

Thus Jesus is present with us—in the persons of needy people, in His Holy Spirit, in His Word, in Holy Communion. He is present as the living Christ. And because He lives, we will live also.

Prayer Suggestion

Pray that Jesus Christ may become a living reality in your life, sharing with you His presence, His power, and the life in Him.

Are the Fires of the Spirit Still Burning?

We are all familiar with the painting *The Spirit of '76*, the original of which hangs in Abbot Hall, Marblehead, Mass. Archibald W. Willard painted it in time for the 1876 centennial of American independence. Having himself been a color bearer in the Civil War, the artist was well qualified to depict the determination of the three men in his painting—two drummers and a fife player—although a hundred years had passed since independence was declared in 1776.

For how many years can one retain the fervor of one's commitment? Is there a limit, an expiration date? It is nearly 2,000 years ago that Jesus lived, taught, suffered, died, and rose again for our salvation. Can we attain to—and retain—the same zeal that His first disciples manifested? Can we as adults, perhaps adults well advanced in years, preserve the spirit of our childhood faith and the love we had for Jesus then? Or must we discard everything from the past and flit from one religious novelty to another?

When the aged Polycarp, a pupil of St. John, was ordered to renounce Christ and offer incense to the emperor, he said, "For 86 years I have served Him, and He has done me no ill; how can I now denounce my King and Savior?" Polycarp couldn't, and didn't.

St. Paul tells the Romans: "Never flag in zeal, be aglow with the Spirit, serve the Lord." And to the Corinthians: "Be steadfast, immovable, always abounding in the work of the Lord." To the Galatians: "Do not grow weary of well-doing."

When we read about Jesus in the four gospels, we are always amazed at His tireless effort and sustained love. Because He so loved us and gave His very life, we cannot help being "aglow with the Spirit."

Prayer Suggestion

Pray that God may grant you a full measure of His Holy Spirit, so that your spirit may never flag.

God, Not Concealed but Revealed

One day, while walking along the seashore, St. Augustine was meditating on the doctrine of the Trinity. It concerned him that he could not comprehend the truth of the three divine Persons united in one undivided being. Then he saw a child digging a hole on the shore, and he heard him say, "I am going to empty the sea into it." St. Augustine then considered that he had been attempting a similar impossibility: putting the vast truth of God's nature into the small receptacle of his mind.

None of us can grasp that God is three in one: Father, Son, and Holy Spirit—three Persons but one God, as the Scriptures teach: "The Lord our God is one Lord." The mystery of the Triune God should not bother us, for in ordinary life we are surrounded by mysteries: life itself, our minds, our bodies, the powers of nature, outer space.

As the nature of God is incomprehensible, so are His power and wisdom. Consequently many of His judgments are unsearchable and His ways inscrutable. St. Paul writes: "No one comprehends the thoughts of God except the Spirit of God," who "searches everything, even the depths of God."

Yet God is not the Great Unknown, not a hidden God, not a stranger to us. We know Him, for He has revealed Himself as our heavenly Father, doing this in Christ, His Son. Truly, "no one has ever seen God; the only Son, who is in the bosom of the Father, He has made Him known." We know the love of God because we know the grace of our Lord Jesus Christ, who offered up Himself on the cross of Calvary to take away our sins and make us God's children and heirs of eternal life.

No, we cannot fully grasp, analyze, or dissect God with our minds, but with our hearts we can love Him who first loved us.

Prayer Suggestion

Pray that you may know and experience more and more of God's great love for you in Christ Jesus.

Putting More Memory into Memorial Day

In his song "The Heart Bowed Down" Michael Wm. Balfe states that memory is a friend to those who grieve. Yes, memory is a wonderful gift of God, for in days of darkness it lets us recall, as the song writer goes on to say, "moments of delight."

Memorial Day is an occasion for going back in our memories to dear departed ones and to thank God anew for all the blessing, all the goodness and truth, all the happy moments He communicated to us through them. This is particularly true of those who gave their lives for their country. What a debt of gratitude we owe them! We honor them by putting their memory back into Memorial Day.

"The memory of the just is blessed" (KJV), says the writer of Proverbs in the Bible. A great blessing comes to us even now as we recall what a dear deceased father, mother, brother, sister, husband, wife, son, or daughter has meant to us. As we follow in their footsteps, we continue to add to their lives, as it were, in serving God and man. It is written concerning the departed: " 'Blessed indeed,' says the Spirit, 'that they may rest from their labors, for their deeds follow them.' "

Even more important is that we follow in the footsteps of Jesus Christ, who "bore our sins in His body on the tree, that we might die to sin and live to righteousness," in the words of St. Peter. Earlier the apostle had said: "To this you have been called, because Christ also suffered for you, leaving you an example, that you should follow in His steps."

Prayer Suggestion

Thank God for all the good that came your way through persons now dead, and ask that God make you the bearer of His Good News to others.

The Praise of God's People

One Thanksgiving Day the general manager of a St. Louis, Mo., television station brought holiday greetings in which he suggested that the audience express gratitude for the community's obvious blessings. One listener objected. He requested equal time to say there was nothing to be thankful for.

When we bring our harvest home and count our blessings, suggesting with the psalmist: "Oh, give thanks to the Lord," some malcontents will say, "We have nothing to be thankful for." They may use whatever opportunities are open to them to deny that God is good and that all blessings flow from Him.

But what is true is true, regardless of what critics say. It is a great privilege to live in the community of God and to be numbered with His people. Life was not all roses for David—he was in constant danger of his life when King Saul hunted him down—yet he declares: "I will tell of Thy name to my brethren; in the midst of the congregation I will praise Thee."

We have so much to praise God for: life and health, home and family, school doors open to all, the opportunity to work and to rest, an abundance of good food to eat, clean water to drink, clothes and shoes, freedom of religion. Most of all, we have a heavenly Father who is good to all and whose tender mercies are over all His works. He is the Giver of life in the fullest sense, as the apostle John testifies: "This is the testimony, that God gave us eternal life, and this life is in His Son"—in His Son Jesus Christ.

Therefore, one and all, let us give thanks to God!

Prayer Suggestion

In your own words, tell God that you are thankful for all His gifts to you, especially for the gift of His own Son, Jesus Christ, the Savior.